MACMILLAN EXAMS

Ready for
First

teacher's book

3rd Edition

Alice Lockyer

Macmillan Education
The Macmillan Building
4 Crinan Street
London N1 9XW
A division of Macmillan Publishers Limited

Companies and representatives throughout the world

ISBN 978-0-230-44010-4

Note to Teachers
Photocopies may be made, for classroom use, of
pages 55, 56, 136, 137, 166, 167 and 168 without the
prior written permission of Macmillan Publishers
Limited. However, please note that the copyright law,
which does not normally permit multiple copying of
published material, applies to the rest of this book.

Original design by Andrew Jones and eMC Design
Page make-up by EXPO Holdings, Malaysia

Author's acknowledgements
Many thanks to my pals Sarah, Helen and Caroline for
jollying me along.

The publishers would like to thank all those who
participated in the development of the book, with special
thanks to Roy Norris and the freelance editor.

The author and publishers are grateful for permission to
reprint the following copyright material:
Adapted from website www.paganini.com, reprinted with
permission of the publisher;
Adapted from website www.rhythmofthedance.com,
reprinted with permission of the publisher;
Material used from website www.cirque-eloize.com;
Material used from website www.tapdogs.com;

These materials may contain links for third party
websites. We have no control over, and are not responsible
for, the contents of such third party websites. Please use
care when accessing them.

Although we have tried to trace and contact copyright
holders before publication, in some cases this has not
been possible. If contacted we will be pleased to rectify
any errors or omissions at the earliest opportunity.

Printed and bound in Thailand

2018 2017 2016 2015 2014
10   9   8   7   6   5   4   3

Contents

Contents map of the Coursebook

Reading	Use of English	Listening	Speaking
Multiple matching (Part 7)	Transformations (Part 4)	1 Multiple matching (Part 3) 2 Multiple choice (Part 1)	Talking about photos (Part 2)
Gapped text (Part 6)	Word formation: Affixes Word formation (Part 3)	1 Sentence completion (Part 2) 2 Multiple choice (Part 4)	
Multiple choice (Part 5)	Word formation: Nouns 1 Word formation (Part 3)	1 Multiple choice (Part 4) 2 Multiple matching (Part 3)	1 Collaborative task (Part 3) 2 Further discussion (Part 4)
Part 3: Word formation			
Gapped text (Part 6)	Word formation: Adjectives ending in *-ing* and *-ed* Transformations (Part 4) Word formation (Part 3)	Preparing for listening: Focus on distractors Multiple choice (Part 1)	Talking about photos (Part 2)
1 Multiple matching (Part 7)	Word formation: *-en* suffix 2 Open cloze (Part 2) Word formation (Part 3) Multiple-choice cloze (Part 1) Transformations (Part 4)	1 Multiple choice (Part 4) 2 Sentence completion (Part 2)	1 Talking about photos (Part 2) 2 Collaborative task (Part 3)
2 Multiple choice (Part 5)	1 Multiple-choice cloze (Part 1) Open cloze: Relative clauses Transformations (Part 4)	1 Multiple matching (Part 3) 2 Multiple choice (Part 1)	1 Collaborative task (Part 3) 2 Interview (Part 1)
Part 7: Multiple matching			
Gapped text (Part 6)	Open cloze (Part 2) Transformations (Part 4)	1 Sentence completion (Part 2) 2 Multiple choice (Part 4)	1 Talking about photos (Part 2) Supermarket psychology 2 Interview (Part 1)
1 Gapped text (Part 6)	Word formation: Adjectives 2 Word formation (Part 3) Transformations (Part 4) Multiple-choice cloze (Part 1)	1 Multiple choice (Part 1) 2 Multiple matching (Part 3)	1 Interview (Part 1) 2 Talking about photos (Part 2)
1 Multiple choice (Part 5) 3 Multiple matching (Part 7)	Word formation: Adverbs 2 Open cloze (Part 2) Multiple-choice cloze (Part 1) Word formation (Part 3) Transformations (Part 4)	1 Multiple choice (Part 4) 2 Sentence completion (Part 2)	Collaborative task (Part 3)
Part 3: Multiple matching		**Part 4: Multiple choice**	
Multiple choice (Part 5)	Transformations (Part 4) Multiple-choice cloze (Part 1)	1 Multiple choice (Part 4) 2 Multiple matching (Part 3)	Talking about photos (Part 2)
1 Multiple matching (Part 7) 2 Gapped text (Part 6)	3 Open cloze (Part 2) Transformations (Part 4)	1 Sentence completion (Part 2) 2 Multiple choice (Part 1)	Collaborative task (Part 3)
1 Multiple matching (Part 7)	2 Open cloze (Part 2) Word formation: Nouns 2 Word formation (Part 3) Transformations (Part 4) Multiple-choice cloze (Part 1)	1 Multiple matching (Part 3) 2 Multiple choice (Part 4)	Talking about photos (Part 2)
Part 3: Collaborative task		**Part 4: Further discussion**	
Gapped text (Part 6)	Word formation: Suffixes *-ible* and *-able* Word formation (Part 3) Transformations (Part 4)	1 Multiple choice (Part 4) 2 Sentence completion (Part 2)	1 Collaborative task (Part 3) 2 Further discussion (Part 4)
1 Multiple choice (Part 5)	Word formation: Suffixes *-ful* and *-less* 2 Open cloze (Part 2) Multiple-choice cloze (Part 1) Transformations (Part 4) Word formation (Part 3)	1 Multiple matching (Part 3) 2 Multiple choice (Part 1)	Talking about photos (Part 2)

Introduction

Ready for First consists of the following components:

- Coursebook (with and without key)
- Macmillan Practice Online
- Teacher's Book with DVD Rom
- Two Audio CDs
- Workbook (with and without key)

Coursebook

Each of the 14 units in the Coursebook provides a balance and variety of activity types aimed at improving students' general English level, as well as developing the language and skills they will need to pass the *Cambridge English: First (FCE)* examination. At the end of every unit, there is a two-page Review section, containing revision activities and exam style tasks, which enable students to practise the new language they have encountered in the unit and, as the course progresses, in previous units.

The book also contains five supplementary 'Ready for …' units, which provide students with information, advice and practice on each of the four papers in the *Cambridge English: First* examination. The Reading and Use of English paper is divided into two sections for the purposes of these units. There is also Ready for Listening, Ready for Speaking and the final unit is Ready for Writing, which includes a comprehensive bank of writing materials. The 'Ready for …' units are situated after every third unit and may be used in the order in which they appear in the book, i.e. Ready for Use of English after Unit 3, Ready for Reading after Unit 6, and so on. However, they are intended very much as a flexible resource which may be exploited at such a time during the course as the teacher feels appropriate.

At the end of the Coursebook, you will find a Wordlist and Grammar reference, each closely linked to the 14 units in the book. There is also an Additional material section, to which students are referred in certain units, and the Listening scripts. The Coursebook is available with or without the answer key.

The following boxes, which appear throughout the Coursebook, provide help and advice to students when they perform the different tasks.

- **What to expect in the exam:** these contain useful information on what students should be prepared to see, hear or do in a particular task in the examination.
- **How to go about it:** these give advice and guidelines on how to deal with different examination task types and specific questions in the unit.
- **Don't forget!:** these provide a reminder of important points to bear in mind when answering a particular question.
- **Useful Language:** these contain vocabulary and structures which students can use when they perform speaking and writing tasks.

Teacher's Book

The Teacher's Book contains teaching notes for each activity in the Coursebook. A typical unit of the Teacher's Book provides you with:

- a summary of examination task types contained in the Coursebook unit
- guidelines and ideas for exploiting the Coursebook material, including further suggestions for warm-up and follow-on activities
- classroom management ideas
- answers to exercises
- scripts for the listening activities
- sample answers for many of the writing exercises, together with the examiner's notes
- photocopiable material on stories and the set text option in the Writing paper, for those teachers who are preparing students for *First for Schools*.

On the DVD-ROM accompanying the Teacher's Book, you will find the scripts for the listening tasks in the Workbook, a complete answer key for the Workbook, and the listening scripts for the practice tests on Macmillan Practice Online. The DVD-ROM also contains:

- **Seven photocopiable progress tests**

These are intended for use after every two units and provide teachers with the opportunity to assess their students' progress on the course at regular intervals. The tests can be downloaded as PDF files, and they are also available in a format which enables you to edit them to meet your students' needs.
Each test follows the same format:
One exam-style Reading exercise
Two exam-style Use of English exercises
One Vocabulary exercise
One exam-style Listening exercise
An exam-style Writing task

- **14 photocopiable activities**

These contain interactive tasks, one for each unit, offering practice of one or more aspect of language from the unit.

- **10 author videos**

In this series of short videos, the author of *Ready for First*, Roy Norris, introduces the different features of the course, and explains the approach taken in the teaching of vocabulary, grammar and the four main skill areas of Reading, Writing, Speaking and Listening. There are also videos on the specific exam-related areas of Use of English and Word formation.

Workbook

The 14 units of the Workbook follow the same order and general topic areas as the Coursebook. They have been designed to provide students with further practice, revision and extension of the language presented in class, as well as examination practice and skills work. Each unit follows the same format:

- **Reading**
To ensure variety, the reading task type in most units of the Workbook is different from that in the corresponding unit of the Coursebook. Students will, however, already be familiar with the reading task type they encounter in the Workbook and are thus provided with an opportunity for revision. In each unit, there is one or more exercise exploiting the language which occurs in the reading text.

- **Vocabulary**
There is usually a combination of puzzle-type exercises (e.g. crosswords, word grids, wordsearches) and more familiar vocabulary exercises (e.g. gap-fills, multiple-choice and matching exercises). These provide revision of the words and phrases seen in the Coursebook unit. Some exercises extend the vocabulary from the topic area by drawing on items from the Wordlist at the end of the Coursebook. On occasions, students are given the opportunity to revise vocabulary presented in earlier units of the Coursebook.

- **Language focus**
This section contains further controlled practice of the grammar presented in class. None of the exercises contains grammar which students have not already encountered in the Coursebook.

- **Use of English**
Most units have three or four exam-style tasks. An attempt has been made to ensure that as much of the language tested in these exercises as possible has already been encountered by students in the corresponding unit, or previous units, of the Coursebook.

- **Writing**
The Workbook contains a complete writing syllabus to complement that in the Coursebook and to ensure that students are fully prepared for the Writing paper of the *Cambridge English: First* examination. Extensive help is given in the form of useful language, model answers and/or planning guidelines. As with the reading sections, the writing task type in any given Workbook unit is usually different from the one in the corresponding Coursebook unit.

- **Listening**
The Listening bank appears at the end of the Workbook and contains one listening activity for each unit. The task type for a particular unit is the same as one of the tasks in the corresponding unit of the Coursebook. Some of the listening activities are followed by a vocabulary exercise based on some of the language used in the recording. The scripts for the listening tasks can be found on the DVD-ROM which accompanies the Teacher's Book.

Also, at the end of the Workbook you will find the following:

- a list of the phrasal verbs encountered in both Coursebook and Workbook
- a list of lexical phrases, including the phrases presented throughout the Coursebook which contain the following verbs: get, take, have, come, give, put, make, do.
- a list of irregular verbs

The Workbook is available with or without the answer key.

Macmillan Practice Online

Each student can access Macmillan Practice Online by going to the 'Ready for' website – www.readyfor-online.com – and entering the unique code which is on the inside back cover of each Coursebook. Students then follow the instructions to create their own log-in and password, which means they can access the *Ready for First* material as and when they like.

The material on Macmillan Practice Online includes the following:
- a video of two candidates performing the tasks contained in the Ready for Speaking unit of the Coursebook, so your students can see what an actual speaking test looks like.
- two practice tests, each with a full Listening and Reading and Use of English paper, as well as a full Writing paper with model answers for each task
- downloadable MP3 audio files for the listening activities in the Coursebook.

Using the course to prepare students for the *Cambridge English: First (FCE)* examination

Whilst *Ready for First* can be used as a general course for students at B2 level of English, one of its main aims is to prepare students for the *Cambridge English: First* examination, an overview of which can be found on pages 4–5 of the Coursebook. A range of support is available in the various components of the course, to give students the best chance possible of passing the exam.

Vocabulary

In most units of the Coursebook, there is at least one section devoted to topic vocabulary, that is, words or phrases which are linked to the theme or themes of the unit. This topic vocabulary is reproduced in the Wordlist at the end of the book, where it is grouped according to the unit in which it appears, together with further items which form part of the same lexical set. Vocabulary activities in the Workbook both revise the topic vocabulary presented in the units, and provide practice of the additional items from the Wordlist. This ensures that students build a sufficient vocabulary store to meet the requirements of the *Cambridge English: First* examination.

As well as individual words, students are encouraged throughout the course to learn whole phrases, a key element in the Reading and Use of English paper, though also of importance in the other three papers of the exam. Attention is given to different types of collocation, and there are regular sections which focus on expressions with verbs such as *get*, *take*, *give* and *put*. These expressions are grouped for reference in the Lexical phrases list at the end of the Workbook. Throughout the book, collocations are shown in bold, and students should ensure they record these and other whole phrases in their notebooks.

In addition, the course contains work on dependent prepositions, affixation (see Use of English below) and phrasal verbs. A variety of different approaches is used to present phrasal verbs, which always appear in the context of a sentence or continuous text as a guide to meaning. An alphabetical list of all the phrasal verbs from the course is included at the end of the Workbook.

Finally, there are three sections – in Units 7, 10 and 13 – which focus on the skill of paraphrasing, using different words to express the same meaning. Paraphrasing is important in all four of the exam papers, especially of course, for the Key word transformations in the Reading and Use of English paper, as well as the Writing and Speaking papers, where students should avoid repeating the same words and expressions.

All elements of vocabulary are revised in the Review sections of the Coursebook, as well as in the Workbook, both in the unit in which they are first presented and in later units, too.

Grammar

Each unit of the Coursebook contains one or more Language focus sections, which generally use contextualized examples from a reading or listening text to present and illustrate a particular grammar point. Students at this level will already be familiar with the majority of the grammar areas which are required for the *Cambridge English: First* examination. Most Language Focus sections, therefore, do not simply give students the grammar rules, but encourage them instead to apply their existing knowledge to example sentences and work out the rules for themselves. To achieve this, they may be invited to answer questions about the examples or perhaps match each example to a rule. Having checked their ideas in the Grammar reference at the end of the book, students then go on to perform written and/or spoken practice activities. Further practice is provided in the Review sections

at the end of each unit, as well as in the relevant unit of the Workbook. This practice often takes the form of exam-style Use of English exercises.

Use of English

The comprehensive nature of the Language focus and Vocabulary sections ensures that students receive the appropriate language input to enable them to deal confidently with the Use of English tasks in the Reading and Use of English paper. In addition, they are provided with plenty of opportunity to practise all four task types, both in the Coursebook and the Workbook. The Ready for Use of English unit of the Coursebook gives useful information on the types of words tested in Part 1, the Multiple-choice cloze, Part 2 the Open cloze and Part 3, the Word formation task.

A key feature of *Ready for First* is the Word formation syllabus, which aims to teach rather than simply test. A systematic approach to word building is adopted, with a number of units each focusing on a different aspect of affixation. Word formation practice exercises test only those items which have been presented in the same unit as the exercise or in earlier units. The effect is therefore accumulative, so that by the end of the course students will have been exposed to all the major areas of affixation tested in Part 3 of the Reading and Use of English paper.

Reading

Texts from a variety of sources (magazines, newspapers, novels, etc.) are used to develop students' reading skills and prepare them for the reading tasks in the Reading and Use of English paper. In Units 1–3 of the Coursebook, students encounter each of the three types of reading task they will be expected to complete in the *Cambridge English: First* exam: Part 5 Multiple choice, Part 6 Gapped text and Part 7 Multiple matching. In these first three units of the book, each reading section is accompanied by a How to go about it box, advising students on the techniques to employ when carrying out the different exam tasks.

The second time they see each of the three task types, in Units 4 to 6, students receive a little less help. This time each reading section is accompanied by a Don't forget! box, which provides students with a brief reminder of the main techniques they learnt in Units 1–3. In the rest of the book, in Units 7–14, students are expected to be independent and almost no further help is given, though of course, they can always be referred back to the relevant help boxes in Units 1–3 before carrying out a particular reading task.

The Ready for Reading unit contains further help and advice for each of the three task types. This comes immediately after Unit 6, although the contents of this unit can be used at any time during the course.

In order to promote sound examination technique, students are encouraged at all times to read through the text for gist (general understanding) first, before they go on to complete the exam-style reading task. They may, for example, be required to answer one or more gist questions, or perhaps check predictions they have made in a pre-reading activity. Once all reading tasks have been carried out, the Reacting to the text sections provide students with the opportunity to discuss the content of the passage and express their own opinions on the issues involved. Further reading practice is provided in each unit of the Workbook.

Writing

All exam writing tasks are covered, both in the Coursebook and the Workbook. The writing sections in both books prepare students thoroughly for each new task and may focus on one or more of the following features: planning answers; help with ideas; paragraph organization; cohesive devices; useful language; appropriate style; checking work for mistakes. Model answers appear throughout the course, and always when students encounter a particular task type for the first time.

In addition, the Teacher's Book and the with-key version of the Coursebook both contain examples of students' answers to many of the writing tasks in the Coursebook. These are accompanied by comments from the examiner. The Ready for Writing includes a writing bank containing examples of each of the different writing tasks that students are likely to encounter in the *Cambridge English: First* exam. For each task type, there is a question and a model answer, with important features highlighted in the margin. This is always followed by a writing task for students to complete, with a Useful language box containing vocabulary and structures they can use for this and other writing tasks of the same type. The writing bank serves both as a reference and also as a source of writing tasks which can be done at any time, with or without the help of the teacher.

For students preparing for *First for Schools*, the Teacher's Book contains supplementary material for the Short story option (pages 55, 136 and 166) and the Set text option (page 167).

Listening

Nearly every unit of the *Ready for First* Coursebook has two exam-style listening tasks, and there are a further 14 tasks, one for each unit, in the Workbook. This makes a total of 45 listenings in the two books. Information on listening in the *Cambridge English: First* exam and guidance on how to tackle the tasks are given in the What to expect and How to go about it boxes, particularly in the earlier stages of the course, when students require most support.

The pre-listening stage is an extremely important one and can greatly influence how successfully students complete the listening task. *Ready for First* therefore includes a number of pre-listening activities intended to raise students' interest in, and activate their knowledge of the subject of the recording, as well as to suggest techniques which can be applied during the examination itself. These activities include discussion questions on the topic, prediction of language and/or information which students are likely to hear, advice on note-taking and raising students' awareness of distractors. And then after the listening, there are questions to encourage further discussion based on what students have heard in the recording.

The Ready for Listening unit on pages 124–127 contains an example of each of the four parts of the Listening paper, together with further help and advice. All the Coursebook listening scripts are included at the end of the book, and the recordings are included as downloadable MP3 audio files on Macmillan Practice Online.

Speaking

There are numerous speaking opportunities in *Ready for First*, both exam-type tasks as well as other non-exam speaking activities.

Guidance is given throughout the Coursebook on how to approach the four parts of the Speaking Paper in the *Cambridge English: First* exam. There are regular How to go about it and Useful language boxes, particularly for Parts 2 and 3, where students need most help with procedure and technique. The Ready for Speaking unit on pages 164–167 contains further useful practice and advice, and includes a recorded speaking test, in which students can compare their own performance in the four Parts of the Speaking paper with that of two candidates who carry out the same tasks. This speaking test can also be seen on video on Macmillan Practice Online.

Clearly, the more speaking practice students have in class, the faster their oral skills will improve and the better prepared they will be for the Speaking paper. *Ready for First* provides regular opportunities for students to speak in pairs, in pre- and post- listening and reading activities, as well as in Vocabulary and Language focus sections. These activities often provide personalization and discussion possibilities, aimed at both improving general fluency and also preparing students for Parts 1 and 4 of the Speaking paper. They are indicated by the special speaking icon, most usually found in the left hand margin.

1 Lifestyle

Content Overview

Themes

The unit is concerned with routines, lifestyles and the topic of clothes. The grammar and vocabulary come directly from the reading and listening exercises and are actively practised through the more controlled grammar exercises and freer speaking and writing tasks.

Exam-related activities

Reading and Use of English
Part 7	Multiple matching
Part 4	Transformations (Review)

Writing
Part 2	Informal letter
Part 2	Article (Review)

Listening
Part 3	Multiple matching
Part 1	Multiple choice

Speaking
Part 2	Talking about photos

Other

Language focus 1:	Habitual behaviour
Language focus 2:	*Be used to, get used to* and *used to*
Vocabulary 1:	Lifestyle
Vocabulary 2:	*Get*
Vocabulary 3:	Clothes

Vocabulary 1: Lifestyle   Page 6

Lead–in
Books closed. Write *lifestyle* on the board and elicit different types from the class, e.g. *a busy lifestyle.* Put students' suggestions on the board.

1a Refer students to the verbs and adjectives and check for understanding, e.g. *Which word describes a lifestyle in which you are often sitting down?* Point out that *life* can be used instead of *lifestyle* in all collocations. Model and check pronunciation of *chaotic, luxurious* and *sedentary.*

1b Give a brief description of your own lifestyle as an example to start students off, e.g. *I've got a very busy lifestyle because I've got two children*

and I work full-time. Encourage students to listen carefully to each other as they do the activity, and point out that this is essential practice in preparing for the *First* exam. Circulate and monitor the activity. Get feedback from each pair when they have finished by asking: *What type of lifestyle does your partner have?* This will check they have been listening.

2 Students discuss the questions in small groups. Circulate and use this activity as a way of getting to know your students. Keep any error correction to a minimum as this might intimidate some students. After the activity, have a brief feedback session with the class by asking a few students to give some information about their group, e.g. *Does anyone in your group want to change their lifestyle? Why?* Write any new or useful vocabulary on the board.

Point out that the collocations in the bullet points are highlighted in **bold**. Explain that this system is used throughout the Coursebook to highlight collocations, and demonstrate this by referring students briefly to Vocabulary 2: *Get* (p11) exercises 1–3 and Vocabulary 2: Sport (p25) exercise 4.

Learner training
Suggest that students buy a notebook to record vocabulary as they go through the course. For homework, they could create a section on lifestyles in their notebooks and write the collocations from exercise 2 with an example sentence for each one.

 **Talking about photos**
Page 7

Lead–in
Books closed. Either show students two flashcards or project two photos onto the screen, e.g. a doctor in a hospital and a gardener. Write the following expressions on the board:
Both pictures show …
In the first picture …, whereas in the second picture …
I get the impression …
I expect …
He/She probably …
I doubt that …
Perhaps …
He/She might/may …

Ask students what they think the people in the flashcards might find difficult about their lifestyles. Explain that they should use the expressions on the board. Elicit answers from various students. At this stage, don't overload them with too much language: contrasting linkers such as *however, while* etc can be introduced later on in the course.

1 Books open. Students read the instructions and the How to go about it and Useful Language boxes. Explain that in the exam, Student A talks for one minute and Student B for about 30 seconds. However, as this is their first experience you can allow them longer.
Students carry out the speaking task using photos 1 and 2 on page 6. Remind them to mention a few of the topics such as daily routine, working hours, etc. Circulate and check students are following the instructions correctly.

2 Students switch roles and carry out the same speaking task, using photos 3 and 4 on page 7. To get some feedback, ask students which lifestyle they chose when they were Student B. Ask some pairs how they feel they performed in this speaking task.

Reading and Use of English
Part 7
Multiple matching
Page 8

This reading continues the theme of lifestyles, using the same jobs as those in the photos on pages 6 and 7. Present tenses, frequency adverbs and the uses of *get* are introduced in a natural way. It provides a springboard for students to talk about their own routines and lifestyles (allowing them to get to know each other as they begin the course). It also links well to the writing task in the review section on page 17, so you could set this writing task for homework.

Lead–in
Write the following words on the board in random order: *craftspeople, rehearse, farm, port, mug, scripts, lambs, crew*. Ask students to match them with the jobs that are represented in the photos.
Pre-teaching vocabulary in this way is a confidence-building activity in the first few classes, but students should gradually be weaned off this as

the course progresses and encouraged to guess unknown words by using contextual clues.

Students read the instructions and the How to go about it box. This is designed to help them with their first multiple matching task. On the next occasion they see this task type, in Unit 5, this advice is summarized in a Don't forget! box.

Once students have read the information in the box, ask them to close their books and summarize the suggested procedure orally with their partner. After this, mention that the text contains distractors and that the students need to read carefully to check that the answers they choose are correct.

Before they do the reading task, check their understanding of the following items of vocabulary in the questions: *untidy* (1), *unpredictable* (3), *keen on* (4). Ask: *What's another way of saying a person is untidy?* (e.g. *not well organized/disorganized*).

If students ask you for the meaning of other vocabulary during the reading activity, encourage them to try and answer the questions without trying to understand every word.

Have class feedback and if students have made mistakes, show the importance of noticing and avoiding distractors, e.g.
B *I would crawl out of bed in the morning and go straight into the garage, which I'd converted into a studio.*
(does not have to go far to get to their place of work)
C *So now I don't get as much exercise as I'd like to.*
(is not particularly keen on taking exercise)
D *I get lonely if I'm away from her for longer than a week or so.*
(used to feel lonely while working)

Alternative approach
If you would like to make the reading more communicative, you could start the activity by asking students to work in groups of four. Each student reads one of the texts and then gives an oral summary of the information to their group.

Answers

Question 4 is answered by the underlined parts in Text A.

Questions **1** and **7** are the other questions answered in Text A. See key below.

1 A *at home there are usually scripts lying all over the place. It's a bit of a mess, I'm ashamed to say.*

2 D *… I can't see myself in any other profession. There's nothing else I'd rather do.*

3 C *I love my job, especially the variety and not knowing what you'll be doing from one day to the next.*

4 A *I'll sometimes go for a run after I get up, though it's not really my idea of fun. None of that fitness business is …*

5 B *I have to get up early and my morning routine is dull and conventional, the same one that's played out in millions of households.*

6 D *My flat overlooks the port, so it's just a short walk to the Ellie May.*

7 A *I always fall asleep as soon as my head hits the pillow.*

8 B *Working at home was such a solitary business and I hated the fact that I would often go for days without speaking to anyone.*

9 C *But being a vet – any type of vet – is not what people think it is. It's not all cuddly lambs and cute little pigs. We have to do some pretty unpleasant things sometimes …*

10 B *I often get to bed later than I would like.*

Reacting to the text

Students discuss the question in pairs. You could finish the activity by telling the class which person you would like to change places with yourself.

Language focus 1: Habitual behaviour

Page 10

A General tendencies

1 When students have read about *tend to* in the Grammar reference on page 209, explain that the structure *used to* + infinitive can only be used for past habits and states which no longer occur or exist now. Stress that we use *usually* with the present simple for present habits. In monolingual

classes, you could ask a student to translate the following sentences:

I usually play tennis twice a week.
I used to play tennis when I was a child.

Answers

use to be

2 Students work in pairs. If your students are fairly strong, they could respond orally. However, if they are weaker, they should write the three statements. Elicit statements from various pairs.

B Frequency adverbs

1a Write the following on the board:
Position of adverbs
1 before the main verb
2 after the verb to be
3 after the auxiliary
Ask students to read the sentences in the book and to match each one with one of the rules on the board. Elicit answers.

1b Note that the adverbs at either end of the scale – (*almost*) *always, rarely, seldom, hardly ever, never* – cannot be placed before the subject in this way.

Answers

1
a immediately before the main verb; after the auxiliary verb and the verb *to be*
b *always* and *never* are incorrectly placed

2 Students do the exercise as suggested. Remind them to use the Grammar reference on page 209. Elicit answers from various students.

Answers

1 correct
2 I usually have my dinner in front of the television.
3 I never spend more than ten minutes doing my English homework.
4 correct
5 I hardly ever play computer games – I prefer reading.
6 correct

3 Ask students to work in pairs. Encourage them to add some extra information to each of their sentences. Their partner could also ask some follow-up questions, e.g. *Where do you normally go? Do you usually go out with your friends or members of your family?* Circulate and help students to self-correct any errors with the use of the adverbs. You could also ask more questions related to the statements and tell them something about yourself. Have class feedback in which you mention some interesting information you have heard about various students.

C *Used to* and *would*

1 Write on the board: *I would crawl out of bed and go straight into the garage.* Ask students what time this is referring to. Elicit that it is a past habit. Ask students whether the sentence could be expressed in a different way. Elicit *used to crawl*.
Focus students' attention on the sentences in the book. Students answer the question. Remind them to refer to the Grammar reference on page 209. Elicit the answer.

Answers

Would + infinitive can refer to past habits, but not states. It is not used with stative verbs such as *have* to refer to the past.

2 Before students do the task, instruct them to read the text quickly to find out how this family's life has changed. Then focus students' attention on the instructions and read the first sentence in the text together. Elicit the answer. Ask students to complete the exercise. Correct the exercise together.

Answers

1 b 2 a 3 a 4 a 5 b 6 c 7 b 8 c 9 c
10 a

3 Write two sentences on the board about things which have changed in your life over the past five years, using *would* and *used to*, e.g. *I used to live in a really small flat, but I have moved to a bigger place outside the city. I would have breakfast in a café near my flat every morning before going to work.*

Ask students to write similar sentences about themselves. Circulate and check that they are using the structures correctly. Then get some feedback by asking a few students to read out one or two of their sentences. Encourage the other students to think of some follow-up questions about the changes in their lives.

Vocabulary 2: *Get*   Page 11

This is the first of a number of sections on verbs which have a variety of different meanings. Other verbs include *take* (Unit 4), *give* (Unit 9), *put* (Unit 11), *make* and *do* (Unit 14). These verbs are common in English and often tested in the *First* exam.

1a Do the exercise as suggested in the book.

Alternative approach
Students work in groups of three. Explain that they are going to have a race to try to remember which of the people from the reading text on pages 8 and 9 said each sentence. Explain that if they can't remember, they should look at the texts. Set a time limit of three minutes. The team with the most correct answers is the winner.

Answers

b	the actor	c	the farm vet
d	the fisherman	e	the potter
f	the actor	g	the fisherman
h	the potter		

1b Students work in pairs. Elicit answers from various students.

Answers

b	get up	c	do exercise
d	become/grow lonely	e	catch the train
f	arrive at/reach the theatre	g	makes us do
h	receive requests/am asked		

Learner training
For homework, suggest that students record these meanings of *get* in their vocabulary notebooks. Considering the meaning of the whole phrase with *get* (and similar verbs) is a useful tool when paraphrasing. Paraphrasing is important in all papers of the *First* exam.

2 This exercise is similar to Reading and Use of English Part 1 in that students have to choose the correct answer from four options.
Do exercise 2 as suggested. When students have finished, ask which sentence the picture is related to, then elicit the answers to the questions from various students.

Answers		
1 touch	**2** chance	**3** paid
4 ready	**5** trouble	**6** over
7 by	**8** on	

3 Students discuss the questions in pairs. Explain that they will have to answer similar questions in Parts 1 and 4 of the Speaking exam.

You could ask students the difference between *anger* and *angry (anger* is the noun, *angry* is the adjective*).* Circulate as the students speak and record any common errors. Write these on the board after the activity and elicit the corrections from various students.

Some of these questions link in well to the writing task in the Review section on page 17.

Vocabulary 3: Clothes   Page 12

Lead–in

Ask students the type of clothes people wear in their country for weddings, work, in their free time, or for different professions.

1 Focus students' attention on the photos. Ask them to work in pairs and to write down the items of clothing. Elicit answers from the whole class.

Answers
1 hat, top hat, suit, jacket, tie, shirt, jeans, trainers, dress

2 Students work in pairs. Monolingual dictionaries could be used. Mention that some of the adjectives can not only be used to describe clothes, but also people and hair, e.g. *scruffy, trendy.* Circulate and if students ask the meaning of a word, encourage another student from a different pair to give a definition. Model and check pronunciation of *unfashionable, scruffy* and *casual.*

Answers
Possible answers:
1 formal, smart
2 scruffy, casual, baggy (jeans), plain (shirt)
3 colourful, sleeveless (dress)

Additional activity

After this activity, get students to play a descriptions game. Organize students into A/B pairs. Student A

describes the clothes of a student in the class and student B has to guess who they are describing. Then they swap roles.

 **Multiple matching**
Page 12

Ask students to read the exam instructions, then focus their attention on the What to expect in the exam box. Ask a few general comprehension questions, e.g. *What should you do during the 30 seconds before listening to the piece? What are distractors?*

Prediction

1–2 Students do exercises 1 and 2 as suggested in the Coursebook.

Answers
A a wedding: guest, witness, priest, best man, in a church, in a registry office
B a birthday party: guest, host, at home, in a disco
C a classical ballet: audience, ballerina, dancer, director, in a concert hall, in an opera house
D a sporting event: spectator, competitor, star, opponent, in a stadium, at a sports centre
E a film premiere: star, audience, director, producer, at a cinema
F an examination: candidate, invigilator, in an examination hall
G a job interview: candidate, interviewer, panel, in an office or other place of work
H a special family meal: guest, host, relative, relations, in-laws, at home, in a restaurant

3 Students work in pairs and have short conversations about each occasion. For example,
A: *If I was going to a wedding I would buy an expensive dress. I would probably wear high-heeled shoes.*
B: *Really? I wouldn't wear high-heeled shoes, because I like dancing and I'd be uncomfortable.*

Listening task

Play the recording twice and let students compare their answers together after the first listening. Explain that they should briefly discuss what they heard if their answers are different.

After they have listened a second time, ask students

what made them choose their answers, in order to see if they can distinguish between the distractors and clues. This will also follow up the prediction work done in the pre-listening stage.

Possible distractors are:

wedding: *trainers and sports top*

birthday: *costume, Coco the clown*

interview: *examination results, serious candidate*

sporting event: *French star, stars of the silent movies, long heavy dresses*

The post-listening question provides an opportunity for personalization. Students work in pairs and discuss the question. Get some brief class feedback.

Point out that the listening script includes language covered in the unit. Draw students' attention to the listening script on page 222 and ask them to work in pairs to underline some examples.

Answers

1 A **2** F **3** D **4** G **5** B (C, E and H not used)

Listening 1: Listening script 1.1–1.5

Speaker 1

After we got the invitation, my mum and I kept having huge rows about what I was going to wear for the big event. She's always criticizing me for my taste in clothes and she'd bought me this long, bright red dress to wear on the day. Of course, I refused. I went instead in a short black skirt, trainers and a sports top, thinking I'd look really cool and trendy. But of course, when we got to the church and I saw all the other guests in their smart new clothes and expensive hats, I just felt really, really stupid and embarrassed. The bride and groom looked quite surprised when they saw me, so I spent most of the time at the reception trying to avoid them.

Speaker 2

We really had no other option but to send her home to get changed, dye her hair back and take out the nose stud. We have rules and the rules are there to prepare young people for the reality of the world of work. I don't know of many jobs where you could turn up with scruffy old clothes, green hair and a pierced nose. We insist on uniform from the first day until the last, and that includes when sitting exams. It's unfair on other candidates who respect the regulations, and distracting for them at a time when they need maximum concentration.

Speaker 3

... Indeed attitudes were already beginning to change in the first half of the century. In 1919, the young French star Suzanne Lenglen caused a sensation at the British championships by wearing a calf-length, sleeveless dress. Her unconventional, yet practical clothing shocked spectators, who were used to seeing women play in the long heavy dresses which were typical of that period. As a result, Lenglen attracted the kind of

attention from the world's press which was normally reserved for the stars of the silent movies. She silenced her critics, however, by beating her opponents and going on to win several major titles.

Speaker 4

He clearly has ability. You only have to look at his examination results to see that. And he used to live in France, which means he probably wouldn't mind changing countries, if we needed him to. No, what concerns me is his appearance. If he's prepared to turn up for something as important as this, wearing what can only be described as casual clothes, what would he be like with our clients? If he really is a serious candidate and we decide to take him on, then he will have to get used to wearing something a little more formal.

Speaker 5

They had to have their little joke, didn't they. 'Jane's having a little celebration at her house for her "coming of age" and she wants everyone to go in fancy dress.' That's what they said. So I thought about it for ages, what I was going to go as and everything. I spent more time thinking about my costume than about what present I was going to get for Jane. Of course, when I turned up at the house dressed as Coco the Clown and everybody else was wearing normal clothes, I don't know who was more surprised, me or Jane.

Additional activity 1

As a post-listening activity, ask students to work in groups of three. Explain that they are going to describe a true or invented situation in which someone's appearance caused them embarrassment. The other students in their group can ask some follow-up questions and decide whether they believe the situation or not.

Additional activity 2

As a post-listening activity, divide students into groups of three. Write the following on the board:

party clothes to the First exam

formal clothes to a football match

a Dracula fancy dress outfit to a wedding

Students should choose one situation each and then invent information to explain why they wore these clothes to the occasion. After the activity they should vote which story was best.

Learner training

Suggest students record some of the vocabulary from the Prediction section in their vocabulary notebooks. You could also model and check the word stress of the following words.

spectator competitor candidate invigilator opponent

Language focus 2: *Be used to, get used to* and *used to* Page 13

1–3 Students work through exercises 1–3 in pairs. Get whole-class feedback.

Answers

1 **1** a **2** b **3** a

2 *Be used to* + -*ing*/noun in the affirmative describes the state in which one no longer finds situations new or strange, e.g. *I am used to the heat* means 'it is no problem for me now'.

Get used to + -*ing*/noun in the affirmative describes the process of reaching normality with a new or strange situation, e.g. *I am getting used to the heat* means 'it is less of a problem for me now than before'.

3 the gerund

Additional activity

The differences between *used to*, *be used to* and *get used to* can be an area of confusion for some students, so you may need to give some further examples. If so, write the following on the board:

1 I've just started working as a nurse and I'm finding it hard to get used to working at night.

2 I have lived in Spain for six years so I am used to eating late in the evening.

3 I used to work in a bank.

Ask students in which sentence:

used to refers to a past state or habit; (3)

the speaker no longer finds the situation new or strange; (2)

the speaker is in the process of adapting to a new situation. (1)

If you have a monolingual class, you could ask students to translate the expressions.

4 If your students are strong you should do this activity orally as suggested in the book. However, if your students are weaker ask them to write out the sentences. Circulate and check students understand the structure. Elicit examples from various students.

5a Find out if any of your students have been to Britain. Elicit one or two aspects of life that they might find difficult to get used to. Then ask them to think of other examples in pairs.

5b Students follow the instructions. Explain that reading through exercises like this to get their general meaning is a good habit to acquire for many sections of the *First* exam.

5c Read through the instructions together and check students understand that some of the gaps can be left blank. Students complete the exercise in pairs. Circulate and help them with any problems.

Elicit answers from various students. If they are still having problems you could ask concept questions for the ones they got wrong, e.g.

Did he find the habit of eating at 1pm strange?

Was cooking for himself one of his past habits?

Does he still find English food strange?

In a monolingual class you could ask students who have grasped the concepts to translate certain expressions for their peers.

Answers

1 get, having	**2** – , cook	**3** is, eating
4 – , write	**5** get, being	**6** be, driving
7 get, driving		

5d Students discuss the question in groups of three. If you have a multilingual class, put students from different countries into each group as this will make the discussion more interesting. Give them some general categories (e.g. *times, food, people's character, transport, relationships*) to help them develop their discussions.

 DVD Resource: Unit 1

Additional activity

As this area of grammar is a complicated one, you should recycle the structures in future classes. One way of doing this is to prepare envelopes with cut up cards. Write a sentence with an error on each numbered card and stick a piece of paper with the correct answers on the back of the envelope. Hand out the envelopes to pairs of students and have them discuss what they think the error is in each sentence. They can then check their answers on the back of the envelope.

You should save these envelopes as they can be reused closer to the exam along with envelopes on other topics which you prepare during the course. If other teachers in your school are teaching the same level you could prepare them as a team and share them.

Writing **Informal letter**
Part 2 Page 14

This section is intended as an introductory training exercise for writing informal letters in Part 2 of the Writing paper. The language presented and information given is also relevant to emails. In the exam, students would read a short extract of a letter, rather than a whole letter, as in this writing section. (Students have exam-style practice of writing informal letters or emails in Unit 7). Notice that the letter includes language from the unit. This will allow students to see structures such as *get used to, getting late, tend to* etc in a natural context.

1 Students do exercise 1 as suggested in the book. Elicit answers from various students. You could also ask some further questions as a way of recycling language studied in the unit, e.g.
How does he feel about milking the cows?
How do they normally spend the day after breakfast?
What time of day did he write the letter?

Answers
Mark wants to know how I am settling in to the new house. He wants to know if I can help him in the summer.

2 Students very often have problems organizing their written work into paragraphs. This section ensures that the purpose of paragraphing and its importance is focused on from the start of the course.
Students do the exercise in pairs. Elicit answers from various students.

Answers
Paragraph 2: to describe how he spends a typical day
Paragraph 3: to give news and invite you to visit
Paragraph 4: to finish and ask for a reply

3 Ask students to read the instructions. Check they understand that three expressions cannot be used. Mention that *Yours sincerely* is used when we know the name of the person and *Yours faithfully* when we use *Dear Sir/Madam.*

Answers	
2	a
3	no, because this expression is too formal
4	c
5	g
6	no, too formal
7	no, too formal
8	d
9	b
10	f

Exam note
It is important that students are aware of appropriate register or level of formality when they are writing. A common problem is for students to misuse or mix the use of formal and informal expressions. Candidates lose marks if they do this.

4 Students do exercise 4 as suggested.

Answers		
1 while	2 as	3 and/so, as well
4 but	5 so	

5 Ask students to read the instructions and to underline the key information they will need to include in their letter. Then focus their attention on the How to go about it box and ask a few questions, e.g. *How could you begin your letter? Should your letter be formal or informal? How should your letter be organized?* Then get students to work in pairs and brainstorm ideas for their letters. Finish by asking a few questions, e.g.
Where is your new house? What's it like? How are you settling in? Is there anything you are finding hard to get used to? What do you do on a typical day?

Suggest they look at the model of an informal letter on page 197 before writing their own.

Sample answer
Dear Mark,
I'm writing to you to tell you that I'm not going to go to your farm in summer because of my new work. However, I'll try to see you as soon as possible.

As you know, I moved to a new house six months ago and since then I've met new people. |

I think that living there is better than I thought and with regard to my new surroundings I must say that they are excellent. I usually get up at half past seven and I went to work. Then I have a breakfast with my friends and I go to improve my English spoken in the afternoon in a specific classe. In the evening, I'm used to going to the cinema because here it's cheaper.

After all, I think is good have a new experience in your life and this is an example to explain it. As far as I'm concerned, I don't know if I'll have to return to my city, but it doesn't matter so much in these moments.

I hope you write me as you did.

All the best,
Luis
186 words

Examiner's comment

Content: Adequate coverage of points.

Communicative achievement: Register is awkward at times – *with regard to my new surroundings* (too formal for the context), and some confusion is evident in the use of *After all* and *As far as I'm concerned*. The overall effect on the target reader would be reasonably positive: the information asked for has been provided and the tone, although inconsistent at times, would not cause problems.

Organization: An abrupt beginning but the letter is organized into paragraphs. Successful use of simple sequencing in the third paragraph – *then, in the afternoon/evening*.

Language: Errors do not obscure communication, but they may distract the reader – *I'm used to going to the cinema* is not appropriate here, the use of *went* instead of *go* in the third paragraph, the omission of the subject in *I think is good* are some examples of inaccuracies. Vocabulary is generally appropriate except for *a breakfast, a specific classe*. Tenses are generally correct – *since then I've met new people*.

Mark*: Good pass

*Note on marking

Each of the four categories is awarded a mark out of 5. These marks are then added up to give a total score out of 20.

For the purposes of this course, the sample answers have been graded according to the following scale: **borderline**, **pass**, **good pass**, and **very good pass**.

Learner training

You might want to set up a correction system. Explain that when students do writing tasks you will use correction symbols in your feedback. These will help them to work out the correct language for themselves. Make a worksheet with different types of errors, e.g. word form, preposition, verb tense etc and decide on your symbols, e.g. word form – WF. Get students to correct the errors and to record the symbols in their notes. When you give them back their first writing task, they should refer to the symbols and try to correct their own work.

 Listening 2 Part 1

Multiple choice
Page 15

Refer students to the instructions and the What to expect in the exam box. Play the recording twice and let students compare their answers after the first listening.

Additional activity

After this you could refer students to the listening script on page 222 and ask them to underline distractors and circle the parts which give them the answers. This will enable you to highlight how distractors are used to make the task more challenging.

Answers
1 C **2** B **3** B **4** C **5** A **6** A **7** B **8** A

Listening 2: Listening script 1.6–1.13

1 You hear two people talking about a friend of theirs.

M = Man   W = Woman

M: How many houses has Mike got now?

W: Four I think. This one here, the flat in Brighton, the country cottage, and …

M: … and the villa in Spain.

W: That's right.

M: Hmm. Easy for some, isn't it?

W: I'm not so sure. I get the impression he's a bit fed up with it all – always moving around. I wouldn't be surprised if he got rid of everything over here and lived in Spain permanently.

M: Is that what he's said he'll do?

W: Well, you know Mike. It's not like him to talk much about his plans. But he did say he might settle down one day – stay in one place. And you know how much he likes Spain.

2 You overhear a man talking to a friend on his mobile phone.

I'm stressed out, to be honest, what with work and the problems with the house and everything. I need to do something to help me relax … Well, I wanted to do yoga, but the class is on Friday and I play squash then. And then I saw they do Pilates on Tuesdays and Thursdays, which would be ideal for me … I know. You did it for a couple of years, didn't you? … So anyway, I was wondering if you could tell me what it was like, what sort of things you did. I had a look on the Internet, but it's always better to talk to someone with first-hand experience.

3 You hear a woman talking about her family's financial situation.

We just about get by, but it's always a struggle to get to the end of the month. Frank – my husband – hasn't had a job for over a year and I've got the two children to look after. Frank said he'll look after the kids and I can go out and look for work. Trouble is, he's useless around the house and he can't cook to save his life. But there's no alternative, really. Both our mums aren't very well these days, so we can't get either of them to come and help out. And we haven't got any family jewels we can sell. So, this weekend I'll be teaching Frank to cook and writing a few application letters.

4 You overhear a man and a woman talking about their morning routine.

W = Woman   M = Man

W: Don't you just hate it when the alarm goes off in the morning?

M: I usually wake up before the alarm goes off. I'm an early riser.

W: That sounds worse. Aren't you tired for the rest of the day?

M: No, I just don't need to sleep so much. I take the dog out for a walk, talk to him about this and that …

W: You talk to your dog?

M: Sure. Much easier than talking to people – he doesn't answer back or ask questions, like people do. I find that much harder to cope with first thing in the morning. I'm the same in the car – most people can't stand the journey to work, but I have a good old chat with myself.

W: Weird.

5 You hear a woman on the radio talking about her experiences in a foreign country.

On my travels, I've got used to eating all sorts of weird and wonderful things, so I was prepared for things like fried insects and scorpions. I don't particularly like them, but I'll eat them if I have to. And it's very hot and humid there, so I was also ready for the rather slow pace of life and relaxed way they go about doing things, like work, for example. What I wasn't expecting was the way they dress

out there. In my experience it's unusual for people in that part of the world to take so much care over what they wear. Colour, style, fashion – it all mattered to them. I was positively scruffy by comparison.

6 You turn on the radio and hear the following.

The world today is faster and more dynamic than when our great-grandparents were alive, but as a result, life is often more stressful and unhealthy. Self-help books offer people the hope of finding a solution to their problems, improving their health and well-being, and generally making their lives better. The author of *Back to basics* says his book will help you achieve all these things in a matter of weeks. He's lying – the only thing it's good for is sending you to sleep, and you'd be wasting your money if you bought it, and your time if you read it.

7 You hear two people talking about the village they both live in.

M = Man   W = Woman

M: Are you enjoying it here in the village?

W: Yes, I am. I think I know nearly everyone now. When I came here last year everyone went out of their way to introduce themselves and make me feel welcome.

M: That's good. So you feel comfortable here, then?

W: Yes, I do. And the children have settled in well, too. I just get a bit nervous about the traffic sometimes.

M: What, on the main road?

W: Yes, and a couple of other spots as well. There are certain places I won't let the children go without me. Some drivers just don't slow down for them.

8 You hear a man talking about his job.

I don't get to wear a uniform – you know, with a cap and all, like they do at some of the other hotels, but I do wear a suit. A decent one – tailor made – not just any old suit. Inside, at the front desk – in reception – they reckon I look smarter than the boss. I'm not so sure about that, but I do like to look good for the guests – I'm the first person they see before they go into the hotel. And I've got this long black overcoat, as well – it can get pretty cold standing outside on the steps in winter, I can tell you.

Learner training

The Workbook can be used in a number of ways. Set activities for homework as you cover various sections of the unit or get students to complete the corresponding unit of their Workbook at the end of each unit in the Coursebook. Explain that they should correct the Workbook themselves and ask you if they have any questions. Whichever method you choose, it's a good idea to ask students to bring in the Workbooks so that you can check they are up to date. Try to keep a record of the units each student has done.

Review 1 Answers Pages 16–17

Reading and Use of English — Part 4

Transformations

1 getting rid of
2 got used to wearing
3 always borrowing my things without
4 is/'s unusual for Simon to
5 not/n't like Helen to be
6 looking forward to seeing

Vocabulary

A Adjectives

2 high-heeled 3 tight-fitting 4 sleeveless
5 baggy 6 long-sleeved

B Expressions crossword

Across
1 thanks 5 forward 8 way
9 love 12 taken
Down
2 know 7 better 11 hear

Expressions with *get*

Across
3 rid 4 on 10 touch
13 paid
Down
1 trouble 3 ready 6 dressed

C People

1 e 2 f 3 a 4 b 5 d 6 c

1 competitor, spectators 2 host, guests
3 bride, groom 4 audience, performers
5 doctor, patient 6 candidates, invigilator

Each unit in the Coursebook has a review section. As this is the first unit, some activities are suggested below. These are designed to give you ideas on how to exploit future reviews.

Additional activities

Transformations Page 16

As this is the first example of a transformations exercise you could do it in class rather than for homework. Ask students to read the instructions and the What to expect in the exam box. You could ask a few comprehension questions. For example, *Can you change the form of the word given in the answer sentence?* (No)

How many words should you use? (between two and five words)
What does 'paraphrase' mean? (to express the same idea using different words)
What aspects of English are tested in transformation? (grammar, vocabulary and collocation)
Students complete the exercise. Elicit answers from various students and go over any problem areas.

Vocabulary A, B and C Pages 16 and 17

Make the review into a class quiz. Ask students to close their books. Divide them into groups of three. Get each group to think of a name, e.g. *The Smart team*, *The Clever Kids*, etc.
Each team uses a piece of paper as a score sheet to write down their answers. Explain that they are allowed a little time to confer for each question. At the end of the quiz, teams swap score sheets. Go through the answers as a class. Count the scores to find the winner. Bring some sweets as a prize.

After the quiz ask students to complete the exercises in the review section for homework.

Part 1 of quiz (A Adjectives)

Write *DRESS* on the board and ask:
Which of the following words does not normally collocate with *dress*?
evening afternoon fancy
You may need to repeat the words. Allow teams some time to confer. Continue by asking about the remaining collocations.

Part 2 of quiz (B Expressions crossword)

Explain that the teams must guess the missing word in sentences related to letter writing. Read out the clues, substituting a 'beep' for the gap. For example,
1 Many (beep) for your letter.
2 I'm looking (beep) to hearing from you.
Allow time between questions for the teams to confer.

Part 3 of quiz (C People)

Give students definitions for the twelve items of vocabulary in Exercise C. The teams must guess what the word is in each case.
1 What do you call a person who watches students during an exam to check they don't cheat? (invigilator)
2 What do you call someone who has guests to their house? (host)

As pronunciation is marked in the Speaking exam, you could also add a few activities like the ones below.

Part 4 of the quiz: Pronunciation from Unit 1
Word stress
Write the following sets of words on the board and ask: *Which is the odd one out?*

0	celebrity	luxurious	variety	information
1	comfortable	maintenance	candidate	opponent
2	spectators	teenager	sedentary	villages
3	candidate	exciting	relaxing	museums

Ask students to look at the sets of words and to decide which word in each group has different word stress. Do the example (0) together: *information* is the odd one out, because the stress is on the third syllable.
Allow time for the teams to confer.
Answers:
1 opponent   2 spectators   3 candidate

Part 5 of the quiz: Pronunciation from Unit 1
Phonemes
Write the following on the board and ask: *Which is the odd one out?*

0	they	day	village
1	chaotic	daily	active
2	buy	quiet	advertisement
3	busy	cottage	scruffy

Ask students to look at the sets of words on the board and to decide which word in each group has a different phoneme. Do the example (0) together: *village* is the odd one out, because the *a* is pronounced /ɪ/.
Answers:
1 active /æ/   2 advertisement /ɪ/   3 scruffy /ʌ/

2 High energy

Content Overview

Themes

The unit deals with the themes of entertainment, music and sport. The listening and reading materials provide a contextualized source for the grammar and vocabulary which will be focused on in the unit.

Exam-related activities

Reading and Use of English

Part 6	Gapped text
Part 3	Word formation (Review)

Writing

Part 2	Letter of application
Part 2	Article

Listening

Part 2	Sentence completion
Part 4	Multiple choice

Other

Language focus 1:	Indirect ways of asking questions
Language focus 2:	Gerunds and infinitives
Vocabulary 1:	Music
Vocabulary 2:	Sport
Word formation:	Affixes

Reading and Speaking   Pages 18 and 19

Lead–in

Books closed. Ask students what shows are on in town at the moment and whether they have been to one recently. Get them to describe what it was like. Books open. Focus students' attention on the photos and ask them which show looks the most original. Let students read the instructions and then brainstorm a few expressions for making suggestions, agreeing and disagreeing, e.g. *Would you like to go … / What about … / I don't really want to … / Yes, that's a good choice.* Write the expressions on the right-hand side of the board and do not rub them off as you will need to refer to them later in the lesson.

Students carry out the speaking and reading task. As feedback, ask various pairs which show they chose. You could also ask if they have ever been in a musical and get them to describe their experience.

Vocabulary 1: Music

1a Elicit the names of the musical instruments in the photos and write them on the board. Mention that *fiddle* is a less formal term for a *violin*. Model and check pronunciation of *violin, viola, cello* etc.

Answers

violin, cello, drums

1b This task focuses on common music-related collocations. Circulate and monitor the activity. Have class feedback. Highlight the word stress of *vocalist, guitarist, record, performance* and *percussion*.

Point out that when *record* is a verb the word stress changes to *record*.

Answers

1	lead	2	a song	3	musician
4	on	5	play	6	live*
7	in	8	instrument		

*pronunciation /laiv/

2 This is a memory activity. Students try to remember the word combinations in exercise 1b.

Alternative activity

Make the exercise more competitive by dividing students into groups of three and asking them to try and memorize the combinations. Student A then acts as a referee, while students B and C close their books. Student A reads out one of the words, e.g. *talented*, and the first of the other two students to complete the phrase correctly scores a point. When students have completed the activity, have class feedback and ask various groups who the winner was.

You could also get students to work in pairs to write four questions using the vocabulary in exercise 1b. Then they ask another pair their questions.

3 This activity is similar to Part 3 of the Speaking exam, where students have to take part in a discussion with another candidate. It tests students' ability to talk about different possibilities, make suggestions, express opinions, give reasons and come to a final decision. Ask students to read the instructions. Check they understand *raise money, workshop* and *donate*. Focus students' attention on the expressions which you wrote on the board earlier in the lesson. Get them to add some more expressions, e.g. *Shall we …, Maybe you're right …, I think it might be better to …,* etc.

Tell students to start the speaking activity. Circulate and record any common errors. In class feedback, ask groups which two events they chose and why they chose them. Write a few of their errors on the board and correct them together.

Conclude the activity by asking if anyone has ever raised money for charity and having them explain how successful they were.

Listening 1

Part 2

Sentence completion
Page 19

This listening continues the theme of entertainment. The radio presenter gives a review of the four shows from the Reading and Speaking activity on pages 18 and 19.

1a When students have read the instructions and information, ask them to close their books. Explain that you are going to read out some statements related to the What to expect in the exam box and that they should work with their partner to decide whether they are true or false. As you read out each statement, allow a short time for students to confer. Ask one pair the answer and then continue with the next statement.

1 You need to write more than three words for each answer. (false)

2 You mustn't make any spelling mistakes. (false)

3 The words you read in the question may not be the same as the words you hear on the recording. (true)

4 The words you need to write are heard on the recording. (true)

5 If you hear information that fits the gap this will definitely be the answer. (false)

1b Ask students to do the exercise in pairs. Explain that this is useful practice for the exam, where they will be given 45 seconds to read the questions. They should use this time to predict the type of answers they will hear. You could write some expressions for hypothesizing on the board, e.g. *perhaps, maybe, it could be, it's probably,* etc.

1c Play the recording twice and let students compare their answers together between listenings.

Answers

1	whole family	**2**	Mexico
3	country and western	**4**	interval
5	1999	**6**	four/4 million
7	Photo/photo gallery	**8**	Rain/rain
9	bikes	**10**	excitement

Listening 1: Listening script 1.14

Hello, Jim Dunne here, with a look at what's on in the area this coming week. And I'm delighted to be able to tell you that *Pagagnini* is in town, with its own special mix of music and comedy. It's great fun and I can guarantee the whole family will enjoy watching these four guys. They play all those bits of classical music that everyone knows, but sometimes can't put a name to – and they have a laugh at the same time.

Pagagnini is actually based in Madrid, but the show tours a lot and I was lucky enough to see it last year with my wife and our two girls when we were in Mexico. They're a really versatile bunch of musicians. At one point, they start using their violins and cellos as guitars, mandolins and even percussion instruments. And they move away from classical into rock, blues and country and western. Very impressive and we're all looking forward to seeing them again. They're on stage for about ninety minutes, but it's a very intense hour and a half, I can tell you. It's exhausting just watching them, and they don't stop for an interval, either.

Now, for those of you who like Irish dancing there's *Rhythm of the Dance* at the Apollo Theatre. Most of you will know about *Riverdance*, which began way back in 1994 – at the Eurovision Song Contest in Dublin, curiously enough. But *Rhythm of the Dance* goes back a long way too. It started out just five years later in 1999 in Norway. It's a similar kind of thing: the traditional music, the step dancing and so on, but there's a theme running through it. It's a kind of history of the Irish Celts. I haven't seen it yet, but I certainly will do – they're clearly very popular. It says here in the publicity that *Rhythm of the Dance* has played to live audiences totalling well over four million in no fewer than forty-four countries. And if you want to find out more about the show, go to their website. There isn't any Reviews section to look at there, but if you click on where it says 'Photo gallery' you get a pretty good idea of what to expect.

Now, the circus is back in town. Not just any circus, but the hugely talented Cirque Éloize from Canada. They're at the Regent Theatre again. The show's called *iD* and it promises to be every bit as good as the one they put on the first time they were there. That one was called *Rain* – as in, the wet stuff that falls from the sky. And there was plenty of water on stage, as you'll remember if you went to see it.

Now I've been looking at the video for *iD* on the show's website and I can tell you it has a totally urban setting. There's hip-hop and breakdance, electronic music and rock, and some of the artists moving around the stage on bikes and Rollerblades™. There are no animals, and no clowns, either. It's not your traditional kind of circus. And judging from the press reviews, it's well worth going to see. One that I have here in front of me says that it's an excellent show, full of originality, energy and excitement.

And if you want even more energy, then those Australian tap dancers, the Tap Dogs are on their way. They'll be at the Orion from Wednesday …

2 Students discuss the question in pairs. Have class feedback and ask a few more questions, e.g. *Have your tastes in entertainment changed in the last five years? Is your country/region famous for any particular type of entertainment?*

Language focus 1: Indirect ways of asking questions   Page 20

Students will have the chance to put this language point into practice in the speaking task in exercise 4a and b. It will also be useful when writing formal letters.

1–3 By looking at the target language and transforming the question into a direct form, students should be able to deduce the rules for forming indirect questions. Mention that the expressions *I'd like to know/we'd be interested to know/I was wondering if* do not need a question mark. Ask them to work through exercises 1, 2 and 3 in pairs. Get class feedback after each of these exercises. In exercise 3, check students understand the meaning of *clown around* (do silly things in order to make people laugh). Circulate and help students with any problems they may have.

Answers

1

1 When did *Rhythm of the Dance* start performing?

2 Why do you call the show *iD*?

3 Are the Tap Dogs planning to come here?

2

a The auxiliary verbs *did* and *do* are not used in the indirect question form. *Start* changes to *started*; *call* does not change, as the second person present simple form is the same as the infinitive form.

b In the direct question form, the auxiliary verb comes before the subject (*Are the Tap Dogs planning …?*).
In the indirect form, the subject comes first, as in the normal word order for a statement (*the Tap Dogs are planning*).

c *If* (or *whether*) has to be added.

3
Possible answers:

a Could you explain why you are called 'Pagagnini'?

b I'd be interested to know when you started performing together.

c Could you tell me if/whether you have ever toured outside of Europe?

d Would you mind telling us what type of music you prefer playing?

e I was wondering if you could tell me how many hours you practise your instrument each day.

f We'd like to know if/whether you clown around when you're off stage as well.

4a Before preparing the roleplays, give an example to show students that they can invent information. Write an indirect question on the board, e.g.
We'd like to know if you have ever made a mistake on stage.
Get a student to ask you the question. Then give your answer, e.g.
Well, actually we've made a lot of mistakes, but the worst was when someone had dropped water on the stage and I slipped and ended up in the front seats of the theatre!
Students prepare their questions. They could refer to the listening script on page 223 for ideas.

4b Before students do the roleplay, brainstorm some expressions which are used for giving yourself time to think. Write the following jumbled expressions on the board and then elicit the correct expressions.
Think let me.
That's an question interesting.
I never have before thought about that.
Encourage students to use these expressions during the roleplay.

Alternative idea
Students work in pairs. They invent a music or dance group and brainstorm information about

themselves. After this they write the name and the type of group on a piece of paper. They pass this to another pair, who has to prepare interview questions. Encourage them to use indirect questions. Then the pairs interview each other.

Writing 1
Part 2
Letter of application
Page 20

Ask students if they have ever applied for a job. Discuss the typical information included in a letter of application.

1 Students work in pairs. Check they understand the meaning of *ignore*. Have class feedback on the candidate's suitability for the job. You could also ask whether the students would like to do the job in the advertisement and why they think they would or would not be suitable.

2–3 Students work through exercises 2 and 3 individually. Check answers as a whole class. Stress that using the correct register is very important in the *First* exam, so they should always think carefully about who the target reader is.

Answers

2

2   I have seen
3   I would like to apply
4   I have also been attending
5   I have no experience
6   a number
7   I feel
8   well-suited to
9   I would love to have the opportunity to
10 I look forward to hearing

3
Although, In addition, as

4 Students discuss the purpose of the paragraphs in pairs. Have class feedback.

Answers

Paragraph 2: relevant skills
Paragraph 3: relevant experience
Paragraph 4: suitability for the job

5 Students read the task. Check they understand the meaning of *volunteer*. Ask a few questions about the information in the How to go about it box on

page 202, e.g. *Should you write a plan? Can you invent information? How many paragraphs could you use? Should you use an informal style? What should you do when you have finished writing the letter?* Students make notes in pairs and write their letters for homework.

Sample answer

Dear Mr Groves,
I have seen your advertisement in the last edition of 'English News' and I would like to apply for the post of volunteer at the pop and rock festival.

After reading the advertisement, I think I have the relevent experience to work at the festival. I am in my first year in the university where, I study music. I play guitar, violin and drums and I am also a member of a rock band that last year my friends and I created.

Furthermore, I have some experience to work with people because I used to have a job as waitress in a busy music café. I enjoyed meeting different people and helping the public in general, and I learned a lot in this position.

I would love to have the opportunity to volunteer at the pop and rock festival. I feel I would be well-suited in this role and I would like to help other people enjoy music as I do. Finally, I believe I would learn a lot from hearing different bands stiles and this would benefit my study.

I look forward to hearing from you.

Yours sincerely,
Claudine Diallo
194 words

Examiner's comment
Content: All points covered and the writer builds on the information given, e.g. *I am also a member of a rock group, I used to have a job as a waitress, I would like to help other people enjoy music.*

Communicative achievement: Register is appropriately formal for a letter of application, and the writer would have a positive effect on the target reader.

Organization: The letter is well organized with suitable paragraphs and the writer uses linking devices, e.g. *After reading, Furthermore, finally.*

Language: Generally accurate. Grammatical errors do not obscure meaning, e.g. *I have some experience* *to work (of working) with people, work as (a) waitress, my study (studies).*

Punctuation and minor spelling mistakes do not distract the reader, e.g. *where, I study, relevant, stiles*. There is a good range of appropriate expressions and vocabulary for the task: *would like to apply for the post of, I used to have a job, opportunity to volunteer, I look forward to hearing, Yours sincerely, apply, drums, busy, well-suited*

Mark*: Very good pass

*Note on marking

Each of the four categories is awarded a mark out of 5. These marks are then added up to give a total score out of 20.

For the purposes of this course, the sample answers have been graded according to the following scale: **borderline**, **pass**, **good pass**, and **very good pass**.

Additional activity

In the next lesson, ask students to exchange their letters. After reading them, they prepare questions and interview each other for the position. Get some feedback from the students, and ask whether they would offer the job to their partner.

Reading and Use of English Part 6

Gapped text
Page 22

Lead–in

Books closed. Ask students what the most popular sport in their country is and whether they play or watch this sport. Ask if rugby is popular in their country. Books open. Focus students' attention on the photographs and elicit some vocabulary, e.g. *score, pass, tackle, goal, kick, team*, etc.

1 Students do exercise 1 in pairs. Have class feedback. Ask if they know anything about the origin of the game. (It started in 1823 when William Webb Ellis broke the rules of football at Rugby school by taking the ball in his arms and running with it.)

Point out that the reading is about Rugby Union, and not Rugby League. The two games are very similar but there are differences in some of the rules relating to tackles.

2 Students do exercise 2 as suggested. Have class feedback. Mention that reading the base text for gist is a good habit as it ensures they have a general idea of the text before doing the matching task.

3 Ask students to read the instructions and the How to go about it box. Mention that they should also check that the verb forms in the missing sentences agree with the ones in the base text. Suggest that they cross out the missing sentences as they choose them, so that they have fewer and fewer choices.

Then students do the reading task. If they ask you the meaning of specific vocabulary, encourage them to guess from context by reading what comes before and after the word. You could refer to the photos during the feedback as these illustrate many of the rules of rugby.

Answers
1 C   **2** F   **3** D   **4** A   **5** G   **6** E   B not used

Additional activity

Write up the following phrasal verbs from the text,

a *team up with* (line 9)

b *be made up of* (line 14)

c *run into* (line 22)

d *end up* (sentence E)

e *run out of* (sentence F).

Students work in pairs. Ask them to look at the phrasal verbs in context and to come up with a definition or a translation.

Answers

a join with other people in order to do something

b consist of; be composed of

c begin to experience

d be in a particular place, after or because of doing something

e use all of something so that none is left

Then ask students to write five sentences using the phrasal verbs, but putting a gap in each sentence in place of the verb. Make sure they jumble the phrasal verbs. Students pass their sentences to another pair who complete them. Students correct each other's sentences. Get feedback from the class and get students to read out some of their sentences.

For homework suggest that students add five words related to sport to their vocabulary notebooks.

Reacting to the text

Students work in pairs to discuss the questions. You could add an extra question, e.g. *How could a sport like rugby help people in other areas of their life, for example at school or work?*

Language focus 2: Gerunds and infinitives
Page 24

1 The language discussed in this section comes directly from the text students have been working on. Ask them to read the sentences and also to refer to the Grammar reference on pages 209–10. By doing this they should be able to work out the rules. You could also highlight examples in the Grammar reference of the gerund as a subject, object and complement.

Answers

a *to score*: the infinitive with *to* is used after certain adjectives, in this case, *hard*(er)
   Note the structure: adjective + *for* someone to do something
b *be done*: an infinitive without *to* because it follows a modal verb, in this case, *can*
   throwing: a gerund is used after a preposition, in this case, *by*
c *passing*: a gerund is used after certain verbs, in this case, *keep*
d *to look*: an infinitive with *to* is used after certain verbs, in this case, *need*

2 Students fill in the gaps and check them with the Grammar reference. Mention that *help* and *can't help* take different forms.

Answers

1 going, to meet
2 smiling, to hit
3 to enjoy, buying
4 to take, studying
5 to let, asking

3 When correcting this exercise, ask whether the sentences where more than one verb is possible change their meaning according to the form used. Give students examples of sentences to illustrate the other meaning of the verbs, e.g.

I stopped drinking coffee, because I could never sleep at night. (gave up)
I remember playing tennis with my grandfather. (recall)

I tried to learn all the new phrasal verbs, but it was impossible! (attempted)

If you have a monolingual class you could ask if the gerund and infinitive in these sentences is the same or different in their language, e.g. *try to do* and *try doing*.

Answers

1 to rain/raining
2 to have
3 to play/playing
4 run/to run
5 to drink
6 using

Additional idea

Students work in pairs. Draw the following table with the verbs on the board.

0	1	2
expect	promise	remember
hope	offer	begin
admit	refuse	forget
agree	finish	manage
3	4	5
want	keen on	can't afford
would like	interested in	can't imagine
feel like	tend to	can't help
decide	fond of	can't stand

Explain that in each of the groups, one of the verbs is grammatically different from the other three. Students decide whether the verbs take the gerund, the infinitive or both, in order to discover which verb is the odd one is out. Do the first one (0) together as an example: *admit* takes the gerund, whereas the others take the infinitive.

Explain that they can use the Grammar reference on pages 209–10 to help them.

Answers

1 finish (+ gerund)
2 manage (the others can take gerund or infinitive)
3 feel like (+ gerund)
4 tend to (+ infinitive)
5 can't afford (+ infinitive)

Learner training

Students find this grammar point tricky, so you will need to recycle it in future lessons.

Suggest that students divide one page of their vocabulary notebook into three columns. In each column they can make lists of verbs that take the gerund, infinitive or both.

4 Elicit the verbs at either end of the scale, then ask students to work in pairs to fill in the rest.

Answers
detest, hate, can't stand, don't like, don't mind, quite like, really enjoy, love, absolutely adore

5 Students do the exercise in pairs. Check that they understand the meaning of *keen* and *fond*.

Answers
interested *in*, fond *of*, good/bad *at*, bored *with*, excited *about*

6 Give the students some examples about yourself, e.g. *I'm really good at cooking curries. I can't stand getting up early in the morning. I started to learn Spanish when I was thirty.* Students then do the exercise individually.

7 Students read the instructions. Ask a student to read out one of the sentences they wrote in exercise 6, and elicit possible follow-up questions from other students. Then students do the exercise in pairs.

Additional activity

Students find prepositions hard to remember so you will need to recycle them frequently throughout the course. As students are writing their sentences in exercise 6, circulate and take some notes on what they have written, e.g. *Victor/fond of watching horror movies; Angela/bad at art*, etc. Keep this information, and in another lesson write a gap-fill where you personalize the sentences. It's more memorable if you write the opposite, e.g. *Angela is really good _____ art.* In the feedback you can ask her to correct the information and illustrate corrective stress, e.g. *No, I'm really **bad** at art.*

 DVD resource: Unit 2

Vocabulary 2: Sport
Page 25

Lead-in

Focus students' attention on the photos. Ask if their country has ever hosted an important sporting event. If so, find out how successful it was.

1 Students do exercise 1 in pairs. Remind them that they can refer back to the reading text on rugby. In feedback, model and practise the pronunciation of *opponent* and *obstacles*. You

could also ask some additional questions about the distractors, e.g.

In which sport do you fire something? (shooting)
In which sport do you use a stick to hit the ball? (hockey)
Which sport do you play on a court? (tennis/squash, etc)

Answers		
a kick, posts	**b** score	**c** passed
d pieces	**d** pitch	

2 Ask students if they do any of the sports in the pictures. They then do exercise 2 as suggested. In feedback, ask if they can work out any rules, e.g. *go* + gerund; *play* + sports with a ball; *do* + other sports.

In some languages it is correct to say *practise sport*. However, in English we say *do* or *play sport*. Explain that we *practise* one aspect of a sport in order to improve, e.g. *I spent the lesson practising my backhand.*

Answers	
do	gymnastics
go	skiing, cycling, swimming
play	volleyball, tennis, basketball, football, golf

3 Students work in groups of three. This will increase the chances of someone in the group knowing the vocabulary. If you have access to monolingual dictionaries, get students to look up the difficult words. This will give them useful practice of reading definitions and seeing the words in context. As you get feedback, ask if there are any words students are still not sure of, and elicit a definition or an example sentence with the word from the rest of the class.

Answers		
3a		
2 football	**3** golf	**4** skiing
5 athletics	**6** cycling	
3b		
1 service	**2** red card	**3** fairway
4 lift	**5** triple jump	**6** gears

4a Students work in pairs. Have class feedback. After this write *beat, win* and *draw* on the board and check students know the meaning.

beat + another player or team; *win* + a game/match/competition; *draw* = have the same score.

Answers					
1	take	**2**	beat	**3**	win
4	hit	**5**	take	**6**	draw

Additional idea
Do a short word stress activity. Draw the word stress table below on the board.

●●	●●●	●●●	●●●

Write *goggles, helmet, referee, peloton, saddle, opponent, racket, athletics* and *hockey* below the table, and ask students to put them into the correct word stress groups. Do an example first with the class. Circulate as students are doing the activity and model any words they are having problems with. Have class feedback and then choral drill the words. This will help with pronunciation and will also help students remember the new words.

Answers

●●	●●●	●●●	●●●
racket	referee	peleton	opponent
goggles			athletics
saddle			
helmet			
hockey			

4b After correcting the exercise, ask which member of their group knew the most about sport.

Answers
1 ice hockey, figure skating, curling
2 Spain
3 silver
4 tennis, badminton, squash
5 five
6 none

5 Students do the roleplay as suggested.

Alternative activity
Students play a yes/no game in groups of three. Student A thinks of a sport. Students B and C ask questions, e.g. *Do you use a ball? Is it a team game? Do you need a racket? Do you usually wear white shorts and a T-shirt?* Student A answers *yes* or *no* until either Student B or C guesses the sport.

Students change roles until each student has had a chance to think of a sport.

Learner training
Remind students to add some of the sports vocabulary to their vocabulary notebooks with either a definition, a translation or an example sentence.

 **Listening 2** Part 4 — **Multiple choice** Page 26

1 Focus students' attention on the photos of strange sports. Students work in pairs. Explain that they must hypothesize about what the contestants have to do, and that they will have to speak for a full minute. Brainstorm useful expressions, e.g. *they might be, must be, could be, it looks as if they are, maybe,* etc. One student in each pair then speaks for a minute. If you have access to the Internet in the classroom, start the activity and time it using a stop watch on the computer screen. If not, you can use the alarm on a mobile phone. Time a second minute for the other student in each pair to speak. In feedback, ask what ideas they came up with and how well they think they performed. Mention that they will have to keep talking for this length of time in Part 1 of the Speaking exam.

2 Ask students to read the instructions and the What to expect in the exam box. Elicit the correct answer (A). Suggest that they underline the key words in the questions or sentence beginnings before listening, as this will help them focus on the information they need to listen for. Do the first question as an example. After they have read the questions ask if there is any vocabulary they don't understand. Possible words might be *skilled, breath, fitness, wrestling.* Encourage students who know the words to give a definition to those who don't. Play the recording twice and let students compare their answers after the first listening.

Answers
1 A **2** B **3** B **4** C **5** C **6** B **7** A

Listening 2: Listening script 1.15

M = Mike Taylor   I = Interviewer

I: Octopushing, elephant polo, ice racing or cheese rolling. Our sports correspondent, Mike Taylor, has been finding out about some of the world's strangest sports. Which is the most unusual one for you, Mike?

M: Well, I think it has to be chess boxing, because it's such a bizarre combination. A match starts off with a four-minute round of speed chess, followed by a three-minute round of boxing. There can be up to six rounds of chess and five of boxing before a **winner** is decided. Now you may think this is just a bit of fun, but when I watched two men competing in a match on German television last year, I was amazed by their level of skill in each of these two very different disciplines. After all, boxing is such an aggressive, violent sport – it's about using the body, whereas chess is all about using the brain. You don't expect a boxer to be good at chess, or a chess **player** to be good in the ring.

I: Have you found any other unusual combinations like that?

M: No, but at the beginning you mentioned octopushing, which is underwater hockey – so it's an unusual setting for a familiar game. I haven't seen it played, but I've read that it's a very exciting **spectator** sport – major tournaments have TV screens which show the images captured by underwater cameras. I've also read that you don't have to be very fit to play. But I'm not convinced, to be honest – it seems physically very demanding to me. The good thing, though, is that because it's a team sport, no individual player has to stay underwater for long periods at a time. People like me who can't hold their breath for very long can keep coming up for air.

I: Hmm, not one for me, though, I'm afraid. What else have you got?

M: Well, there's wife carrying. That's where **competitors** race over a 250-metre course with a woman on their back. The female **participant** has to weigh more than 49 kilos, but she doesn't actually have to be the man's wife. So it would be more accurate to call it 'woman carrying', I suppose. Anyway, if she isn't heavy enough she has to wear a rucksack with some kind of weight in it. The regulations are surprisingly strict.

I: Now that sounds alright. Fancy carrying me, Mike?

M: Er … no. Bad back, I'm afraid. Actually, there are quite a few sports like this one that rather irritate me.

I: Why's that?

MT: Well, they're a bit ridiculous, to be honest. Wife carrying, retro running, pea shooting, egg throwing … they all seem very childish to me. I'm sorry if that upsets **listeners**, but they're just not sports I'd want to do or even watch.

I: So which one is the silliest?

M: Well, it has to be toe wrestling, where you have to force your opponent's foot to the ground. It's fine for kids, and a toe wrestling competition is the kind of thing you might expect them to organize in the school playground. But for grown men and women to hold a World Championship every year, and then for **organizers** to apply for toe wrestling to become an Olympic sport – well, it's too daft for words. I'm just pleased the application wasn't accepted.

I: Alright. But you seem to like chess boxing and octopushing. Are there any more that impress you?

M: Well, how about the Man Versus Horse Marathon, which takes place every July in Wales? Human **runners** race cross-country against **riders** on horseback for twenty-two miles – that's around thirty-five kilometres – and on two occasions in the last thirty years, a human **contestant** has won. Now that's not as astonishing as it might seem – horses are fast in short races but not so good over long distances. But it does seem a little unfair that the human victories are not mentioned in the same breath as some of the world's more famous sporting achievements. These people are heroes, but they're virtually unknown outside Wales.

I: Yes, it's the first time I've heard of the race. You're a runner, aren't you, Mike?

M: I was, but I damaged my knee when I was skiing and had to stop. I was a real enthusiast – used to run for a couple of hours after work every evening – but even then, I wouldn't have beaten a horse, that's for sure.

I: There's no shame in that! Right, thanks Mike. Time now for …

3 Ask students to discuss the questions in pairs. If you have a multilingual group, get students to tell the whole class about their country's strange sport.

Alternative idea

Students work in groups of three. They each choose a different sport from the listening and pretend that they want to try it. They read the listening script for their sport. Then they have to convince the other members of their group that the sport is interesting. Encourage the students to ask each other questions during the activity, e.g. *Is it dangerous? Do you have to be fit? What are the rules?* Explain that they can invent information.

Word formation: Affixes   Page 27

1 This is the first in a series of exercises in the book aimed at exposing students to the different aspects of word formation.

Books closed. Write *win*, *spectate* and *participate* on the board. Ask students if they know how to form the words for people from these verbs, and elicit answers. Then tell them to open their books and do exercise 1.

Answers

boxer, player, spectator, competitor, participant, listener, organizer, runner, rider, contestant

2 After students have completed the noun formation, ask them to mark the word stress on all the words, e.g. *employ/employee*. Model and drill the pronunciation.

Answers

employee/trainee, electrician/politician, novelist/scientist, mountaineer/engineer

3 Look at the example and then do number 2 together, so that students realize all three prefixes are the same in each group. After the exercise, ask if they can see any general rules.
In many words beginning with *l*, *m* or *r* the initial consonant is doubled after the *i*. Words beginning in *p* are usually made negative by adding *im*, but notice that the negative prefix for *pleasant* is *un*. These are only general guidelines – it is always worth checking if unsure.

Answers

1	un	**2**	in	**3**	il	**4** im
5	im	**6**	ir	**7**	dis	

4 Students do the exercise in pairs. If you think your students will find this hard, you could write the definitions on the board in jumbled order and ask students to match them to the words.
after   too little/not enough   wrongly   again
too much/excessive(ly)   before   outside or beyond
very big   very small   former

Answers

under	too little/not enough
over	too much/excessive(ly)
pre	before
post	after
hyper	very big
micro	very small
mis	wrongly
re	again
ex	former
extra	outside or beyond

Additional activity
Students work in pairs. Ask them to write five questions using the words from exercises 1, 2, 3 and 4, e.g. *What qualities do you need to be a good mountaineer? Do you prefer being a spectator or a participant in sports?* Circulate and help students with any problems. Then students join with another pair and ask their questions.

 Writing 2 Part 2   **Article**
Page 27

Students read the instructions. Check that they understand the expression *take something up*. Ask who will read the article and what style they should use. Refer them to the model of an article on page 202 and ask them to read this and complete the activities. Ask some follow-up questions, e.g. *Does the writer use full or contracted forms? Are the linkers formal or informal? Does the writer use any questions?* Students answer the questions on page 27 for paragraphs 1 to 4 in pairs. Then they should spend some time writing notes for each paragraph. Explain that in the *First* exam, they will be awarded marks for their use of vocabulary, so they need to include words related to the sport they choose. Students write the article for homework. In the next lesson they could read another student's article and give it a mark out of five for vocabulary.

Answers

2
Paragraph 1 c   Paragraph 2 a
Paragraph 3 d   Paragraph 4 b

3
It is written for readers of *International Sports Weekly* magazine.

4 The style is informal.
a Contractions: *doesn't, you've, you'll, I'm, you're, don't, they're*
b Informal linkers: *So, And, Also*
c Direct questions: *Have you ever seen a smile on the face of a long distance runner? So what is the attraction of running?*
d Phrasal verbs: *give up, take up, put off*

5
1 c **2** a **3** b

Sample answer

In the world, as I know, there are a lot of sports that are very interesting and everyone can occupy with them like, for example, football, basketball, volleyball and so on. But in my opinion, the most famous and the most interesting, in the world, is football. Firstly, I extremely fond of this kind of entertainment (I say this because for me and my friends, football is the same thing with the entertainment).

We play football everyday and everywhere. We love it and anything else apart from football is boring for us. Once again I love it. Secondly, football has many particularities. Special equipment and special clothes are usuful. Although the professionals teams play in big football courts, the children play football everywhere. If you want to become a good and a famous football player you must go into training everyday with many efforts but because of the injuries you must be careful.

For all these reasons, I have the impression that this particular sport is lovely and I believe that there is nobody who watch this sport.

By Loukas Geronikolaou
178 words

Examiner's comment

Content: Adequate coverage of points 1 and 3 but point 2 (*why do you like it?*) not really dealt with. The question incites a personal response but the information given is mostly rather general again.

Communicative achievement: Consistently neutral register in an acceptable article format. The message would not be entirely clear to the target reader; certainly some enthusiasm conveyed, but why does the writer like football so much? Some awkwardness of expressions may distract target reader, and the final sentence is obscure.

Organization: Four paragraphs including an introduction and conclusion. Conventional paragraph links (*Firstly, Secondly*). Some sentence links (*although, if, because of*).

Language: Reasonably accurate. One missing verb (*I extremely fond of* – a slip?), one spelling mistake (*usuful*), one false agreement (*professionals teams*). The problem is awkwardness rather than pure inaccuracy (positive error). Final sentence doesn't communicate. Doesn't have all the vocabulary (*occupy with them, many particularities, big football courts*) though makes good attempts (*fond of, anything else apart from football, go into training, because of the injuries*). Some variety of structures, some complex sentences.

Mark*: Pass

*Note on marking
Each of the four categories is awarded a mark out of 5. These marks are then added up to give a total score out of 20.

For the purposes of this course, the sample answers have been graded according to the following scale: **borderline**, **pass**, **good pass**, and **very good pass**.

Review 2 Answers Pages 28–29

Word formation

1

1	undersleep	2	overlittle	3	oversing
4	missucceed	5	dislove	6	unglad

2

1	undercharged	2	overgrown
3	overslept	4	misspelt/misspelled
5	disappearance	6	uncommon

Reading and Use of English — Part 3

Word formation

1	spectators	2	distance
3	participants	4	walker
5	extraordinary	6	performance
7	unlikely	8	physically

Gerunds and infinitives

1	to write	2	getting	3	tapping
4	to have	5	talking	6	to study
7	to open	8	putting		

Vocabulary

A Sport

1	course, hole	2	referee, pitch
3	hit/get, racket/racquet	4	lift, slope(s)/run(s)
5	part, place	6	beat, draw

B Music

1	on the radio	2	play a tune
3	in the charts	4	session musicians
5	in tune	6	mime a song
7	on tour	8	play a track

Additional activity
The review could be adapted to make a quiz similar to the one suggested in Unit 1.

 Progress Test 1

3 A change for the better?

Content Overview

Themes

Technology and the associated changes in society are the themes of this unit. As with previous units the grammar and vocabulary are clearly contextualized and linked to the reading, listening, speaking and writing tasks.

Exam-related activities

Reading and Use of English

Part 5	Multiple choice

Writing

Part 1	Essay
Part 2	Article (Review)

Reading and Use of English

Part 3	Word formation (Review)

Listening

Part 4	Multiple choice
Part 3	Multiple matching

Speaking

Part 3	Collaborative task
Part 4	Further discussion

Other

Language focus 1:	Comparisons
Language focus 2:	Articles
Vocabulary:	Technology
Word formation:	Nouns 1

Vocabulary: Technology — Page 30

Lead–in

Books closed. Students work in pairs to note down the technological devices they use in a typical day and to find three which they have in common. Get feedback from the class. Ask various pairs what their common devices were and which of these they would find it hardest to live without.

Books open. Focus students' attention on the photos and ask them to name the items. Ask if there is any object that they don't use. Get them to explain why they don't use it.

1 Ask students to read the instructions. Model the first conversation with a student in the class by asking the questions and responding. Use expressions for showing interest, e.g. *Me too.*

Me neither. Do you … ? I prefer … . Really? Then write the useful expressions on the board and explain that students should use these to show interest in their partner's opinions. Then ask students to talk about the other alternatives in pairs. Circulate and join in with different conversations. Get some feedback from the class by asking various students how their partner responded to the different choices, e.g. *Silvie, can you tell us how Isaac logs on to the Internet?*

2 Focus students' attention on the text message in the visual and ask them to read what it says out loud, helping them as necessary. Then ask them to read the instructions for the exercise. Look at the first phrase together and elicit the complete sentence: *I have got to go.* Students do the exercise. Correct it together and explain that LOL/ROFL don't really have a literal meaning, they just express amusement in the same way as a smiley face icon. Ask if they know any other textspeak and whether they think textspeak is affecting people's ability to spell well.

Answers			
2	bye	3	out
4	by	5	know
6	in my opinion	7	happy birthday
8	for your information	9	on
10	I see what you mean		

 **Reading and Use of English** Part 5 — **Multiple choice** Page 30

This reading continues the theme of technology and illustrates its effect on family life.

1 Students read the paragraph and the question. Get some brief feedback on the possible effects of the experiment. Do not elaborate too much, as some of the details are dealt with in questions 4–6 and students will have a chance to discuss this in the Reacting to the text section.

2 Pre-teach *IM* (instant messaging), *SMS* (short message service, i.e. text message) and *shrug*. Students then do exercise 2 as suggested. If students ask the meaning of vocabulary, encourage them to try to work it out from context.

Get brief feedback to see which of the points they discussed in exercise 1 are mentioned.

3 Students read the instructions and the How to go about it box on page 31. Then ask them the following questions:
Why should you read the whole text before looking at the questions? (to get an overall understanding)
Do the questions appear in the same order as the information in the text? (Yes)
Do you lose marks for incorrect answers? (No)
Ask students to read the questions, and check that they understand the vocabulary, e.g. *pond, tearful,* and *took turns.* They then answer the questions. Check the answers together, and if students have chosen the wrong option, ask them which part of the text they thought the answer came from. Warn them to be careful of distractors.

Learner training
Suggest that students underline the section where they found the answer. This makes the feedback stage more efficient, and also trains students to find the exact answers in the text.

Answers

1 B 2 D 3 A 4 C 5 B 6 D

Students read the What to expect in the exam box on page 32. Ask *Which type of question might come last?* (A question testing global understanding).

Reacting to the text
Elicit a few useful expressions for giving opinions and write them on the board. You could also add the following language which came up in the reading text: *the main cause of, create, enable me to, devote more time to, pay more attention to.* Then students discuss the questions in pairs.

Language focus 1: Comparisons Page 33

This task is designed to see how much students already know. Students read the instructions. Check they understand them by asking: *What do you have to do with the words in brackets? Do you have to write one word only?* They then complete the sentences. Either ask them to look back at the text to check their answers, or check the answers together as class.

Answers

1 more, less
2 longer, more complex
3 more, than, more efficiently, more quickly
4 most militant, youngest
5 least, most

A Comparative and superlative forms
Refer students to the Grammar reference on pages 210 and 211. Students do exercises 1–4 in pairs. Go through the answers as a class.

Answers

1
The comparative of adjectives with one syllable, like *long* and *young*, is formed by adding the suffix -er (*longer, younger*).
The comparative of most adjectives with two or more syllables is formed by preceding the adjective with the word more (*more complex, more militant*).

2
cleaner, the cleanest
hotter, the hottest
stranger, the strangest
happier, the happiest
more clever, the most clever *or* cleverer, the cleverest
better, the best
worse, the worst
farther, the farthest *or* further, the furthest

3
The comparative of adverbs like *quickly* or *efficiently* are usually formed by preceding the adverb with the word *more*, not by adding the suffix -er.

4
big differences: *much, significantly, a lot*
small differences: *a bit, a little, slightly*

B Other comparative structures

1–2 Read through the explanations and then ask some questions to check students' understanding:
What can I say …
… if I am tall and my sister is also tall. (Tell students to use *as*: *I am as tall as my sister.*)

... if my brother is rich, but I have less money. (Tell students to use *so*: *I am not so rich as my brother.*)
... if I thought my boss was good, but now I realize she isn't. (Tell students to use *such*: *She isn't such a good boss as I thought.*)
... if every time I buy my son more toys he becomes more badly behaved. (Tell students to use *the*: *The more toys I buy my son, the more badly behaved he becomes/the worse he behaves.*)

1 This exercise exposes students to pairs of sentences with similar meaning but using different structures, rather like a completed transformation exercise. This will prepare them for the transformation exercise which follows.

Answers

1 c   2 a   3 e   4 b   5 f   6 d

2 Students do the exercise as suggested. Circulate and help students if they have any problems. Give them clues, e.g. Question 1: *What's the comparative adjective of bad?*
Question 2: *You've had a lot of holidays, so should you use comparative or superlative?*

Answers

1   was far worse than
2   the least enjoyable holiday
3   are not as many
4   you work now, the less
5   is/'s the same height as
6   quite as much experience as

3a Students write an example for each category.

3b Students read the instructions. Elicit the expressions they might need for giving an opinion, agreeing and disagreeing, and write appropriate suggestions on the board. You might include the following:
I'm afraid I don't really agree.
Do you really think so?
Yes, but don't you think ...
Well yes, but it depends on ...
I suppose you're right ...
Roleplay the example dialogue with two students, then ask them to discuss their choices in their groups. Encourage students to use the expressions from the board and a variety of comparative forms during their conversations. Stress that the objective

is to practise the target language and to argue as much as possible, not to finish quickly! Circulate and join in with some of the conversations. Get feedback from the class. Ask who was the most convincing member of each group.

Additional activity
For homework, students write eight sentences comparing some of the following: members of their family, friends, their high school teachers, bars and restaurants in their town or rooms in their house. Insist that they write a different type of comparative sentence each time. You can then check their writing for accuracy.
The writing task from the review on page 40 could also be used at this point, if not needed for review purposes at the end of the unit. Students brainstorm ideas in pairs. Encourage them to use a variety of comparative structures. Remind them look at the model of an article on page 196.

 DVD resource: Unit 3

Word formation: Nouns 1   Page 34

1 Students read the instructions. Do the first word together as it is quite tricky, then ask students to continue in pairs. Students can either check their answers in the reading text, or you could correct them as a class.

Answers

1   consciousness, curiosity
2   entertainment
3   attention, conversations
4   evidence

2 Check students understand that the last word in each group requires a spelling change. Correct the exercise together. Ask students to spell the words out loud where there is a spelling change.

Answers

1   enjoyment, treatment, government, argument
2   originality, popularity, majority, ability
3   appearance, performance, annoyance, tolerance
4   sadness, weakness, carelessness, loneliness
5   information, resignation, presentation, explanation
6   difference, existence, dependence, obedience

Additional activity

Practise word stress so that students see some common patterns. Draw this table on the board.

● ● **●** ●	**●** ● ● ●	**●** ● ●	● **●** ●	**●** ●
information				

Ask students to look at the answers from exercise 2 and match them to the stress patterns in the table. Elicit the word stress of the first few nouns from the class, and write them on the board in the correct column. Then students should work in pairs and add the remaining nouns. Circulate and model words students have problems with. Check the answers and then choral drill each column.

Answers

● ● **●** ●	**●** ● ● ●	**●** ● ●	● **●** ●	**●** ●
information	ability	carelessness	appearance	sadness
conversation	majority	government	prediction	treatment
explanation	obedience	argument	enjoyment	weakness
resignation		loneliness	annoyance	
presentation		tolerance	conversion	
			reaction	
			performance	
			existence	
			dependence	

3 Students should read the whole of each paragraph before filling in any words. Explain that this will help them decide if the missing words are singular, plural, positive or negative. Mention that in this text, all the words are nouns, but that in the exam there will be a variety of word forms. Students do the exercise in pairs. Circulate and help them with spelling if necessary. Correct together.

Answers

1 amusement, collection, similarities, thickness
2 activities, payment, permission
3 generosity, decisions, disappointment
4 dissatisfaction, differences, description, occurrence

 **Listening 1**
Part 4

Multiple choice
Page 35

1 Focus students' attention on the visuals. Ask them to write a list of the different uses for robots in pairs. Circulate and suggest general areas if students are having problems, e.g. *domestic, work, education, entertainment, health, security.* Elicit ideas from round the class and respond, e.g. *That's a great idea. I'd love one of them!*

2 Refer students to the How to go about it box. Then let them read the listening questions and underline key words. Check they understand *monotonous, display* and *toy.* Remind them again about distractors, explaining that they shouldn't choose an answer simply because they have heard a word from this option. Instead, they should listen to the whole segment before making a decision. Play the recording twice and let students compare their answers together after the first listening. When correcting, ask students why they decided on their answers. Students discuss the follow-up question in pairs.

Answers

How to go about it
Suggested answers:
2 How does Keith <u>describe his work</u>?
3 What is the <u>possible result</u> of having <u>robots</u> that can <u>display and detect emotions</u>?
4 What does Keith say about <u>robots in films</u>?
5 Keith expresses <u>concern</u> that <u>robots</u> might <u>cause</u> us …
6 Keith says that <u>progress</u> in the <u>robotics industry</u> …
7 What does Keith say about <u>humanoid robots</u>?

1 B   **2** C   **3** A   **4** A   **5** C   **6** B   **7** C

Listening 1: Listening script 1.16

P = Presenter   K = Keith Wells

P: My guest today is robot scientist Keith Wells. Keith's company, ELA Robotics, hit the news a few years ago with their Home Help robot, the first of its kind to be able to perform more than one domestic task. What are you working on these days, Keith?

K: I can't really tell you that, I'm afraid. It's not that I don't want to, it's just that we've all been given our instructions and signed an agreement not to give anything away until it actually comes onto the market. I don't quite know when that will be, but probably some time early next year.

P: OK, well we'll look forward to that. In the meantime, perhaps you could tell us what you think are the most important applications of robots in our lives. Why are they useful?

K: Well, they help us to do what we call 'the three D's'. That's anything which is dull, dirty or dangerous. They can be used in the home or in the car manufacturing industry, to do dull or monotonous work; they're used for doing dirty jobs like mining or cleaning toxic waste; and then they have applications in the military or in the dangerous business of space travel. Of course, that's not an exhaustive list, but it gives you an idea of the range of different uses they have – and also of the variety involved in my line of work.

P: Yes, indeed. Let's talk if we may about one area in particular, though, the more humanoid robots, the ones with a recognizable human form. What are the latest developments there?

K: Hmm, yes, the ones being built now are able to see, hear, touch and even smell and taste. Others can show a range of emotional states, such as sadness, joy, anger and even comical surprise. They can even recognize emotions in humans, by interpreting people's body-language – the postures they adopt, the gestures they make. The hope is that people will be more willing to welcome robots like these into their homes, and they could act as companions and home helps for the sick or the elderly.

P: Amazing. But isn't all this a little bit worrying – robots with emotions? Isn't there a danger of science fiction becoming science fact, with robots taking over?

K: Yes, unfortunately, robots do get rather a bad press sometimes, don't they? Particularly in films and video games where they're either objects of humour and ridicule which we laugh at or else they're menacing characters which threaten to destroy the whole human race. But no, there is actually an ethical code which sets out what we can and can't do in robot design – and one thing we won't do is allow ourselves to lose control over our creations.

P: Don't you think, though, that robots will make us lazy, that we'll no longer want to do anything that requires any effort?

K: I think the car's already done that to us. It's made us physically very lazy. We don't walk so much as we used to and our bodies have suffered as a result. I think robots could well have the same effect on our brains. If we let intelligent robots do all of our thinking for us, there is a danger we won't be able to make any of our own decisions, that we'll become mentally lazy. And that, I think, is just as worrying.

P: Do you really think that the day will come when most homes have their own robot?

K: If you think back to just thirty years or so ago, few of us then would have predicted that we'd soon have a personal computer in our home, be logging onto the Internet and downloading hundreds of songs and videos onto a thing called an MP4 player. So why shouldn't we all have robots? We've been talking about them for nearly a century now and certainly, their initial development wasn't quite as fast as we thought it would be. But now, with advanced computer technology available, very rapid changes are taking place in robot design.

P: Yes, I remember those rather clumsy-looking machines at the end of the 1990s.

K: That's right. The first humanoid robots could do very little, then later models learnt to sit down and stand up, then talk, walk around, dance and so on. It's rather like watching a child grow. Through television and other media, the public is slowly growing accustomed to the idea of robots as a reality, and when they eventually become widely available, people will be ready for them.

P: Thank you, Keith. It's been fascinating having you on the programme.

Additional activity

Students work in groups of four. They imagine they are entrepreneurs and decide on a type of robot that they would like to produce. They should consider their market, costs, price, promotion methods and sales outlets. Give each student a letter, A, B, C or D. Then ask all the A's to form one group, all the B's another group, etc. In these new groups, students present their idea for a robot and then the group discuss which is the best. Get feedback from the class and vote on the best robot in the class.

 **Speaking 1** Part 3

Collaborative task
Page 36

1 Students read the instructions and the How to go about it box. As this is the first time students have done a full Part 3 of the Speaking exam, ask some true/false questions to check they understand the tasks, e.g.
You have to discuss changes that have taken place over the last ten years. (False)
You have to choose one area which has experienced the most positive changes. (False)
You should interact with your partner. (True)
There will be pictures to help you in the Speaking exam. (False)
You must not make your decisions for task 2 while you are doing task 1. (True)
You don't have to agree with your partner when making your final decision. (True)
The timing for the different tasks is flexible. (False)

Focus students' attention on the Useful language box. Mention that most of the structures are from Units 1–3. (The present perfect isn't covered until Unit 7, but students should already be able to use it at this stage). Explain that they will be awarded points for their range of grammar, so they should use a variety of structures. Points are also awarded for communicative interaction, so they should listen and respond appropriately to their partner. Stress that they must be polite when disagreeing. Explain that you will allow them more than three minutes as this is the first time they have done a Part 3 task. Mention that the pictures are designed to help them, but they can talk about other aspects of each topic, e.g. in the Travel section they could mention low-cost airlines.

Circulate and write down some good examples of language. Take feedback from the class. Ask one pair which two changes they chose as being most positive and see if the other students chose the same two. Write the examples of good language on the board as positive feedback.

 **Speaking 2** Part 4 | **Further discussion**
Page 37

Students read the instructions and the How to go about it box. Ask them some questions, e.g.
Is it a good idea to give yes/no answers? (No, you should give full answers)
Should you interact with your partner in this section? (Yes)
Students do the task. Circulate and write down a few common errors. Write these on the board after students have finished speaking. Take feedback from the class and correct the common errors together.

Language focus 2: Articles   Page 37

This section is designed to find out which areas cause problems. The cloze test is followed by analysis of the uses of the definite and indefinite articles and when no article is used.

1 Ask students to read the text and answer the questions in exercise 1. Explain that reading the text before filling in the gaps will help them understand the overall gist. Elicit answers from the class.

Answers

Travel and transport and Communication

2 Students do exercise 2 as suggested.

Answers

1	–	2	The	3	–	4	the
5	the	6	the	7	the	8	A
9	–	10	a	11	–	12	the
13	an	14	–	15	–	16	a
17	the	18	the	19	a	20	the

3 Students match the rules from the Grammar reference to the answers in exercise 2.

Answers

Question	Grammar reference section
The definite article	
2, 20	A1
4	A4
6, 17	A5a
5	A5b
7	A7
18	A10
12	A12
The indefinite article	
19	B2
8, 16	B4
10, 13	B5
No article	
1, 11	C1a
3, 9, 14	C1b
15	C4

Alternative approach

Students work in pairs. If you have a multilingual class, try and get students with the same language to work together. Do exercise 1 as suggested in the Coursebook. After this, refer students to the Grammar reference on pages 211–12. Ask them to read the rules and to underline the ones which are different from their own language. Get feedback from the class. Ask whether articles are used more or less in their language than in English. Get some examples of differences from various pairs. Students complete the gaps in the text, referring back to the Grammar reference when necessary.

 **Listening 2** Part 3 | **Multiple matching**
Page 38

The follow-up task with this listening is designed to make students aware of distractors.

1 Ask students to read the instructions and the How to go about it box, then to read the options and underline the key words. Before listening, ask a few students which words they have underlined. Play the recording twice for students to answer. Don't allow time after the first listening for the students to discuss their answers, because they will discuss distractors in exercises 2 and 3.

Answers

How to go about it

Possible answers:

B Too many changes

C insufficient

D should have been consulted

E for selfish reasons

F Most parents support

G unexpected benefits

H Most teachers, unnecessary

1 E **2** D **3** H **4** C **5** A B, F and G not used

2 Ask students to follow the instructions, then check the answers together as a class.

Answers

Possible answers:

1 *… she has her own interests in mind rather than those of the kids. It's just another of her schemes to get publicity for herself.*

2 *… he has a habit of making changes without bothering to find out what anyone else thinks first … he could have let us have some say in the matter before going ahead.*

3 *Most parents won't read the comments anyway – they're just interested in the marks. It's a waste of time as far as I'm concerned, and I know the majority of my colleagues feel the same.*

4 *Mixing up the classes like that – splitting up the troublemakers – is a step in the right direction, but it doesn't go far enough.*

5 *The ceiling's enormously high and the acoustics are terrible for the piano. Plus I practically have to shout to make myself heard, so my throat is suffering. And then the sun streams in during the afternoon and sends the kids to sleep.*

Listening 2: Listening script 1.17–1.21

Speaker 1

Apparently, teenagers need more sleep than the rest of us, so next year we're starting lessons at 10, rather than 9 every day. The head says the kids will be more awake, more receptive during class if they come in an hour later. It's a fairly radical idea and it's attracting a lot of attention from the press. The head's given three newspaper interviews already – all of which goes to confirm my belief that she has her own interests in mind rather than those of the kids. It's just another of her schemes to get publicity for herself. Perhaps I should have spoken out at the consultation meeting, but she's got the support of the whole teaching staff, and they don't care that her motives are all wrong.

Speaker 2

I'm really fed up with our head of department. We all are. As well as having absolutely no interpersonal skills, he has a habit of making changes without bothering to find out what anyone else thinks first. He told us in a meeting last week that we're going to be using a different coursebook for Year 8 next term, and he's ordered three class sets already. Now, I'm not saying that a change wasn't necessary – I think we're all a bit tired of the book we're using at the moment – but I do think he could have let us have some say in the matter before going ahead. It's no way to run a department.

Speaker 3

I teach maths to as many as two hundred students in one year, so I'm not at all pleased about the changes to report writing. Until now, a student's end-of-term report consisted of a mark for each subject, and then the class tutor made a summarizing comment at the end. With the new system, each subject teacher has to write a comment as well. It'll take ages! The head says the tutor's comment isn't enough to give parents a full picture of how their child's getting on, but as long as it's carefully written, it's fine. Most parents won't read the comments anyway – they're just interested in the marks. It's a waste of time as far as I'm concerned, and I know the majority of my colleagues feel the same.

Speaker 4

The situation in Year 10 is not much better than it was before. Mixing up the classes like that – splitting up the troublemakers – is a step in the right direction but it doesn't go far enough. They're still there, and they're still causing disruption to lessons. The head should have asked the parents to come in and got the kids to make certain guarantees in front of them, made them promise to improve their behaviour and so on. Then if the promises aren't kept, expel them from the school. We told her that, but she said expelling them would just create problems for other schools. She needs to be much tougher.

Speaker 5

There's some building work going on outside the music room, so you can imagine how difficult it is to teach in there. The windows are double glazed, but they're not enough to keep out the noise, so I've been moved – along with my piano – to a room on the other side of the school. Now I've changed rooms many times before, but never to one as bad as this. The ceiling's enormously high and the acoustics are terrible for the piano. Plus I practically have to shout to make myself heard, so my throat is suffering. And then the sun streams in during the afternoon and sends the kids to sleep. I'm telling you, as soon as the work's finished, I'm moving straight back to my old room.

3 Explain that this exercise will help students see how distractors are used. Suggest that they underline the distractors in a different colour to the real answers in exercise 2.

Answers

Possible answers:

2 *Now I'm not saying that a change wasn't necessary ...*

3 *The head says the tutor's comment isn't enough to give parents a full picture of how their child's getting on ...*

4 *... she said expelling them would just create problems for other schools.*

5 *Now I've changed rooms many times before ...*

4 Tell students about a change in your life then ask them to discuss changes in their own life in pairs. In class feedback ask various pairs to describe the changes their partner has experienced.

Additional activity

Students work in pairs. Ask them to underline the following phrasal verbs in the listening script and to try and work out their meaning from context.

Speaker 1: spoken out

Speaker 2: find out, going ahead

Speaker 3: getting on

Speaker 4: splitting up

Speaker 5: going on

Possible answers

spoken out – said firmly and publicly what I thought

find out – discover

going ahead – taking action, proceeding

getting on – progressing

splitting up – separating

going on – happening, being done

Correct the answers together and suggest students add these phrasal verbs along with their definitions to their vocabulary notebooks.

5 Do the exercise on expressions with *as ... as* on page 203.

Answers

1

| 1 | well | 2 | many | 3 | long | 4 | far | 5 | soon |

2

1 in addition to

2 the surprisingly large number of

3 provided

4 in my opinion

5 immediately

Additional activity

After completing the exercise write these sentence beginnings on the board:

You can borrow the car as ...

Playing video games is a complete waste of time as ...

She's a brilliant student. She speaks German and Chinese fluently as ...

Could you hand in your composition as ...

I went to the demonstration, there were as ...

Students work in pairs. Ask them to complete the sentences with their own ideas. Explain that they should use the expressions with *as ... as*. Circulate and correct the sentences. Get some class feedback by asking various students to read out a sentence.

 **Writing** **Part 1** | **Essay** Page 38

This essay task gives students the opportunity to practise a balanced essay type. They will have further practice on this in Unit 5. In Units 8 and 11, a one-sided model is shown. Both are presented in the Ready for Writing section.

It's worth bearing in mind that high schools in many countries dedicate more time to grammar than to writing in their mother tongue, so you may find that students are not used to planning a structured essay.

1 Ask students to read the instructions and example answer, then discuss the questions with a partner. Get some feedback from the class.

2 Ask students to identify the writer's own idea.

Answers

The safety aspects

3 Students should work individually first before comparing their answers with their partner. This will give them time to think and concentrate.

Answers

Paragraph 2: advantages/positive aspects of change

Paragraph 3: disadvantages/negative aspects of change

Paragraph 4: conclusion

4a–b Students work in pairs to complete the tables.

Answers

4a

on the negative side	on the positive side
on the one hand	on the other hand

4b

Adding information	Expressing result	Concluding
In addition (to this)	Consequently	On balance
What is more	As a result	To sum up
Furthermore	–	In conclusion
Moreover		
Firstly/Secondly/Finally		

5 Refer students to Additional Materials on page 203. Ask them to read the instructions and the How to go about it box. If you prefer, you could offer students a choice of essay titles, e.g. *The mobile phone has greatly improved our lives today.* or *Technology has improved life for the consumer.* or *Technology has improved the quality of education.* As some students may not be used to planning an essay, ask them to brainstorm ideas for each section with their partner. Circulate and offer further ideas where necessary.

If you feel it is necessary, remind students not to copy from the Internet.

Learner training

When you mark the essays, take one error from each student's work and make a worksheet. Underline the error and add your correction symbol after the sentence (you may need to semi-correct some sentences so that they only have one mistake). When you hand back their work, give them the worksheet and get them to correct the sentences. Students will appreciate this personal touch.

Sample answer

The Internet is part of our lives and many people could not imagine how would be the world without it. However, it is not sure that we must have it to enjoy the life completely.

Firstly, in my opinion it is much better to speak with your friends personally and don't get in touch with them online all the time. The only way to keep your friends and have a good relationship with them is see them regularly, rather than chating on networking sites. Similarly, I prefer to go to the shops to buy instead of do it online. There is no sustitute for the personal treat which you can find when you are in a real shop or a market.

In addition, it can be a little sad to spend all your day to play online games or watch films which you download. It is something special when you go to the cinema or sit with your family playing a table game.

To sum up, the best way to enjoy the life is without the Internet, since a computer cannot give you the good relations you have when you speak, shop and play with another people.

Maria Sanz
197 words

Examiner's comment

Content: Adequate coverage of points 1 and 2. However, the candidate's own idea is not completely clear.

Communicative achievement: Language is generally appropriately formal, and despite frequent errors, the message is generally clear and well organized, so the target reader would be sufficiently informed.

Organization: Linking devices used effectively e.g. *However, firstly, similarly, in addition, to sum up.* Well organized, but the second and third paragraphs could be combined.

Language: In general, the frequent errors do not obscure meaning; however, they do distract the reader: *how would be the world* (what the world would be like), misuse of definite article – *enjoy the life*, problems with infinitives and gerunds – *don't* (not to) *get in touch, is* (to) *see them regularly, the shops to buy instead of do* (doing) *it online*, misuse of determiners – *another* (other) *people.* At times, vocabulary errors lead to confusion, e.g. *the personal treat which you can find, playing a table game.* There are also two spelling mistakes, but these do not distract the reader, *sustitute, chating.* There is an adequate range of vocabulary for the task, e.g. *get in touch, relationships, networking sites, download.* Some use of more complex language, e.g. *The only way to keep your friends, rather than chating on networking sites.* However, frequent errors with more basic structures.

Mark*: Pass

*Note on marking
Each of the four categories is awarded a mark out of 5. These marks are then added up to give a total score out of 20.

For the purposes of this course, the sample answers have been graded according to the following scale: **borderline**, **pass**, **good pass**, and **very good pass**.

Review 3 Answers Pages 40–41

Vocabulary: Technology

2 laptop		**3** headset	
4 landline		**5** download	
6 netbook		**7** multitasking	

Expressions with *as ... as*

1 long	**2** soon	**3** far	**4** well
5 many			

Comparisons

1

1 the	**2** most	**3** in	**4** many
5 much	**6** nearly	**7** lot	**8** so
9 by	**10** less		

Articles

3 in **the** home
4 spend ~~the~~ more
5 killed **the** art
6 write ~~the~~ emails
7 **the** less
8 **the** mobile phone
9 put in **a**
10 on **the** train
11 watched **a** young couple
12 not just **the** young
13 **a** high percentage
14 into ~~the~~ your phone
15 I'm **the** one
16 to **the** mountains

Reading and Use of English
Part 3

Word formation

1 earliest	**2** inventor
3 researchers	**4** existence
5 equipment	**6** collection
7 assistant	**8** responsibilities

Ready for Use of English

Reading and Use of English paper

Part 1	Multiple-choice cloze
Part 2	Open cloze
Part 3	Word formation

This is the first of five 'Ready for …' units which focus on the five different skills areas tested in the First exam: Use of English, Reading, Listening, Speaking and Writing. In each of the 'Ready for …' units, there is a clear explanation of the different kinds of exercise types students can expect to find in the exam. This serves to give students an overview and summary of each paper. They are provided with and reminded of the useful strategies which can be used in the exam to help improve their performance.

Possible approaches to using the 'Ready for …' unit material

Although the material is designed for classroom use, it is also suitable for individual study, so some or all of this could be set for homework. The method you choose will depend on the length of your course. Make sure you consider this carefully at the beginning so that you don't run out of time at the end.

Remind students that they will only be looking at three of the four Use of English tasks in this 'Ready for …' unit. As stated in the Coursebook, information on the content of Part 4 (Transformations) appears at frequent intervals throughout the book.

Introduction   Page 42

The emphasis in this unit is on teaching students rather than testing them. The unit starts with a true/false activity about the content and mechanics of the various exercises. This serves to give students an overall picture of the Use of English tasks in the Reading and Use of English paper.

What do you know about the Use of English tasks?   Page 42

Students do the activity as suggested. Get feedback from the class and go through the answers carefully. Pay special attention to statement 7, as some countries use a system of deducting points for

incorrect answers. For statement 8, mention that you must write one word in the gap even if the sentence is correct as it stands.

Answers

1 **False** All except Part 4 (Transformations) for which the six questions are unrelated.
2 **True** Students should read for gist first. Looking first at the title and predicting the content of the text will help their overall understanding.
3 **False** There is one mark for each correct answer except in Part 4 (Transformations): in this part, two marks are given for a completely correct answer, one mark if it is partly correct.
4 **True**
5 **True**
6 **True** Unfortunately, some students do this in the exam. If they write the answer to the example where the answer to the first question should go, all their answers will be in the wrong space.
7 **False** Marks are not deducted for incorrect answers. If students are unsure, they should eliminate any alternatives they consider to be clearly wrong and then, if they still cannot decide on the correct answer, make a sensible guess.
8 **False** Only one word. Note that contractions (e.g. *can't, won't, I've*) and hyphenated words (e.g. *one-way*) count as two words.
9 **True** No half marks are given in this paper (although one mark out of a possible two can be given in Part 4 – see 3 above).
10 **True**

Part 1: Multiple-choice cloze   Page 42

Students follow the instructions in the What to expect in the exam box. As you go through feedback, draw their attention to question 3 and remind them to record words that collocate together in their vocabulary notebooks.

Answers

1 A   2 C   3a D   3b C   4 B   5 D

1 Elicit suggestions from the class. Students read the text to check their predictions. Get feedback from the class and ask if students think 'bookcrossing' is a good idea.

2 Students do the cloze activity. Check the answers as a class.

Answers
1 A 2 B 3 D 4 A 5 C 6 C 7 D 8 B

Part 2: Open cloze   Page 44

The first text gives students an example of a completed cloze and asks them to think about the kinds of words that they need to write in this type of exam exercise. They then do an exam-style cloze.

Optional lead–in
Books closed. Brainstorm the types of words which students typically need to write in the gaps in a cloze activity, e.g. articles, prepositions, relative pronouns, etc. Write students' suggestions on the board.

1 Ask the question and elicit ideas from the class.

2 Students work individually. Get class feedback and find out which of their points were mentioned. Then ask them to read What to expect in the exam and to follow the instructions. If they ask the meaning of any words encourage them to guess these from the context.

Answers	
Type of word	**Number and example**
Articles	**3** a
Auxiliary verbs	**8** are
Linking words	**6** although
Negative words	**2** not
Possessive adjectives	
(*my, your, his,* etc.)	**1** their
Prepositions	**7** to
Relative pronouns	**4** which
Words in comparisons	**5** than

3 Draw students' attention to the photo of the wolf and ask them what they would do if they encountered a pack of wolves. Then get them to read the open cloze once to see if their ideas are the same as Walter Eikrem's. After this, students follow the instructions for exercise 3. Circulate and elicit the type of word which is missing if students have any problems.

Answers			
1 where	2 a	3 have	4 What
5 the	6 At	7 to	8 by

Part 3: Word formation   Page 45

1 Students read the What to expect in the exam box and the instructions. Check for understanding and instruct them to do exercise 1. Get class feedback, asking students to spell the answers out loud. Write the words up on the board to ensure that all students can see the correct spellings. Model and check the pronunciation of *humorous, employees, uncomfortable* and *extraordinary*.

Answers	
1 humorous	2 employees
3 tighten	4 increasingly
5 uncomfortable	6 heat
7 saucepan	8 extraordinary

2 Students do the activity in pairs.

Answers
1 adjective; spelling change required (the 'u' in 'humour' is dropped)
2 noun in the plural
3 verb
4 adverb
5 negative adjective
6 noun; spelling change required
7 compound noun
8 adjective

3 Students work individually and then check their predictions in pairs.

4 Students now do the Word formation activity. Check the answers as a class, asking students to spell the words out loud. Model and check the pronunciation of *strength* and *disastrous*.

Answers	
1 magicians	2 interested
3 ability	4 independent
5 strength	6 easily
7 careless	8 disastrous

4 A good story

Content Overview

Themes

The unit is concerned with films and novels. The reading, listening, grammar and vocabulary are closely linked to these themes. Students learn to write reports and reviews.

Exam-related activities

Reading and Use of English

Part 6	Gapped text
Part 4	Transformations (Review)
Part 3	Word formation (Review)

Writing

Part 2	Review × 2
Part 2	Report

Listening

Part 1	Multiple choice

Speaking

Part 2	Talking about photos

Other

Language focus 1: *So* and *such*
Language focus 2: Past tenses
Vocabulary 1:   Films
Vocabulary 2:   *Take*
Word formation: Adjectives ending in *-ing* and *-ed*

Vocabulary 1: Films   Page 46

1 Students do exercise 1 in pairs. If they have seen the films ask if they would recommend them. Elicit suggestions for other good films to see, and ask what type of films they are.

Answers
A science fiction film; action film
B historical drama
C comedy
D fantasy film

2 This section aims to clarify words which some students misuse. Students do exercise 2A and B individually. Model and check the pronunciation of *terrifying*. Ask students to give you an example of a terrible, terrific and terrifying film they have seen,

but don't discuss them in detail as they will talk about a frightening film in exercise 5.

Answers					
A	**1** terrific	**2** terrifying	**3** terrible
B	**1** review	**2** critic	**3** criticism

3 Tell students to ignore the underlining as they read the review for the first time.

4 Students do exercise 4 as suggested. Encourage them to guess any new vocabulary from the context. During the correction stage, model and check the pronunciation of *performance, characters* and *science fiction*.

Answers			
1 set		**2** cast
3 stars		**4** role
5 performance		**6** plot
7 main characters		**8** special effects

Learner training
Remind students to add the film vocabulary to their vocabulary note books.

5 Pre-teach *gripping*. Model the activity with one student by asking them to talk about a film they didn't enjoy, then responding and asking follow-up questions, e.g. *Why didn't you like it? Didn't you think X performed well? I loved the special effects. I suppose you're right about the plot*, etc. Get students to continue the activity in groups of three in case one of them is not a cinema-goer.

Additional activity 1
Write up some statements related to the theme of films and encourage the groups to continue their discussion.
Hollywood produces the best films.
High budget films are always better than low budget films.
The film is never as good as the book.
Dubbed films are never as good as the original version.

Additional activity 2
Students work in groups of four. Explain that they are going to prepare a film quiz. Each team should choose a name, for example, The Stars. Write a few ideas for questions on the board.
Which film was set in _____ and tells the story of _____?

Who plays the lead role in the film _____?
In which film is there a scene where _____?
Which film is based on the novel _____?
Encourage them to use as much of the vocabulary
from exercise 3 as possible. You could allow them
to use their mobiles to search the Internet for ideas.
Tell them to use famous films rather than more
obscure ones. Each team uses a piece of paper as
a score sheet to write down their answers. Explain
that they are allowed a little time to confer for each
question, but they can't use their mobiles to find
the answers. The teams take it in turns to ask their
questions. At the end of the quiz, teams swap score
sheets. Go through the answers as a class. Count
the scores to find the winner.

Language focus 1: *So and such*   Page 47

1   Students do exercise 1 as suggested. Write *I
haven't eaten such good food for a long time* and *Our
neighbours are such friendly people* on the board and
ask why the article is not used. Elicit that the article
is not needed with uncountable or plural nouns.

Answers

a   Both words intensify the adjective or (adjective
+) noun that follow.
b   *so* + adjective (or adverb)
such + (indefinite article +) adjective + noun

2   Students read the Grammar reference on page
212 and do exercise 2 as suggested. Circulate and
help students with any problems.

Answers

1   were so good that
2   was such bad weather
3   was such an absorbing
4   were so many people

Word formation: Adjectives ending in *-ing* and *-ed*   Page 48

In some languages, the same word can be used to
describe both feelings and the thing or person that
produces those feelings. Consequently students
often have problems using *-ing* and *-ed* adjectives
correctly in English.
Read the examples together and give some more
examples. Tell students you went to see a film, and

mime someone watching a film and yawning. Ask
what the film was like and elicit *the film was boring.*
Then ask *How did I feel?* and elicit *you were bored.*

Alternative approach
Books closed. Write the example sentences from
the Coursebook on the board. Ask the following
questions:
*Which type of adjective do we use to describe the
thing or person that produces a feeling?*
(present participle or *-ing* adjective.)
*Which type of adjective do we use to describe how we
feel about something?*
(past participle or *-ed* adjective.)
How can we form an adverb from these adjectives?
(by adding *-ly* to the present participle.)

1   Students work individually to find the *-ing* and
-ed adjectives and adverbs.

Answers

**To describe how we feel about something or
someone**
... you will not feel <u>disappointed</u>.
Also: *The plot is <u>complicated</u>.*
**To describe the thing or person that produces
the feeling**
*... one of the most <u>entertaining</u> science fiction
films I have seen.*
The plot ... is ... at times <u>confusing</u>.
... the special effects are <u>stunning</u>.
**Adverbs formed from present participle
adjectives**
<u>surprisingly</u> competent
<u>convincingly</u> choreographed

2   This aspect of pronunciation causes problems
for many students, as the combinations of sounds
produced (consonant clusters) may not exist in
their own language. Pronunciation of the *-ed* ending
depends on the pronunciation of the final sound
(not letter) of the infinitive.
The general rules are:
1   Is the final sound of the infinitive voiced?
(See *surprise* in column 1)
2   Is the final sound unvoiced?
(See *embarrass* in column 2)
3   Is the final sound /t/ or /d/?
(See *excite* in column 3)

Write the example from the Coursebook on the board.

/d/	/t/	/ɪd/
surprised	embarrassed	excited

If students have difficulty telling if the sound is voiced or unvoiced, get them to cover their ears with their hands and say the infinitive form of the words from column 1 and 2. If they can hear the sound amplified, it is voiced, and if they cannot hear any amplification, it is unvoiced. Then go on to highlight the rule for column 3.

Do the first few words together, eliciting the answers from various students. Then ask them to work in pairs to complete the rest of the exercise. Circulate and refer back to the general rules if they are having difficulties. Check the answers together. Choral drill the words in each column.

Answers

/d/	/t/	/ɪd/
annoyed	astonished	frustrated
tired	impressed	disappointed
amused	relaxed	disgusted
bored		fascinated
frightened		
terrified		

3–4 Students work through exercises 3 and 4 individually and then compare their answers in pairs. After this check answers as a class.

Answers

3

Impress – impressive (adj)

4

Suggested answers:

1	tiring	2	amused
3	annoying	4	disappointingly
5	fascinating	6	disgusting
7	Astonishingly		

Additional activity

Students work in groups of three. Ask them to talk about …

… a time when they felt annoyed/frustrated/tired/ disappointed/bored/relaxed

… something they find disgusting/astonishing/ amusing/fascinating/frightening.

Encourage them to show interest in each

other's comments. Circulate and correct any *-ed* pronunciation issues. Get some feedback from the class.

 Writing 1 Part 2   **Review**   Page 48

Students complete the activities in the How to go about it box, then write their review.

Answers

1 c **2** a **3** d **4** b

Sample answer

The last film I've seen on DVD was 'The Holiday' and it was alright. It is supposed it is a romantic comedy with Cameron Diaz, Kate Winslet, Jude Law and Jack Black and it is nice to watch but it is not a type of film that it makes you to laugh a lot.

The film is about two women very different. They are Iris, who is playing by Kate Winslet and Amanda (Cameron Diaz) and they decide to change houses for a holiday. Iris's house is a small one in England and Amanda's is enormous in Hollywood. Amanda falls in love to Iris's brother, who is widower, and Iris falls in love to Amanda's neighbour, who is componist. Kate Winslet is a bit disappointed in the role of Iris because she is normally very good actress. I like very much the photography and the music.

I would recommend the film to people who they are tires and they do not want to watch a complicate film. It is also very good for a rainy afternoon on Sunday of winter.

By David Benoa
180 words

Examiner's comment

Content: Reasonable realization of the task, though rather a large section of the review is devoted to a simplistic summary of the plot.

Communicative achievement: Both register and format are appropriate to the task. The target reader may have some difficulty following the review due to the number of errors.

Organization: Adequate paragraphing. Some sentences poorly organized, e.g. second sentence of first paragraph.

Language: A large number of distracting errors, e.g. *it is supposed it is a romantic comedy, two women very different, who is playing by Kate Winslet*, and use of relative clauses. *Disappointed* is used incorrectly (*disappointing*), and it is not clear what is meant by *componist* (*composer?*). A very limited range of structures and vocabulary, particularly when expressing opinions, e.g. *very good* (twice) and *nice to watch*.

Mark*: Borderline

*Note on marking
Each of the four categories is awarded a mark out of 5. These marks are then added up to give a total score out of 20.
For the purposes of this course, the sample answers have been graded according to the following scale: **borderline**, **pass**, **good pass**, and **very good pass**.

Alternative approach
Students make notes for their film review, as suggested in the How to go about it box. Circulate and check all the students are writing detailed notes. Then explain that they are going to roleplay a film critics' cocktail party where they mingle and ask other critics about the films they have reviewed. Write some possible questions which they can ask each other on the board, e.g. *Which film are you reviewing? What type of film is it? Were any of the actors particularly impressive? Was the plot convincing?* etc. Then students stand up and mingle. You could join in and ask students about their films. Take feedback from the class and get students to vote on the best film.

Talking about photos
Page 49

Ask students to read the instructions and the Don't forget! box. Remind them to answer the question at the top of each pair of pictures. Ask if they can remember the useful expressions they used to describe the photos in Unit 1, and elicit some of these from various students. Explain that Student A has one minute and Student B has thirty seconds, and suggest that they time each other. Check they understand that this is a monologue and that they shouldn't interrupt their partner.
Circulate and write down some common errors.
Get feedback from the class. Ask various pairs how

they felt about speaking for a full minute. Write the errors on the board and correct them together.

Preparing for listening: Focus on distractors   Page 50

1–2 The aim of this section is to show how distractors are worked into listening exercises. The AB alternatives in exercise 2 mimic the ABC options in Part 1 of the listening exam.
Students do exercises 1 and 2 as suggested. As you get feedback, check students understand the linkers.

Answers
1
2 d **3** a **4** e **5** b
2
1 B **2** B **3** A **4** B **5** B

Multiple choice
Page 50

Students read the instructions and the Don't forget! box. Play the recording twice and let them compare their answers after the first listening. If students have made mistakes you could read out the correct section of the listening script, e.g. in question 1: *I mean, 'politeness' is just not a word he understands.*

Answers
1 C **2** B **3** C **4** A **5** B **6** A **7** B **8** C

Listening: Listening script 1.22–1.29

1 Listen to this woman talking about an actor.

I used to think he was so good looking – those sparkling blue eyes and that sexy smile – but now of course the wrinkles have taken over and he's lost it completely. Call me old-fashioned, but I really don't think that somebody of his age should be wearing tight trousers and flowery shirts. It's obscene. And the way he talks to the press! I mean, 'politeness' is just not a word he understands. I'm not surprised they get upset and give him bad reviews.

2 You overhear this conversation between two friends.

M = Man   W = Woman

M: So, have you decided which film we're going to see, then?

W: Well, I really wanted to see the new Fiona Miller film which everyone is raving about.

M: Oh, please, no! I couldn't stand another costume drama.

W: No, this one's very different from her others. She plays the part of an out of work spy who decides to turn to crime and begin a life as a jewel thief. But anyway, Katie says it's not her cup of tea, so I'm afraid it's 'get your handkerchief ready for another tear-jerker'. You know the plot already: boy meets girl, girl meets another boy, first boy gets upset – all that kind of nonsense.

3 You hear a man telling a woman about a storytelling course he attended.

W = Woman   M = Man

W: So what made you decide to do a storytelling course?

M: Well, a friend of mine who did it last year recommended it to me. She thought I might enjoy it – and she was right. It was great fun, really laid-back and everyone was very supportive. It gave me the courage I needed – and the self-belief – to be able to stand up and speak in front of a group of people.

W: So are you going to be leaving us to take up a career as a storyteller, then?

M: No, I like working here too much.

W: Ha-ha! That's a good story.

4 You hear an actress talking about her performance in a play.

Drained, darling, absolutely drained. And have you read what the critics wrote about it? I don't know how anyone could say it was 'disappointing'. I mean, OK, so it's not the most exciting part I've ever had to play but I gave it my all, absolutely everything. One look at my face will tell you just how utterly exhausted I am. I could sleep for a week.

5 You overhear this man talking on the telephone.

What do you think we should get him? ... An atlas! That's not very much ... I know he's interested in geography, but he's been with the company for nearly 25 years. I really don't think an atlas would express our appreciation for all he's done for the firm. He's been like a father to us all ... I don't know, something that will remind him of us in his retirement, something he can use on a regular basis. How about an e-book reader or a decent video camera – that kind of thing?

6 You hear a young woman talking to her friend about a film.

M = Man   W = Woman

M: What was it like?

W: Oh, don't ask. I certainly wouldn't recommend it to anyone.

M: Too violent for you, was it?

W: Hmm ... Quite the opposite. I mean, at first there was the usual dose of gratuitous violence – basically what you'd expect from that type of film, and partly why I went to see it. After that, though, not a great deal happened. From what I can remember – when I wasn't falling asleep, that is – the script seemed to focus on an analysis of the protagonist's inner self.

M: A kind of 'non-action film', then.

W: Exactly.

7 You hear a woman telephoning a bookshop.

Hello, yes, it's about a book I bought in your shop last week. A Katharine Adams novel. I just wanted to point out that there were one or two pages missing ... No, no, there's really no need to apologize. I mean it's not as if it was the last page or anything. And I got the gist of what was happening without the pages. I just thought you ought to know so you can check the rest of your stock, or talk to the publishers or something ... That's OK ... Yes, pages 60 to 64 ...

8 You hear this young man talking on the phone.

Well, we were born in the same month, but I'm a Leo, as you know, whereas her birthday's at the beginning of July, which makes her a Cancer. I don't know if that's good or bad. We certainly seem to laugh at the same things; the same jokes, the same comedy programmes ... Sorry? ... Oh, next Friday. We're going to a jazz concert, although I can't say it's my favourite type of music. She's really into it, and she wanted me to go, so ...

Vocabulary 2: *Take*   Page 51

This section looks at the meaning of phrasal verbs with *take* and some common expressions that use *take*. Gerunds and infinitives and other verb forms are also revised.

A Phrasal verbs with *take*

1 Elicit answers from the whole class.

2 Students read the text and then decide on the best title in pairs. Elicit an answer from the whole class.

3 Students work in pairs. Check the answers as a whole class.

Additional activity

Ask some questions about the text to check students' understanding of the phrasal verbs.
Who does Roisin take after?
In what way does she take after him?
What did she take up when she was eight?
Did she take to dancing quickly or slowly?
Which part of her body takes over when she dances?
Why did her teacher take her aside?
What did she find hard to take in?
When did her career take off?
How did her career take off?
Write the phrasal verbs on the board in the same order as above (and as in the text). Students retell the story in pairs including all the phrasal verbs.

Answers

1   start (a new job or activity)
2   c
3   **a** resemble
    b start doing
    c start to like
    d gain control
    e move away from other people to talk
    f accept as true
    g start to become successful
    h employ

B Expressions with *take*

1 Pre-teach *stray cat*. Check that students know they have to use *take* in the correct form in each gap, then ask them to do the gap-fill, ignoring the A, B, C, D lettering.

Answers

2	take	3	taking/having taken
4	to take	5	took
6	had taken	7	takes
8	are taking		

2–4 These exercises encourage students to notice which words make up these expressions. Students do exercises 2–4 as suggested.

Answers

2
2   take (me) to school
3   taking (his) advice
4   take (any of) the blame
5   took (more) interest in (the children)
6   taken pity on (it)
7   takes (a great deal of) courage
8   taking so long to (do this exercise)

3
1 D   2 A   3 C   4 B

4
to take pride in something C (3)
to be taken to hospital A (2)
to take a joke B (4)
to take the infinitive D (1)

5 If you think your students will find this too open-ended you could provide more ideas, e.g. a story about taking up a new sport.

Reading and Use of English
Part 6

Gapped text
Page 52

Lead–in
Focus students' attention on the photos. Ask if they have read any of the books or seen a film based on the book. Find out whether they enjoyed it.

1 Students do exercise 1a and 1b as suggested. Ask whether they have ever read any book in English, and elicit some feedback.

Answers

1 C   2 E   3 A   4 H   5 B   6 F   7 D   8 G

2 Do exercise 2 as suggested. Encourage students to guess any difficult vocabulary from the context.

Answers

1   It is an extract from a crime novel.
2   The narrator is angry because she had been trying to forget her father and now he has 'come back into her life'.
3   She wants to know why no one has been punished for the murder of her father.

3 Students read the instructions and the Don't forget! box. Remind them to look carefully at the sentences before and after the gap. Students could compare their answers in pairs and discuss any differences. Correct the exercise. If students have the wrong answer, get students who have the correct answer to explain why they chose this option.

Answers

1 F   2 C   3 E   4 A   5 B   6 G

Reacting to the text
Write up some expressions for hypothesizing on the board.
She probably discovers the secretary … , I expect the murderer … , Maybe her father …
Students discuss the question in pairs.

Learner training
If you have any graded readers in your school, bring them into class. Ask students if they have ever read an English novel. Explain that reading is an excellent way of learning new vocabulary

and consolidating grammar. Let students browse through some of the books. Encourage them to buy a book or borrow one from a library and read it. Once they have read their books, they can do Writing task 2 on page 57 of the Coursebook. They can also discuss their books in groups of four, then exchange books.

Language focus 2: Past tenses   Page 53

1–2 Students do exercise 1 and 2 in pairs.

Answers

1
1 past continuous
2 past perfect
3 past continuous + past simple
4 past simple (×3)
5 past perfect continuous

2
1 d 2 b 3 e 4 a 5 c

3 Students discuss the differences in pairs. Ask students to draw time lines next to each sentence. Go through the pairs of sentences together. If necessary, ask some concept questions to prompt them, e.g. *In which sentence did he read the newspaper after breakfast? In which sentence did he read the newspaper and eat at the same time?* Ask whether there was any vocabulary that they didn't understand, e.g. *to drop a bombshell,* and explain the meaning (to say something that has dramatic consequences).

Answers

1a He read the newspaper *during* his breakfast. (past continuous)
b He read the newspaper *after* his breakfast. (past perfect)
2a I heard about it *while* I was listening to the news on the radio. (past continuous)
b I heard about it, and *as a result* I listened to the news on the radio. (past simple)
3a I no longer live in Oxford. (past simple)
b I had been living in Oxford for six years *when* … (past perfect continuous – the speaker may or may not live in Oxford now)

4 Students answer the questions in exercise 4.

Answers

While can be used in place of *when* in 1a and 2a. It emphasizes that the two things happened at the same time, but does not change the meaning. *As soon as* can be used in place of *when* in 1b and 2b. It emphasizes that the action in the main clause happened immediately after the action in the clause introduced by *as soon as*.

5 Explain that students should read the relevant sections on page 212 of the Grammar reference as they work through this exercise. You might need to give them a few more examples of *in the end* and *at the end,* e.g. *Darcy and Elizabeth get married _____ of the book. They don't get on very well at first, but _____ they fall in love and get married.*

Answers

a at the end   **b** in the end   **c** at last
In sentence **b**, *eventually* can be used instead of *in the end*.

6 Explain the difference between *during* and *for,* and *after* and *afterwards,* as these are typical problem areas. Make sure students understand that *during* needs to be followed by a noun and tells us when something happened, and *for* is followed by a period of time and tells us how long something went on for. Write on the board: *I went to Italy during the holidays. I stayed for two weeks.*
Ask: *How long did I stay in Italy? When did I go to Italy?*
Check students know that *afterwards* means *after that.* Students then do exercise 6 as suggested.

Answers

1 A   2 C   3 B   4 C   5 B   6 C

7 Pre-teach *blush, ponytail, nephew* and *beard.* Students complete the texts.

Answers

Bus blush

1	was travelling	2	were having
3	saw	4	was sitting
5	ran	6	sat
7	had never seen	8	smiled
9	didn't/did not stop	10	(had) got

Face paint

11	had been asking	12	agreed
13	were playing	14	fell
15	had arranged	16	kept
17	saw	18	burst
19	discovered	20	had drawn

Alternative approach

Pre-teach *blush, ponytail, nephew* and *beard*.
Students work in A/B pairs. Student A reads Bus
blush and student B reads Face paint. Students A
and B retell the stories to each other. After this they
fill in the verbs in each story. Correct the stories
together.

Writing 2
Part 2

Report
Page 54

 If you have students who are interested in
preparing for the *First for Schools* version of the
exam, turn to pages 55 and 56 at the end of this
unit for short story preparation and exercises
(photocopiable).

1 Students read the instructions. Ask: *How many
of the topics do you have to write about? What is the
purpose of the report?* Then ask various students to
say briefly what their city offers visitors.

2 This exercise shows different ways of expressing
purpose and extends students' lexical store for
introductions to reports. Students will have further
practice of this in Unit 14. The important skill of
paraphrasing is also developed and will be dealt
with again in Units 7, 10 and 13.
Check students understand *aim* and *provide*.
Students do exercise 2 as suggested.

Answers

1	ways	2	aim	3	aims
4	terms	5	contains	6	provide
7	make	8	order		

3–5 Students do the exercises as suggested.

Answers

3
The report is for the local mayor and is written in
an appropriately formal style.

4
Cinemas: The condition of the cinemas *create[s] a
bad impression on anyone visiting our town.*
Theatres and concert halls: These *offer both
resident and tourist a wide variety of plays and
concerts* but many *overseas visitors do not attend
shows because of the high prices of tickets.*
Recommendations: One suggestion is for some
original version films to be shown *particularly for
the benefit of English-speaking tourists.* The other
recommends *discounts on theatre and concert
tickets for the many young people who come here
to study.*

5a
recommend + should + infinitive without *to*
suggest + gerund
b
Possible answers:
create a bad impression on
anyone visiting our town
there is not much choice in terms of
we are fortunate enough to have
offer ... a wide variety of
visitors comment on
particularly for the benefit of

6 Students read the instructions and the How
to go about it box. Ask a few questions to check
students understand the procedure before they
write their reports.
*What should you include at the beginning of each
paragraph?* (A short title)
*Should the report offer recommendations for
improving facilities for the local residents?* (No, for
visitors to the area)
Can you invent information? (Yes)
What style should you use? (Formal)

⊙ DVD resource: Unit 4

Sample answer
<u>Report about parks and gardens</u> <u>Introduction</u> The aim of this report is to describe what our town offers visitors in terms of parks and gardens. It also makes recommendations for improving these facilities in order to encourage more people to visit the town.

Parks

This town has an excess of 70,000 habitants, but there are only two quite large parks where people can run and play. In addition, only one of the parks 'The Queen's Park', has sports facilities, for example football pitch or tennis court. Moreover, both parks, 'The Queen's Park' and 'The North's Park', are both in the north of the town, the south only has a small park.

Gardens

There are some small parks with flowers and trees that they are good for sitting and eating lunch if you are a worker. However, there is nothing in the town centre, where many people are, including business people and tourists.

Recommendations

I suggest puting sports facilities in 'The North's Park' and make another park in the south. I also recommend to have a garden with flowers in the town centre where the people could enjoy and eat their lunch.

Richard
191 words

Examiner's comment

Content: The report starts well with a clear introduction. However, there is little mention made of visitors. The candidate aims the report at people in general and workers, and only briefly mentions tourists.

Communicative achievement: Appropriately formal with clear headings. Despite some inadequacies of content, the reader would be sufficiently informed.

Organization: The report is clearly divided into appropriate sections. Linking devices are used effectively, e.g. *in order to, in addition, moreover, however*.

Language: Some awkward use of language, e.g. *there are only two quite small parks, both parks … are both*. There are also some basic errors, e.g. misuse of possessive 's', *the North's Park*, problems with gerunds – *I suggest make (making), recommend to have (having)*, omission of reflexive pronoun – *people could enjoy (themselves)*, use of double subject – *that they are good*. Some errors with word formation and spelling, but these do not distract the reader, e.g. *habitants, putting*. Suitable use of

vocabulary for the task, e.g. *aim, facilities, football pitch, tennis court*. Some use of more complex structures, e.g. *also makes recommendations for improving, in order to encourage more people to visit, suggest putting*, but in general the language is very simple.

Mark*: Pass

*Note on marking
Each of the four categories is awarded a mark out of 5. These marks are then added up to give a total score out of 20.
For the purposes of this course, the sample answers have been graded according to the following scale: **borderline**, **pass**, **good pass**, and **very good pass**.

Review 4 Answers Pages 56–57

Reading and Use of English Part 4 — **Transformations**

1   soon as the meeting had
2   the time we got to
3   leave until he (had) put
4   not to take him on
5   not take/have/show much interest in
6   never read such a funny

Correcting mistakes

2   part, As for ~~as~~
3   much, the
4   ~~had~~ came, was
5   took ~~to~~ your advice, a

Vocabulary: Cinema

1	cast	2	role
3	critics, reviews	4	plot
5	scene		

Reading and Use of English Part 3 — **Word formation**

1
to attract new students to the *Storytime School of Storytelling*

2

1	interested	2	librarians
3	confidence	4	creativity
5	fascinating	6	performances
7	surprisingly	8	unlimited/limitless

Learner training

Now that you are well into the course, you could prepare a short questionnaire to find out how students feel they are progressing. Ask whether:

- the pace of the class is correct
- they would like to do more or less of particular activities
- they feel their English is improving
- they have done all the homework.

Include a section for any other comments.

Study the questionnaires and have class feedback in the next lesson. Discuss any issues openly and try to find solutions if there are any problems. For example, if some students feel the pace is too fast whilst others feel it is too slow, you could bring in coloured cards. Ask students who feel the class is too slow to take a green card, students who feel it is too fast should take a red card and those who are happy with the pace should take a yellow card. Then ask them to move and sit with students who have a different coloured card. This will mean that stronger students can help weaker ones.
Encourage students to always tell you if they have any problems.

 Progress Test 2

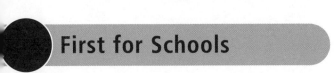

First for Schools

Writing Part 2   **Short story**

This photocopiable is intended for those students who are preparing for the *First for Schools* exam. It replaces the Writing section (Report) on pages 54 and 55 of the Coursebook.

1 Read the following Writing Part 2 instructions.

You have seen this announcement in an international magazine for teenagers.

> **Story competition**
>
> For this month's competition, we would like you to write a story which begins with this sentence:
>
> *It was a big mistake not to go home straight away.*
>
> Your story should include:
> • bad weather
> • a pleasant surprise
>
> The best entry will win a year's subscription to the magazine.

Write your **story** in **140–190** words.

2 Read the two sample answers **A** and **B** and decide which is the better entry.

A

It was a big mistake not to go home straight away. My friend and I stayed at school to play chess. At 3.30 when school finished it was sunny. When we finished our game at 4.15, it was raining very hard. What a mistake! 'Why didn't we go home at 3.30?' my friend said. We decided to stay at school and play more chess and wait for the sun, and we played and played and we waited and waited, the rain did not stop, my friend remembered he had his mobile phone and he phoned his mum, she did not answer, maybe she did not have her mobile phone with her, normally she was with her mobile phone all the time - that was not a very pleasant surprise for us. Then a teacher came and said, 'You have to go home now, it's very late.' So we went home and got very wet. We arrived at my home and it stopped raining. 'That's typical,' I said.

B

It was a big mistake not to go home straight away. My sister and I had just been to the cinema and when we came out we were thrilled to see it was snowing. Although it was getting late, we just couldn't resist making a snowman.

However, by the time we arrived at the bus stop, we had missed the last bus. Unfortunately, we couldn't afford to get a taxi back to our village and our parents had gone away for the weekend, so we had to set off on foot in the snow.

After we had been walking for nearly an hour we were both freezing cold and exhausted. It was snowing so heavily that we could hardly make out where we were going and we had both fallen over several times in the deep snow.

Just as our situation was becoming desperate, a car pulled up beside us and my mother opened the window. 'Would you like a lift?' she asked. My parents had had to come home because of the poor weather conditions. It was such a surprise and a relief to see them again.

3 The box below shows the criteria which an examiner would use when marking these competition entries. Decide how well each story satisfies the criteria by answering the questions in each category. Give examples from the stories to support your opinions.

Content:	Have the instructions in the question been followed?
Range:	Have a variety of past tenses been used? Is there a wide range of vocabulary and structures?
Organization and cohesion:	Are the ideas and events organized logically? Are linking devices used well?
Style:	Is the story written using suitably neutral language? (neither too formal nor too informal)
Target reader:	Would the story have a chance of winning the competition?

4 Your teacher has asked you to write a story for the school's English magazine.
It must begin with this sentence:
Amy started to panic when she found herself stuck in a traffic jam.
Your story must include:
- a hat
- a meal

Write your **story** in **140–190** words.

> **How to go about it**
>
> - Think of a general outline for your story.
>   Here is an example:
>   1 *boyfriend's birthday – meeting him in a restaurant – going to be late*
>   2 *tries to phone him – no signal – worried he'll be angry*
>   3 *passes broken-down car causing traffic jam – owner wearing a hat like boyfriend's*
>   4 *arrives at restaurant – boyfriend not there – he phones – his is the broken-down car*
>
>   Now think of another possible storyline. Remember, your story has to include a meal and a hat.
> - Make a plan, organizing your ideas into logical paragraphs.
>
>   Opening: Set the scene (e.g. **1** in the example outline above).
>   Main events: One or two paragraphs on what happened (e.g. **2** and **3** above).
>   Ending: This could refer back to something earlier in the story (e.g. **4** above).
> - In your story, include a variety of past tenses, a range of relevant vocabulary and appropriate linking words.
> - Make sure your story begins with the given sentence and includes the two given elements (*a hat* and *a meal*)

Now you are ready to write your story in **140–190** words.

Teacher's notes

1 Students read the instructions. Tell them not to look at the sample answers yet. Ask them to brainstorm possible ideas for a story in pairs. Then elicit their ideas as a whole class.

2 Students work individually.

Answers

2
B is the better entry.
It follows the instructions in the question.
It is organized into clear and logical paragraphs.
It uses a variety of past tenses appropriately.
It includes a range of vocabulary and linking devices.

3 Students work in pairs. Draw the table below on the board and ask them to copy it.

	Sample A	Sample B
Content		
Range		
Organization and cohesion		
Style		
Target reader		

Ask students to use the questions to fill in the table for the two samples. Feedback as a whole class and elicit additional detail, e.g. *What is the problem with the content of sample A?* It turns a pleasant surprise into something negative.

Note
The criteria on page 193 of the Coursebook are all important points for students to bear in mind when preparing for the Writing paper in the *First* exam. While the official terms used by Cambridge English are phrased slightly differently, the same features are considered: Content, Communicative achievement (including appropriate register for the target reader), Organization, Language (including accuracy and range).
The Cambridge English terms are used in the Examiner's comments on the sample answers in this Teacher's Book. These headings are also used in the analysis of the model Writing tasks in the two practice tests which are on the Ready for First Practice Online site.

Answers

3
Content:
B Yes.
A Not entirely. It begins with the given sentence and includes bad weather, but it turns *a pleasant surprise* into a negative: *that was not a very pleasant surprise for us*.

Range:
B Tenses: Yes, past perfect simple and continuous, past simple and continuous.
B Vocabulary and structures: Yes, *thrilled, couldn't resist making a snowman, couldn't afford to get a taxi back, set off on foot, freezing cold and exhausted, could hardly make out*, etc.
A Tenses: No, almost exclusively the past simple, and one example of the past continuous (*it was raining*).
A Vocabulary and structures: There is some evidence of good use of vocabulary and structure (e.g. *stayed at school to play chess, it was raining very hard*), though generally the language is quite basic and repetitive (e.g. *play, wait, mobile phone*).

Organization and cohesion:
B Yes. Use of tenses and paragraphs helps organize events.
B Yes. Linking devices include: *when, although, however, by the time, so, after, just as*.
A The order of the events is clear, but these are not organized into paragraphs. One paragraph for a story of this length is not acceptable.
A Linking words are limited: *when, then, so*. The sentence beginning *We decided to stay at school … is overlong and joins ideas with a series of commas rather than linking devices.

Style:
B Yes.
A Yes.

Target reader:
B Yes, for all the reasons given above.
A No, for all the reasons given above.

4 Students read the information and instructions. Then ask them to think of an idea for the story in pairs and write a plan. Ask various students to give a brief summary of their story to the whole class. Students write their story for homework. In the next lesson, you could get them to swap stories and fill in a marking criteria table like the one previously used.

5 Doing what you have to

Content Overview

Themes

The unit is concerned with school rules, household chores, being a parent and the world of work. The grammar and vocabulary are related to these themes.

Exam-related activities

Reading and Use of English

Part 7	Multiple matching
Part 2	Open cloze
Part 4	Transformations (Review)
Part 3	Word formation (Review)
Part 1	Multiple-choice cloze (Review)

Writing

Part 1	Essay

Listening

Part 4	Multiple choice
Part 2	Sentence completion

Speaking

Part 2	Talking about photos
Part 3	Collaborative task

Other

Language focus 1:	Obligation, necessity and permission
Language focus 2:	Noun phrases
Vocabulary:	The world of work
Word formation:	-en suffix

Speaking 1
Part 2

Talking about photos
Page 58

Lead–in

Books closed. Ask students if discipline is a problem in high schools in their country. Elicit some of the problems and find out whether they think the situation is getting worse.

1 Books open. Ask students to read the instructions and carry out the task. As this is the first activity in the unit, you can be flexible with the time. Get some class feedback and find out what students said in the question for Student B (which student is behaving worse). Ask the class if anybody has ever done any of the things shown and find out how they feel about the use of mobile phones in class. Do they think there are any circumstances when students should be allowed to use their mobile phones?

2 Students change roles and discuss photographs 3 and 4 in the same way.

Reading and Use of English 1
Part 7

Multiple matching
Page 58

1 Check students can use *agree* and *disagree* correctly (in some languages it is an adjective not a verb). Give examples of correct use (*I agree with* + noun or *I agree that* + clause) and point out errors like *I am agree*. Then ask students to read the questions. Write up some general areas for them to consider, e.g. in class, homework, exams, moving around the school, lunch time, break time. Ask one member of each group to take notes. Having to write their ideas down will encourage them to think of a wider range of rules and punishments and will help in the feedback stage. Students discuss the questions in groups of three. Get some class feedback.

2 Ask students to read the instructions and the Don't forget! box. Suggest they work in pairs to underline key words in the statements. Check students understand *forbidden* and *ban*.

Alternative approach

Students work in groups of four. Each student reads a different part of the text (A, B, C or D) and summarizes the information orally for their partners. Then they read the remaining sections and do the matching task.

Reacting to the text

Elicit some expressions for agreeing and disagreeing and write them on the board. You could add the ones which come up in the reading, e.g. *that's just silly/I can't see why/they should/I think it's unfair*, etc. Draw student's attention to the last point in the Don't forget! box, and encourage them to use the expressions on the board to help them develop their opinions.

Answers

1 C *According to the head teacher, in a busy school piercings present 'a very real risk of accidents'. I can't see why …*

2 A *They didn't let us drink water in the classroom either... to the end of the paragraph.*

3 D *... all rules, whatever they are, help to ... get children ready for the real world.*

4 B *David doesn't have to wear a tie if he doesn't want to, even though it's part of the uniform. That's just silly.*

5 C *It seems I agreed to all this when I signed the school rules document at the beginning of last term, but I honestly wasn't aware of any ban on tiny metal objects in the nose.*

6 B *It's very confusing ... Everything was black and white in those days ...*

7 A *... and sometimes this got in the way of learning.*

8 D *Discipline there has gone downhill in the last few years and the kids seem to do what they want.*

9 C *I was still furious when they made her take it out and sent her home for the day: they humiliated her in front of her classmates ...*

10 B *I almost wrote to the school about it, but my son advised me against it.*

Language focus 1: Obligation, necessity and permission

Page 60

1 Students work in pairs. During feedback you might need to highlight the meaning and form of *have to*, as this is a typical problem area. Write on the board:
I had to wear a jacket and tie.
David doesn't have to wear a tie.
Ask students to make the affirmative, negative and question forms, e.g. *I had to wear/I didn't have to wear/Did you have to wear?* etc. Ask concept questions to check they understand the meaning of *don't have to*, e.g. *Is it necessary for David to wear a tie?* (No).

Answers

a

1	could (do)	5	can (be used)

b

1	couldn't do	3	didn't let us drink
5	cannot be used	7	isn't allowed to wear
9	weren't allowed to have		

c

2	had to wear	4	have to drink
8	made her take		

d

6	doesn't have to wear
10	don't need to be convinced

2 You could give a few more examples as students are usually surprised by this aspect of obligation, e.g. *You must come round to dinner some time. I have to wear a uniform at my school.*

Answers

a a teacher (to students)

b one student to another

- *Must* expresses the authority of the speaker, i.e. the obligation comes from the teacher and it is the teacher who is imposing the obligation (the speaker's internal obligation).

- *Have to* is used to show that the authority does not come from the speaker but from someone else, i.e. the teacher (external obligation).

3 Students work in pairs. Circulate and help them with any problems. Correct the answers together and then ask a few more concept questions, as some students find this grammar point tricky.
Which modal do we use to give strong advice? (must)
Which modal do we use for strong obligations imposed by the speaker? (must)
Does 'must' have a past form? (no)
Which form do we use to talk about an obligation in the past? (had to)
Which form do we use to refer to strong obligations imposed by another person? (have to)
How can we express a lack of obligation? (don't have to)

Answers

1 I don't have to/don't need to tidy ...
2 Do you have to ...?/Must you ...?
3 Last week I had to go ...
4 Were you allowed to watch ...?
5 Now I have to start ...
6 But you don't have to ...
7 You need to prepare ...
8 You really should go/You really must go ...

Additional activity

Model and practise the pronunciation of *must* and *mustn't*, paying attention to strong and weak forms. Choral drill the following sentences.

You mustn't eat in the library. /ˈmʌsənt/

You must eat your vegetables. /məst/

Must I sign this? /mʌst

4 Before doing the exercises, ask students to read about permission in the Grammar reference section on page 213. Then circulate and help students as they do exercises 4a and b.

During feedback, ask a few concept questions.

Is let *used in the passive?* (No)

Which verb do we use instead of let? (*be allowed to*)

Which verb form do we use after make *in the passive?* (infinitive with *to*)

Answers			
4a 1	allowed to drink (*let* is not possible in the passive)		
2	made to take		
b 1	allowed	**2** let	**3** made/makes

5 Check students understand the meaning of *supposed to* because it may be a false friend. Ask students to work individually, as this will allow you to see if they really understand the structures. Circulate and help with any problems.

Answers		
1 should	**2** mustn't	**3** need
4 don't have to	**5** ought	**6** supposed to
7 have to	**8** better	

6 Students discuss the questions in groups of three. If you have a multilingual group, they could give some information about things a visitor to their country should know, e.g. *In Japan, you have to take your shoes off when you come into the house.*

 **DVD resource: Unit 5**

Word formation: -*en* suffix   Page 61

1a Write *tight* on the board. Ask how we can change it into a verb. Elicit *tighten*. Focus students' attention on the examples in the Coursebook. Elicit the rule for when to use the double consonant.

Answers			
weaken	sweeten	deafen	fatten
brighten	widen	worsen	sadden

1b Write *strong* on the board. Elicit the noun *strength*. Ask how the verb is formed: *strengthen*. Do the exercise and have students spell the words out loud in the class feedback. Model and check the pronunciation of *heighten, lengthen, strengthen*.

Answers		
Adjective	**Noun**	**Verb**
strong	strength	strengthen
long	length	lengthen
high	height	heighten

2–3 Students work in pairs to complete the sentences, then discuss the questions. Get some class feedback. Don't go into too much detail about question 5, as these topics are covered in more depth at a later point in the Coursebook.

Answers		
2 brighten	**3** sweeten	**4** deafening
5 worsened	**6** strengths	**7** lengthen
8 heights		

Reading and Use of English 2
Part 2

Open cloze   Page 62

1 Students work in pairs. Get feedback from the class and check they understand why each quotation is amusing.

2 Pre-teach *chores*. Students work in groups of three. Circulate and join in with the conversations.

3 Focus students' attention on the visual. Check they understand *flat*. Ask if they think the book would be useful to any of the students in their groups.

4 Do exercise 4 as suggested. Explain that reading the whole cloze first, before completing the task, is a good habit as it will help them understand the general gist before they look at the details.

5 Students read the instructions and the How to go about it box. Ask them how many words they have to put in each gap (one). Remind them that grammar words are missing from the cloze tests, e.g. prepositions, relative pronouns, linking devices, etc. Students work individually. Check the answers as a class.

Answers

1	so	2	on
3	to	4	Although/Though
5	what/which	6	not
7	in	8	made

Listening 1
Part 4

Multiple choice

Page 63

1 If possible, get students to sit next to someone of a different age or nationality. Then ask students to discuss the question in groups of three. Get feedback from students of different ages or from different countries as their answers will probably vary.

2 Students read the instructions and questions. Encourage them to underline key words. Play the recording twice and get students to compare their answers in pairs after the first listening. Ask whether they think Deborah's advice is good. Correct the answers together.

Answers

1 A 2 C 3 B 4 C 5 A 6 B 7 B

Listening 1: Listening script 1.30

D = Deborah Chilton   I = Interviewer

I: Few of us would admit to actually enjoying doing the housework, so getting our teenage children to do their fair share is no easy task. Deborah Chilton, the author of a new parenting book, *The Stress Free Guide to Bringing up Teenagers*, is here to give us a few pointers. Deborah, where do we start?

D: Well, as you say, it's not easy, but if we're aware of what we're trying to achieve and why, then the battle is half won. Getting teenagers to contribute to housework has so many benefits. It's an ideal way of teaching them what it means to belong to a family and a community. They also learn to take on more responsibility as they approach adulthood, and they pick up some useful skills on the way, too. Knowing all this gives parents the strength they need to see their goals through.

I: Right. And at what age should teenagers begin helping out with the housework?

D: Long before they reach adolescence. Teenagers are naturally resistant to being told what to do, and suddenly asking them at fourteen or fifteen to take on chores when they've never done anything to help before – well, let's just say it doesn't meet with a very positive reaction. Parents often fail to take advantage of the fact that young children are quite happy to make their bed, tidy their room, lay the table or wash the dishes. So get them started early and you'll find it easier later on.

I: And what sort of things can teenagers do?

D: Cleaning, washing, ironing. Anything, really. Planning and cooking a meal each week is excellent training, and teaches teenagers how much time and effort goes into putting food on the table. Whatever they do, just be sure to explain to them carefully how to do it first. My son once almost tried to wash the toaster in the sink while it was still plugged in!

I: Oh dear!

D: Yes. Teenagers will make mistakes, and that's part of the learning process. But it's best to try and avoid them before they actually happen.

I: Indeed. And what if your teenage son or daughter decides not to do a chore? What then?

D: Well, it's a good idea to make their contribution something that's important to them as well. That way, if it's not done, they're the ones to suffer. So for example, if they don't do the washing, they won't have clean clothes for a party; if they don't do the shopping, they can't eat. They'll get the idea eventually.

I: So you wouldn't consider handing out punishments?

D: Only as a last resort. They tend to cause bad feeling and resentment. If things don't get better, sit down together and remind them of their duty to other family members and the need to work as a team. And for the same reasons, don't give financial rewards for completing chores. Housework is an obligation, rather than a choice, and no one gets paid for doing it.

I: Hmm. If only we did! So, housework has to be done, and that's it.

D: Yes, but there's still room for some negotiation. Understandably, teenagers like to feel they have at least some say in the matter. So whilst the chore itself is not negotiable, when it is carried out might be. In fact, rather than say to your teenage child 'could you load the dishwasher?' – to which they could answer 'no' – ask them instead 'would you like to load the dishwasher before or after the film?' That way there's an element of choice, and the job gets done sooner or later.

I: Very clever. I like that.

D: Yes. And I would just like to say, that although domestic duties can be a pain, they can also be a welcome distraction. Teenagers generally have a lot on their minds, whether it's schoolwork, friendship problems or boyfriend/girlfriend issues. Vacuuming the carpet, cutting the grass or cleaning the car provides an alternative focus and helps take a teenager's mind off his or her daily concerns.

I: Certainly. And that's a very positive note to finish on. Deborah, thank you for coming in ...

3 Discuss the question as a class. Ask if they have ever been paid for doing household chores.

Speaking 2
Part 3

Collaborative task
Page 63

1–2 Ask students to read the instructions and the Don't forget! box. Make sure they don't start doing the task yet. Check they understand *fairness*. Ask some questions, e.g.
Do you have to talk about all the qualities? (Yes)
What do you have to do in Part 2? (decide on the two most important qualities)
Read through the Useful language box together. Encourage students to use these expressions when they are doing the task. Look briefly at the expressions previously studied on page 36 of the Coursebook. Explain that students will usually do the Speaking exam in pairs, but occasionally it is carried out in a group of three, so they can complete this task in groups of three. Use the same mixed age/nationality groups from those set up for the listening activity.
Circulate and record any errors. Get class feedback and find out if they agreed on the two most important qualities. Ask if they used the expressions from the Useful language box. Write some of their errors on the board and correct them together.

Vocabulary: The world of work Page 64

This section deals with expressions and collocations related to work.

1a Write: *I have an interesting work/job* on the board and ask which word is correct. Elicit that the countable noun *job* is correct and that *work* is not correct because it is uncountable. Point out that *work* can be used before the verbs in exercise 1a, but without an indefinite article. Students then complete the activity.

1b After students have done the exercise, check their understanding by asking:
Which verb means …
… it is your decision to leave? (resign)
… you lose your job, because you did something wrong? (sack)
… you lose your job, because the company is having problems? (made redundant)

Answers
1a
1 be out of a job
2 look for a job
3 apply for a job
4 go for an interview for a job
5 get a job
1b
1 made redundant
2 resigned
3 sacked

2 In some languages the noun *career* is a false friend, and the words *earn* and *win* are the same. After completing the exercise, point out that we study a *subject* not a *career* and that undergraduate studies at university are known as a *degree*. Point out that we *win* a competition or a game, but we *earn* money in a job.

Answers	
a *study a career*	is **not** possible
b *earn a competition*	is **not** possible

3 Students discuss the differences in pairs. As feedback, read out the definitions in the wrong order and get students to say which expression you are describing.

Answers
1a *to work part-time* – when you are contracted to work fewer hours than a normal working week, e.g. 21 hours per week or 3 days a week (a part-time job)
b *to work full-time* – when you are contracted to work a full working week, e.g. 35 hours per week (a full-time job)
2a *to work overtime* – to work supplementary hours for which you are paid extra
b *to work long hours* – to work for many hours each day
3a *to work flexitime* – to work with a flexible timetable: within limits you decide when you start and when you finish, as long as you work the required total number of hours each month
b *to work shifts* – to work for a set period (e.g. 12 am to 8 am) before other workers replace you for the next set period (e.g. 8 am to 4 pm)

Additional activity

Students work in pairs. They write five questions using the vocabulary and expressions from exercises 1 to 3, e.g. *How should I prepare for a job interview? Do you think it's more important to enjoy your work or to earn a high salary?* etc. Then they join with another pair and ask them their questions.

4 Students do the exercises as suggested. Model and check the pronunciation of *surgeon*.

Answers

a   chef, hairdresser, surgeon, dustman, hotel receptionist

Alternative activity

Ask one student to choose a job from the photos. Tell them not to say which job they have chosen. Ask them *yes/no* questions to find out which job they chose, e.g. *Do you have to be patient to do this job? Is it satisfying? Do you need a lot of qualifications? Do you travel a lot?* etc. Get another student to guess the job. Students play the game in groups of three. They can either use the jobs in the photos or other jobs. Encourage them to use the Useful language box.

Listening 2
Part 2
Sentence completion
Page 65

1 Students discuss the questions in pairs.

2 Students read the instructions and choose the correct options in the Don't forget! box. This provides useful exam information and also uses the language studied in the unit.

Answers

- You *don't need to* write more than three words for each answer.
- You *should* write a word or phrase that you actually hear. You *don't need to* rephrase.
- Minor spelling errors *can* be made, but the words you write *need to* be recognizable, so you *should* check your spelling.
- You *can* expect to hear the answers in the same order as the questions.

Students read the sentences for questions 1–10 and predict the answers in pairs. Check they understand *recruit* and *vulnerable*. Play the recording twice and

get students to compare their answers in pairs after the first listening. Ask whether they were surprised by any of the information.

Answers

1   academic qualifications
2   people
3   back *and* legs
4   three
5   four days
6   wear full uniform
7   elderly *and* disabled
8   evening
9   several hours
10   satisfying

Listening 2: Listening script 1.31

Right, let's start by talking about the selection procedure. What do you have to do in order to become a firefighter? Well, it's a fairly rigorous process, with a range of different tests. We don't insist on any academic qualifications, but potential recruits do have to take a short educational test. Now this test is aimed at assessing basic literacy and numeracy, or in other words, reading, writing and arithmetic. But we also look at a candidate's people skills, because community work, dealing with the public, is such an important part of the job nowadays. And I'll say a bit more about that later.

Now you may be surprised to hear that firefighters no longer have to be a minimum height. Instead, they do a series of physical tests, which are designed to measure things like how tightly they can grip things, or whether their back and legs are strong enough. If they **get through** this stage they **go on to** the next one, the practical awareness day, which involves fitness tests, checks to see if claustrophobia is a problem and practical tasks such as ladder climbing.

Of course, both sexes are accepted into the force, though I have to say, women are still very much in the minority. In case you're wondering, we've had up to five women working with us at Hove Fire Station at any one time in the past. At the moment, though, there are just three on the workforce.

OK, what's next? Well, as you know, firefighters are on call 24 hours a day, so let me just say a little bit about how the shift system works. At Hove we operate an eight-day rota. That means a firefighter works two nine-hour day shifts, followed by two fifteen-hour night shifts. And then we get four days off before starting again. It's a continuous cycle.

Er, a typical shift begins with the Watch Parade, which is where one shift **hands over** to the next. Now this is a fairly formal affair and it's compulsory for everyone to wear full uniform. After that – if it's a day shift – mornings are **taken up with** training and equipment checks. We have to make sure that vital equipment such as our breathing apparatus is in perfect working order.

And our fire engines, of course, have to be checked from top to bottom, too. Er, afternoons are usually **given over to** community safety work, which is what I mentioned at the beginning. So, for example, we do a lot of home safety visits, where we give advice to vulnerable people, such as the elderly and disabled, on how to keep their homes safe. And we'll fit smoke alarms if they haven't got them installed already.

One question I often get asked at these talks is 'What is your busiest time?' Well, we tend to get **called out** more in the evening, rather than during the day. That's the time when shops and other business premises are left unattended, and also when most people are at home, cooking and so on. As you might expect, the majority of fires are domestic ones. The fires themselves often take only minutes to **put out**, but **clearing up** afterwards can take several hours. We have to do everything we can to prevent the danger of a fire re-igniting, so that means taking all the floors up, getting flammable things like carpets out of the building, and so on.

So what's it like being a firefighter? Well, obviously it's dangerous work and any firefighter who said that he had never felt frightened would be fooling himself and you. But it's all a matter of control. It's what we've been trained for and we learn to control feelings such as fear. But quite apart from the danger and the drama of the job, it's obviously very satisfying being out on the street, knowing that you're helping the public, doing something useful. I certainly don't think I'd be able to do any other job.

3 Some students may have found the listening task quite challenging, so reading through the script and working with the phrasal verbs will help with confidence building.

Answers

get through – pass a test or stage of something

go on to – do something after you have finished doing something else

take up with – (*always passive*) be busy doing something

give over to – (*usually passive*) use something for a particular purpose

call out – ask a person or organization that provides a service to come and deal with something for you

put out – make something stop burning, extinguish

clear up – make a place tidy

4 Elicit some responses from the class.

Learner training

Students add the phrasal verbs to their vocabulary notebooks.

Language focus 2: Noun phrases Page 66

Books closed. Write the following on the board:

a Sunday	*equipment*
work	*newspaper*
a series of	*force*
the fire fighter's	*tests*

Ask students to match the words (*a Sunday newspaper, workforce, a series of tests, the fire fighter's equipment*). Explain that these are all noun phrases.

1 Books open. Students work in pairs to do the exercise as suggested. Correct the answers together. Pay special attention to the use of '*s* or *s*' in C and D as students often have difficulty with this. Mention that the first word in a noun phrase is stressed.

Answers

1 workforce
2 a series of tests
3 the top of the ladder
4 a candidate's back and legs
5 a Sunday newspaper
6 next Friday's meeting
7 four weeks' work
8 wine bottle

2–3 Students work in pairs. Encourage them to use expressions of agreeing and disagreeing in exercise 3.

Answers

1 start of the day, cups of coffee
2 holiday job, leisure time
3 night shift, month's holiday
4 world of work, waste of time
5 job opportunities, young person's chances
6 work experience, workplace

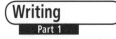 **Writing** Part 1 | **Essay**
Pages 66 and 67

1 Students read the instructions and the essay question. Then ask them to work in pairs and to think of two ideas for each of the 'Things to write about'.

2 Students do exercise 2 as suggested. You could also ask which of the ideas that they came up with in exercise 1 were mentioned in the model letter.

Answers

a The writer has dedicated most of the essay to the first point: *contact with people*. Little has been said about *working hours* and in the last paragraph, the writer has misinterpreted what is meant by *your own idea*: the third point in Part 1 Writing questions invites students to introduce an idea of their own that relates to the essay question.

b The language is repetitive, with the result that some of the writer's ideas are not expressed very coherently. In the second paragraph alone, *talk to* is used four times; there are two more examples in the third paragraph, where *work(ing) all the time* is also repeated.

c The style is too informal, too conversational for an essay. As well as contractions (*I'd, can't, it's*, etc) there are a number of informal words such as *OK, really, loads of, a bit* (lonely) and *pretty* (boring). Short sentences such as *No one else* and *I think so, anyway* are also very conversational and an example of poor organization of ideas.

d There is evidence of linking, but again this is often informal and limited to *if* (four times), *so* (three times), *but* (twice), *anyway* (twice) and even *OK*.

3 Students work individually to correct the mistakes. Take class feedback. Ask students to spell the words out loud.

Answers

ofice	office
their's only you	there's only you
helthy	healthy
oppinions	opinions
lonley	lonely
your at home	you're at home
poeple	people
intresting	interesting
realy	really
brakes	breaks

Learner training
Remind students to use a dictionary or to run a spellcheck before handing in any essay. Suggest that they record words which they weren't sure of, because they will not be able to use a dictionary in the exam.

4 Students read the instructions and the Don't forget! box. Ask if they can remember any of the linking devices and expressions for introducing and concluding which they studied in Unit 3 on page 39. Look back at these together. If you decide to set the second essay question, ask students to brainstorm ideas in pairs.

Sample answer

Often our parents and grandparents say that the life was more difficult before than now. Personally, I think this is true for some things but not for everything.

For example, on one side the health of people is better now becuase there are more medicins and hospitals and doctors can get better the people easier. In the past the old people could die from illness which today are not very hard. As well, more children goes to school now – before, children started to work with twelve or younger. In some countrys old people cannot read or write very well becuase they left the school early. On another side, the work is still a problem like it was before. Perhaps it is worse now, becuase the unemployment is high and the young people have problems to find a job.

In conclusion, I think life is better for young people now, not harder, becuase they have a better health, they go to the school and if they can become a job then they do not have to work many hours.

Mario Prim
178 words

Examiner's comment

Content: Adequate coverage of 1 and 2, and candidate has added their own idea.

Communicative achievement: There is appropriately formal register and format. Although the target reader would be sufficiently informed, the frequent inaccuracies would create a negative effect.

Organization: Has introduction and conclusion, but starts the second paragraph with an example and gives their personal opinion in the introduction. Misuse of linking devices e.g. *on another side, as well*.

Language: Frequent errors distract the reader, e.g. misuse of definite article – *the life, the school, the work, on one side*, false agreement – *children goes to school*, confusion with gerunds and infinitives – *problems to find a job*, problems with uncountable nouns – *a better health*. At times errors lead to confusion, e.g. *doctors can get better the people easier, if they can become a job, very hard (serious)*. There are three spelling mistakes, but these do not obscure meaning – *becuase, medicins, countrys*. Limited use of vocabulary and cohesive devices. Language is simple and contains frequent inaccuracies.

Mark*: Borderline

*Note on marking

Each of the four categories is awarded a mark out of 5. These marks are then added up to give a total score out of 20.

For the purposes of this course, the sample answers have been graded according to the following scale: **borderline**, **pass**, **good pass**, and **very good pass**.

Additional activity

Make a revision activity. Write the transformation sentences from the exercise on page 69 onto cards. Put them in an envelope and write *obligation, necessity and permission* on the front and stick the answers on the back. Bring these, along with other envelopes which you will prepare in later units, to a lesson towards the end of the course. Students work in pairs, they choose an envelope and work through the cards. Remind them not to write on the cards.

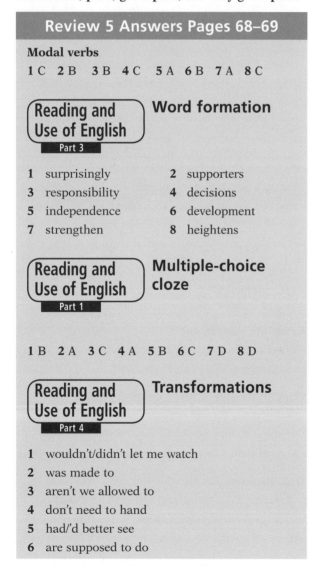

Review 5 Answers Pages 68–69

Modal verbs

1 C   2 B   3 B   4 C   5 A   6 B   7 A   8 C

Reading and Use of English Part 3 — **Word formation**

1 surprisingly	**2** supporters
3 responsibility	**4** decisions
5 independence	**6** development
7 strengthen	**8** heightens

Reading and Use of English Part 1 — **Multiple-choice cloze**

1 B   2 A   3 C   4 A   5 B   6 C   7 D   8 D

Reading and Use of English Part 4 — **Transformations**

1 wouldn't/didn't let me watch
2 was made to
3 aren't we allowed to
4 don't need to hand
5 had/'d better see
6 are supposed to do

6 Relative relationships

Content Overview

Themes

The unit is about relationships within and outside the family. Students also review and extend their vocabulary related to describing people.

Exam-related activities

Reading and Use of English

Part 1	Multiple-choice cloze
Part 5	Multiple choice
Part 4	Transformations (Review)

Writing

Part 2	Article
Part 2	Email (Review)

Listening

Part 3	Multiple matching
Part 1	Multiple choice

Speaking

Part 3	Collaborative task
Part 1	Interview

Other

Language focus 1: Defining relative clauses
Language focus 2: Non-defining relative clauses
Language focus 3: Causative passive with *have*
 and *get*
Vocabulary 1: Phrasal verbs
Vocabulary 2: Describing people

Vocabulary 1: Phrasal verbs   Page 70

Lead–in

Focus students' attention on the photos. Ask how the people are feeling in each one. Elicit *having a row* (/raʊ/).

Students discuss the two questions in pairs. Get feedback on their ideas and ask if they agree with each other. Write up any new vocabulary on the board.

A Romance

1 Students should be familiar with some of the phrasal verbs in this exercise. The context will help them to guess the others. Get them to do the exercise individually, so that they focus on the meaning of each verb.

---

2 Students match the verbs from exercise 1 to their meanings. Remind them to write down the infinitive form of the verb.

Answers
1 to fall out with somebody
2 to split up with somebody
3 to be going out with somebody
4 to get on with somebody
5 to fall for somebody
6 to get over somebody

3 Students work in pairs to memorize the example sentences.

B Family

1–2 Students work out the meaning of the phrasal verbs in pairs. Elicit definitions during class feedback. Mention that *grow up* is an intransitive verb (it does not take a direct object) and therefore cannot be used in the passive. Model and check the pronunciation of *brought*.

Answers
1
1 to take care of a child until he or she becomes an adult
2 to change from being a baby or young child to being an older child or adult
3 to tolerate or accept unpleasant behaviour by someone without complaining
4 to criticize someone angrily for doing something wrong
5 to admire and respect someone
6 to make someone disappointed
2
1 to bring somebody up
2 to grow up
3 to put up with something
4 to tell somebody off
5 to look up to somebody
6 to let somebody down

3 Students do exercise 3 as suggested. Circulate and check students' gapped sentences are correct.

Alternative approach

Students work in pairs. Ask them to write five questions using some of the phrasal verbs from exercises A and B. Give them an example: *Where were you brought up?* Circulate and check their questions are correct. Students join with another pair and ask and answer their questions. Encourage them to add extra information. In class feedback, ask students to tell you something interesting they found out about their partners.

 **Collaborative task**
Page 71

1–2 Students read the instructions and the Useful language box. Check they understand the meaning of *arise*. Before they start, get them to write down useful phrasal verbs and vocabulary next to each of the categories, to use during the task, e.g. Boyfriends and girlfriends: *split up with, fall out with*. Remind them that tasks 1 and 2 should be done separately, and mention that part of the marks for the Speaking exam will be based on their range of vocabulary. After they have completed the tasks, comment on students' performance in terms of vocabulary.

 **Multiple matching**
Page 71

1 Students read the instructions and the Don't forget! box. Allow time for them to underline the key words. Check they understand the meaning of *lack*. Mention that they will hear some of the phrasal verbs from Vocabulary 1 (*tell off, get on, look up to, get over, fall out with, split up, put up with*). Pre-teach *can't bear* and *can't stand*. The listening also includes language on past habits which was studied in Unit 1.

Answers
1 C   2 B   3 F   4 H   5 E
(A, D and G not used)

Listening 1: Listening script 1.32–1.36

Speaker 1
Before Paul started school, he used to come round to us every morning while his mother, Lynda – my daughter-in-law – was at work. He was a lovely child but, like most boys, he had almost limitless energy and at times

he was rather difficult to control. We only had to look after him for four hours each day, but it completely wore us out. His mother would tell us off for letting him watch too much television – she said Paul needed to work his energy off in the park or on long walks. Easy for her to say, but we weren't getting any younger and watching television was a useful survival strategy. I remember arguing with Lynda on more than one occasion about this.

Speaker 2
I shared a flat once with someone who used to get annoyed about the silliest of things. He seemed quite pleasant at first, and we got on fine for a while. But that's because we hardly saw each other – he had an evening job in a bar and I worked during the day in a supermarket. When I got to know him better, though, I realized just how difficult he could be. Things had to be done his way and his way alone. He was obsessive about tidiness and he couldn't bear it if I left anything lying on the floor. He'd also tell me off for cooking food that made the house smell or for singing in the shower. I had to move out in the end. I couldn't stand it.

Speaker 3
Julie was a friend as well as a colleague. I looked up to her and admired her self-belief and quiet determination. It came as no surprise when she was promoted to senior manager and I wasn't. I didn't think it was unfair or anything. She deserved it. Of course I was disappointed, but I got over it quickly enough. But Julie was now my boss and it soon became clear that she wasn't good at managing people. She bullied and shouted, and upset most people in the department, including me. To her credit, she realized she wasn't suited to the job and she asked for a transfer. But I haven't spoken to her since she left.

Speaker 4
My brother, Mike, and I often don't see eye to eye with each other, but it's never really affected our relationship. We've always got on very well, despite having very different ideas and opinions about things. Recently, though, something's come between us that's changed all that. The money we inherited from our grandmother wasn't divided equally between us. She left me more because I'm married with two children and Mike's single. At least that's what she said in her will. Understandably, I suppose, Mike thinks it's a bit unfair and feels hard done by. We haven't exactly fallen out with each other, but there's certainly a tension between us that wasn't there before.

Speaker 5
We split up around about this time last year, just before he went off to India. I'd always been very tolerant and understanding – I knew how much John's work meant to him and I'd put up with the situation for as long as I could. But we both realized these long periods of separation weren't good for the relationship. Not being able to make any plans for the future inevitably caused friction, so we decided to end it. We still see each other from time to time, and it's good because there's not the same tension between us that there used to be.

2 Students work in pairs. Refer them to the recording script on pages 226–27 and ask them to read the details about the speaker they identify with most, and then explain their reasons for sympathizing with that speaker.

Language focus 1: Defining relative clauses
Page 72

1–5 Students follow the instructions for exercises 1–5. Correct each exercise before allowing students to move onto the next so that you can clear up any problems.

Refer to the Grammar reference on page 214 and draw students' attention to the use of *the reason why*. Mention that we cannot say *the reason because*. This is a typical error in some languages.

Answers

1

in the first sentence – *that*
in the second sentence – *which*
They cannot be omitted because they are the subject of the verb in the relative clause.

2

The money (that/which) **we** *inherited* from our grandmother wasn't divided equally between us.
Note: In this sentence, the subject of the verb in *italics* in the relative clause is we: the underlined relative pronouns are the object of the verb in the relative clause. They can be omitted because they are object relative pronouns.

3

The first sentence is more formal. The relative pronoun can be omitted in the second sentence.

4

a where **b** why **c** when **d** whose

5

1 where/in which (formal)
2 that/which
3 whose
4 that/which/ –
5 who/that
6 that/which
7 that/which/–
8 when/that/in which/–

6 Give students time to write their sentences. Before they discuss them with their partner, elicit

some expressions for agreeing and disagreeing and write these on the board, e.g. *Me too/Me neither/ So do I/Neither do I/So would I/Neither would I.* Encourage students to use some of these as they compare their sentences.

Additional activity
At the beginning of the next lesson do the following activity. Write ten sentences which contain relative pronouns. Photocopy one set for each group of three students and cut each sheet up into sentences. Cut the sentences in half and get students to match them. For example:
Let's go back to that night club … where they play great dance music.
That's the girl … who's going out with my brother.
I'll never forget the day … when I first saw my husband.

 DVD resource: Unit 6

 **Interview**
Page 72

Students read the instructions and the How to go about it box. Ask if the following statements are true or false:
It's fine to give 'yes' or 'no' answers to the examiner's questions. (False)
Try to give reasons for your answers. (True)
You should pre-prepare long answers. (False)
Check their understanding of *take after* (students have covered this on page 51). Students work in pairs to ask and answer the questions. Circulate to monitor their speaking, and write down any pronunciation errors you hear. In feedback, comment on how you feel they developed their answers. Write their pronunciation errors on the board. Model and choral drill these.

Reading and Use of English 1 **Multiple-choice cloze**
Part 1   Page 73

1 Students work in pairs to discuss the questions. Get feedback from the class. Mention a wedding you have been to and say how you felt.

2 Students read the instructions and the How to go about it box. Ask some questions, e.g.
What should you do before you start to fill in the correct options? (Read the whole text.)

Are any words underlined in the real exam? (No)
Check they understand *stare* and *glance* by miming.
Students work individually. Question 2 is a typical
problem area for students, so during feedback
mention that *number* goes with countable nouns,
amount with uncountable nouns and that *quantity*
can go with both, although it is generally associated
with weight or volume.

Answers
1 B   2 D   3 A   4 D   5 C   6 A   7 B   8 D

3 Students discuss the question in pairs.

Alternative activity

If you think most of your students will have the
same opinion, you could change the activity. Have
a mini debate about rent-a-person agencies. Divide
the class into A/B pairs. Tell Student A to argue for
and Student B to argue against. Encourage them
to use language of disagreement. They can use the
ideas from the cloze test.

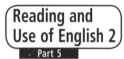

Multiple choice
Pages 74–75

1 Start by describing one of your own aunts or
uncles. Then students do the activity in pairs.

2 Students read the instructions and the Don't
forget! box. Remind them to always give an answer,
as marks are not deducted in the exam for incorrect
answers. Check students understand *show off*, *sharp
edges* and *niece*. Focus students' attention on the
photo. Ask what type of relationship you think the
writer has with her aunt. Students complete the
task and then compare their answers in pairs. You
could point out some useful vocabulary and get
students to explain the meaning, e.g. *to cut corners*
(line 43); *to get at someone* (line 70); *to stand up for
yourself* (line 71).

Answers
1 A   2 B   3 C   4 D   5 A   6 B

Reacting to the text

Ask the whole class the question and get one
student to answer. Elicit any other suggestions from
the class.

Language focus 2: Non-defining relative clauses
Page 76

1–2 Students read the information and complete
the rules.

Answers
2
a   cannot
b   cannot
c   are

3 Write the following sentences on the board and
elicit the missing words.
We went to Claridges Hotel, ____ my brother works.
(where)
*Come round for a coffee at the weekend, ____ I'm not
so busy.* (when)
My niece is always untidy, ____ really annoys me.
(which)

Check students understand that *which* can refer to
the whole of the main clause and that the relative
adverb *where* is used after nouns which refer to a
place, and *when* after a time. They then do exercise
3. Remind students to use *who* and *whose* as well.

Answers
3
1   We spent the weekend in York, where my mother was born.
2   My best friend, who always said she wanted to stay single, has just got married.
3   My oldest sister, whose husband is German, lives in Munich.
4   The best time to visit Iceland is in summer, when the average temperature is around ten degrees.
5   He has to work on Saturdays, which he isn't very happy about.

Open cloze: Relative clauses
Page 76

Look at the instructions together and then ask
students to read the text without writing anything,
so that they understand the gist. When they
finish you could yawn and see if any students do
the same. Ask what the research says about the
relationship between you and your students, i.e. if
they yawned, there is a closer relationship! Students
should complete the gaps individually.

Answers

1	which/that/–	2	which/that
3	who/that	4	who
5	which/that	6	where
7	whose	8	which
9	who/that	10	when

Vocabulary 2: Describing people   Page 77

A Personality

1 Students work in pairs to classify the adjectives. Circulate and help them with adjectives they don't know. Give a definition, e.g. *a lazy person is someone who doesn't like working hard*. Get feedback from the class. Model and check the pronunciation.

Answers

Positive: sociable, reliable, sincere, cheerful, polite, tolerant, patient, decisive, mature, sensible, adventurous, practical, sensitive
Negative: bad-tempered, lazy, selfish, moody, mean

2 Do the first few adjectives together then ask students to complete the exercise in pairs. In feedback, ask if they can see any rule for adjectives beginning with *p* and *m* (they all take *im*). Mention that *cheerful* does have an opposite prefix *cheerless*, but point out that this generally collocates with a place or the weather and not a person, e.g. *their living room is a rather cheerless place*.

Answers

un-: unsociable, unadventurous, unselfish, unreliable
in-: intolerant, insincere, indecisive, insensitive
im-: impatient, impolite, impractical, immature
different word: mean/generous, cheerful/miserable, sensible/silly or foolish, bad-tempered/sweet-tempered or calm, lazy/hard-working, selfish/selfless, moody/even-tempered

3 Model the activity first by describing two people you know. To make it more interesting you could use one you get along with well and one you don't. As students do the activity, circulate and note down any pronunciation issues. In feedback ask a few students who they talked about and find out whether they have a good relationship with them.

B Appearance

Ask students one general question about the photos. Do not discuss them in detail as they will do this in exercise 3.

1 Check students understand *complexion* as this is a false friend in some languages. Students do the exercise in pairs. If necessary, they can use monolingual dictionaries.

Answers

1	bald	2	pierced	3	thinning
4	well-built				

2 Elicit the differences in meaning from various students.

Answers

2a
All the adjectives describe weighing too much.
Fat has negative connotations in many parts of the world.
Plump is more positive and can mean either weighing a little too much or can be used as a 'polite' way of describing someone who is fat.
Overweight is factual and of the three, is the most neutral.

2b
Thin means having little fat on the body; it is descriptive and neutral.
Slim means being attractively thin and has positive connotations.
Skinny means being unattractively thin and has negative connotations.

3 Write the following on the board:
She looks like a cheerful person.
She looks scruffy.
She looks as if she has alternative ideas.
Elicit the rules for *looks* and *looks like*.
looks + adjective
looks like + noun
looks as if + clause
Point out that *looks like* + clause is commonly used with the same meaning as *looks as if*, but has traditionally been seen as incorrect. Encourage students to use this language when they compare the photos. They could also include expressions of comparison from Unit 3, page 33. Circulate and correct some of their errors. In feedback, ask a few students who they would like to meet.

Listening 2
Part 1
Multiple choice
Page 78

This listening recycles the vocabulary of descriptions and includes phrasal verbs from various units (*turn to, get on with, take aside, take on, sort out* and *get rid of*). It also introduces the causative *have*.

Ask students to read the instructions. Play the recording twice and let students compare their answers together after the first listening.

Answers
1 B **2** C **3** B **4** A **5** B **6** A **7** B **8** C

Listening 2: Listening script 1.37–1.44

1 You hear a woman on the radio talking about her father.

I always got on very well with my mother. I felt I could turn to her for advice, share confidences with her, because she understood my problems. With my father it was different. I found it difficult to talk to him, and when we did speak, you could feel the tension between us. I think it was partly because I take after him so much – I inherited my lack of confidence from him for one thing – and I blamed him for my own weaknesses.

2 You overhear a man talking about a former teacher.

After the first lesson we all thought he was a bit mad. But he was just different. Most of the other teachers in the school were really serious and uninspiring. They'd speak, we'd take notes and that was about it. It was deadly dull. But Hilton-Dennis would jump around the room, waving his arms about and jabbering away in Italian at us. He seemed to really enjoy what he was doing, and I took to him almost straight away. He managed to communicate his passion for the subject and he got a lot of people interested in learning the language.

3 You hear a woman complaining about one of her employees.

W = Woman   M = Man

W: I'm going to have to have a word with Simon again. If it's not one thing, it's another.

M: Is Simon the scruffy one?

W: Yes, he is. That's not what worries me, though. He doesn't have any contact with the public, so I don't mind what he looks like.

M: So has he been rude again?

W: No, we managed to sort that one out. I took him aside just before Christmas and had a long talk with him. He's been quite pleasant since then. But I need reliable people who turn up on time and he's been late

for work three times this last fortnight. I'm beginning to regret taking him on.

4 You hear part of a radio programme in which a man is giving advice.

Unfortunately, there's not always a direct relationship between hard work and good performance at school. Think how demotivating it must be for a young person to spend hours on homework and then get low marks for their trouble. Something like that can seriously affect their self-esteem and their confidence. So they may look for other ways to feel good about themselves. Let's imagine they come to you and say they want to have their nose pierced or get a tattoo done. Would you let them? Maybe not, but perhaps you should at least consider their motives for wanting to do so.

5 You overhear a woman talking on the phone about some clothes.

We're getting rid of anything we don't need before we move. We've got so much rubbish in our house, and there's not a lot of room in the new flat ... Well, there are Hannah's old baby clothes, for a start. I've held on to them for years, just in case Hannah started a family of her own. But it doesn't look as if that's going to happen now ... No, I haven't got the heart to put them in the bin, and I can't imagine anyone wanting to buy them. Can you? ... Well, I'll probably take them round to Marina's. She knows lots of young mothers – I'm sure one of them will be delighted to have them.

6 You hear a man and a woman talking about a person in a photograph.

W = Woman   M = Man

W: It's a lovely photo. She looks so relaxed and cheerful – as if she's really enjoying it all.

M: Yeah, it's my mum's favourite. She's had it framed and it's up on the wall in her living room. She was starting to think she might never see her daughter in a wedding dress, so it's got pride of place above the telly. Lucy doesn't like it though.

W: Why not?

M: She says you can see all her wrinkles. She's a bit sensitive about her age.

W: Oh dear. So, anyway, do you think there'll be a photo of you above your mum's telly one day? Little brother in a wedding suit?

M: Don't you start!

7 You hear an elderly woman talking to a man about her new neighbours.

M = Man   W = Woman

M: So how are the new neighbours?

W: Well, I must say I'm quite pleased so far. It's early days, of course – they've only been there for a couple of weeks. But they do seem better than the last ones. All those weekend parties. Such an unpleasant family.

M: Have you invited them round yet?

W: Well, no, I haven't had a chance. You see, they've asked me to go to their house on two occasions already – and one of those was for lunch.

M: That's very sociable of them.

W: Yes, it is, isn't it? As I say, I'm rather pleased. They've even offered to come and cut my grass for me.

8 You hear a man talking on the radio about a musician who influenced him.

People are surprised when I mention him as an influence. He played Blues Rock and my music's always in the New Age section. I suppose if he'd moved into Progressive Rock, there might have been some similarity. But he hated all that stuff, and probably would have hated what I do, too. And OK, I have the same kind of knee-length hair, but his was a fashion statement – mine's there because I can't be bothered to get it cut. No, it's the atmosphere he created on stage that I'm referring to – moody, some people call it. Soulful. No moving around – just let the guitar do the talking.

Additional activity

Write the questions below on the board and tell students they contain phrasal verbs from the listening.

Who do you usually turn to for advice? Why? (ask/rely on)

Are you good at sorting out your own problems? (solving)

Have you ever had a teacher who you took to straight away? Why? (liked/got on with)

Have you ever had a teacher who you really didn't get on with? Why? (have a good relationship with)

Has a teacher ever taken you aside and warned you about your behaviour? (have a private talk)

Do you find it annoying when your family or friends turn up late? (arrive)

Ask students to read the questions and write a synonym or definition of the phrasal verbs. Check their answers as a whole class. Then ask them to discuss the questions in pairs. Circulate and join in with students' discussions. Get feedback from the class. Mention interesting facts about different students and ask them to explain what they said to the whole class, e.g. *Maria, can you tell us what made your art teacher so inspiring?*

Language focus 3: Causative passive with *have* and *get*   Page 78

Lead–in

Write *piercing* on the board and ask the students what it means, e.g. *a nose piercing, an ear piercing*. Organize them into pairs and ask them to briefly discuss with their partners if they would ever consider getting a piercing. Get some feedback from a few pairs.

1 Students do the activities in pairs.

After students have read the Grammar reference on page 214 make sure they noticed that the causative *have* can also be used for events which are outside of the speaker's control, e.g. *John had his car stolen last week.* Mention that we don't usually use causative *get* with the present perfect as it could be confused with *have got* for possession.

Answers
1a
Extract 4: pierced, done
Extract 6: framed
1b
the past participle
1c
1a He repaired the car himself.
b Someone/A mechanic repaired it for him.
2a He cut his own hair.
b Someone/A hairdresser cut it for him.

2 This exercise tests whether students can use causative *have* in a variety of tenses. Circulate and make sure students are writing the tenses correctly. If they have made an error, try to elicit the correct form, e.g. in question 2 ask: *What verb form do we use after a preposition?* (Gerund)

Answers
2 having, shaved
3 have, taken
4 had, filled
5 having, restyled
6 has had, broken

3 Look at the example together. Students then work in pairs to ask and answer the questions, giving detailed answers. Circulate and correct any errors with the causative *have*. Get feedback from the class. Ask students what their partner said about some of the questions.

 **Writing** Part 2   **Article** page 79

1 Read the instructions and the notice. Ask a couple of students who they think has influenced them most.

2 Ask the students to read the model answer quickly, ignoring the errors for now, to find the correct picture.

Answers

The third illustration

3 Students work in pairs to correct the mistakes. Circulate to make sure they are not trying to correct sentences which do not contain an error. Indicate where the errors are if they are having difficulties.

Answers

3

Paragraph 1: says to me/tells me (says me), in the end (at the end)

Paragraph 2: fallen (fell), problems don't (problems they don't), in a better mood (in better mood)

Paragraph 3: She is always cheerful (Always she is cheerful)

Paragraph 4: so small (such small), look up to (look up at)

4–5 Students do the activities in pairs.

Answers

4

a The first sentence follows on directly from a catchy title. The use of direct speech also adds colour.

b The writer plays with the meaning of *live up to* and ends by comparing her small size and big influence.

5

a *She has a straight back and a determined look on her face. She's always cheerful and I've never seen her in a bad temper … she's nearly half my size and so small that she sometimes wears children's clothes*

b *turn out, fallen out with, sort … out, look up to*

c *And, So, And although, But despite this, So even though*

6 Students read the instructions and the Don't forget! box. Then ask them to close their books and give their partner three pieces of advice on how to write a good article. They then write their own articles.

Learner training

When you correct the articles, choose a good example and photocopy it for each pair of students (check that the student who wrote it is happy about other students reading it, and keep it anonymous if necessary).

Review 6 answers Pages 80–81

Relative clauses

1 Lady Gaga, whose real name is Stefani Joanne Angelina Germanotta, was born on March 28 1986.
Non-defining (the name itself defines the person)

2 What's the name of the village where you got married?
Defining – *where* cannot be omitted

3 He hasn't given me back the book that I lent him.
Defining – *that* can be omitted

4 She told me that Vasilis had failed his driving test, which didn't surprise me at all.
Non-defining – *which* refers to the whole clause

5 That song always reminds me of the time when I was working in Brazil.
Defining – *when* can be omitted

6 He's the only person in this class whose first name begins with 'Z'.
Defining – *whose* cannot be omitted

7 Emma received a phone call from her Managing Director, who had been impressed by her sales performance.
Non-defining – she has, we assume, only one Managing Director

8 Few written records have survived so it is a period of history about which we know very little.
Defining – *which* cannot be omitted as it follows a preposition. The sentence could be changed to: *Few written records have survived so it is a period of history **which** we know very little **about**.*
In this case, *which* could be omitted.

Vocabulary

A Describing people

Across

1	unsociable	3	green	6	generous
8	ear	9	in	10	selfish
11	skinny	12	bad	14	pale

Down

1	un	2	cheerful	4	hair
5	mean	7	sensible	10	slim
11	shy	13	dis		

B Phrasal verbs

1	let down	2	told off
3	brought up	4	looked up
5	get on	6	fell for
7	falling out	8	got over

Reading and Use of English
Part 4

Transformations

1 to put up with
2 whose example you should
3 of the most sincere
4 are having the roof repaired
5 had his tonsils taken out
6 to have it done by

 Progress Test 3

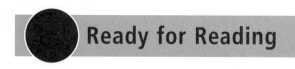

Ready for Reading

In this Ready for Reading unit, students gain an overall picture of the Reading tasks in the Reading and Use of English paper. They are provided with and reminded of the useful strategies they should use to help improve their performance.

Lead–in

Write the following text types on the board under the title *Reading strategies* and ask students to think about how they would read each one. Then they should match the pairs of text types that have similar reading strategies. Ask students to justify their answers.

1 *Instructions for using a mobile phone*
2 *A telephone directory*
3 *A novel*
4 *A dictionary*
5 *A letter from a friend*
6 *Information about how to apply for a visa to the USA*

Answers

1 and **6** require very careful reading and detailed understanding of every word (intensive reading).
2 and **4** require reasonably fast reading and looking for the information you need while ignoring the rest (scanning). It is not necessary to start at the beginning of the text and read all the way through to the end.
3 and **5** require you to start at the beginning and read through. A general understanding of the text is needed, but it is not necessary to understand every single word (skimming).

Introduction   Page 82

Students read the introduction. Explain that the different tasks for each text will require them to use the reading strategies they have just discussed: intensive reading, scanning and skimming.

Part 5: Multiple Choice   Page 82

1 Students read the information and the text and answer the questions. Ask if they have ever been walking in summer in the mountains. What was their experience like?

---

or f book page.

Answers

The purpose of the text is to give advice to people who go walking in hot weather. *or website,* You might find it in a specialist magazine for walkers or people who like outdoor activities. It could also come from the travel section of a newspaper.

2–3 Students discuss possible meanings in pairs.

Answers

2
pump (verb) – move liquid or gas in a particular direction, e.g. blood around the body
intake (noun) – the amount you eat or drink
raging (adjective) – very strong or severe
swig (noun) – a quick drink of a liquid *similar to sip.*
palatable (adjective) – having a pleasant or acceptable taste

3
swell (verb) – to become bigger
blister (noun) – a swelling on the surface of the skin, which contains a clear liquid
leak (verb) – (in this case) the water gets or enters into your boots
rash (noun) – lots of red spots on your skin
breeze (noun) – a light wind
deceptive (adjective) – from the verb 'deceive'; something which tricks you, which makes you believe something which is not true

4 Students work individually to choose the options. Get feedback from the class. Refer them to the detailed explanation of the answers in the key on pages 254–55.
Ask how they would do a similar task in their own language, e.g. would they read the text first for general meaning or look at the questions and then read the text? Explain that they should use the technique which is most effective for them.

Answers

4
1 C   2 D   3 A   4 D   5 B   6 B

1

A Not stated. The writer says that *The majority of mountain rescue statistics are made up from summer walkers suffering heart attacks* but this does not mean that heat is the main cause of heart attacks in general.

B Not stated. The writer implies merely that if you are not fit you will suffer the effects of heat even more.

C Correct answer. *The answer is to keep up your water intake and keep taking regular swigs from your water bottle.*

D Not stated.

2

A Not stated.

B No. It replaces the body salts lost through sweating, but it doesn't prevent their loss.

C No. It is a treatment for diarrhoea, not a prevention.

D Correct answer. *Dioralyte will do the job just as well.*

3

A Correct answer. *Extra sweating makes the skin softer and increases the chance of blisters forming, in the same way as when water leaks into your boots and gets to your feet.*

B No: *… cool water … reduces swelling and helps … comfort.*

C No. Your boots feel tight because the heat makes your feet swell. It does not mean they are the wrong size.

D Not stated.

4

A Not stated. *The answer, if this does develop, is to try and stay cool* is a distractor.

B The writer says walkers should ideally wear *lightweight and loose-fitting* clothing. He does not suggest that loose-fitting clothing is usually very light.

C Not stated.

D Correct answer. *Tight clothing … may even lead to the formation of an irritating rash known as 'prickly heat' on your skin.*

5

B Correct answer. *It's understandable to want to remove any extraneous clothing when it's extremely hot…*

6

A Not stated: *… a good strong sun cream should therefore be applied* is a distractor.

B Correct answer. *… deceptive. It might not feel so hot, so you probably won't notice the damage being done.*

C Not stated: *harmless* and *damage* are distractors.

D A breeze is not a strong wind. *an apparently harmless breeze.*

Additional activity

Students do a roleplay in pairs. Student A is an experienced walker, while Student B wants to go walking and needs advice. Write the following useful phrases on the board:
It's essential/important to …
You should always …
Don't forget to …
You need to …
One mistake that many people make is to …
You mustn't …
Students act out the roleplay using language of advice.

Part 6: Gapped text   Page 84

1 Students read the explanation and the What to expect in the exam box. Ask the following questions.
What does this task test? (Your understanding of the way texts are structured.)
What should you look at carefully? (What comes before and after the gap.)
How many marks do you receive for each correct answer? (two marks)

2–3 Students do the prediction activity and then check their ideas in the text. Ask why it is a good idea to predict what you will read before starting.

4 Students read the instructions and the How to go about it box. They should work individually to match the sentences with the gaps, and then compare answers with their partner.

Answers

1 C   2 G   3 A   4 E   5 F   6 D

Additional activity

Students do a roleplay similar to the one above, but they should swap roles so student B is giving advice this time. Student B lives in Kakutsk and Student A is a visitor and needs advice on how to survive the cold. They should use the same useful language from the board as before.

5 Students discuss the question in pairs.

Part 7: Multiple matching   Page 86

1 Students read the explanation. Ask which reading strategy they will need to use (scanning).

2 Students discuss the questions in small groups. Get feedback from the class. Ask whether they would recommend any of the novels and, for question 2, whether the film was as good as the book.

3 Students read the instructions and the How to go about it and What to expect in the exam boxes. They should underline key words in the statements and compare these with their partner before reading the texts. Remind them to underline relevant parts of the text as they read. Get feedback from the class.

If possible, prepare for the task beforehand by underlining the relevant sections of the text and writing the number of the statement next to these underlined sections. If you have access to a scanner, scan the page and project this during feedback so that you can explain clearly why each statement goes with a particular text.

Answers
How to go about it
5 I read the <u>original version</u> of this story <u>as a child</u>.
6 It shows a <u>way of life</u> which <u>unfortunately</u> does <u>not exist now</u>.
7 It <u>reminds</u> me of <u>a certain period</u> of my life.
8 The story proved to be very <u>educational</u>.
9 Children will find it <u>easier to read</u> than the other books in this selection.
10 The <u>beginning</u> of the book <u>gave me ideas</u> for the <u>start of my latest work</u>.

3

1 A *I ordered it on the Internet ... with the audiobook ... The CD arrived first ... In the end I didn't bother with the book*

2 D *Stevenson writes with a good deal of humour anyway, something which many aren't expecting when they read the book for the first time.*

3 B *... the great affection with which Mark Twain writes about his protagonists, Tom and his friend Huckleberry Finn, who both come across as cheeky, but likeable rogues.*

4 A

5 C *Of all the books here that I read when I was growing up, this was the only one which wasn't adapted or abridged in any way.*

6 B *... it's sad to think that young children can no longer play like Tom and his friends, that they no longer have the freedom to go off in search of adventure ...*

7 E *brings back memories of my teenage years, when I lived in a house on a river bank.*

8 A *We learnt a lot about how hard life was for the gold prospectors and the girls were motivated to find out more.*

9 C *Being more modern than the rest ... the language is still fairly accessible for younger readers and there's less danger of them becoming frustrated with the style.*

10 E *... the first chapter, when Mole first meets Rat, provided the inspiration for the opening of my most recent novel Harvest Mouse.*

4 Students work in groups of three. If you haven't already set up a class library you could do so after this activity.

7 Value for money

Content Overview

Themes

The themes of this unit are shopping and living in different places. The skill of paraphrasing is also developed.

Exam-related activities

Reading and use of English

Part 6	Gapped text
Part 2	Open cloze (Review)
Part 4	Transformations (Review)

Writing

Part 2	Email
Part 1	Essay (Review)

Listening

Part 2	Sentence completion
Part 4	Multiple choice

Speaking

Part 2	Talking about photos
Part 1	Interview

Other

Language focus 1: Present perfect simple
Language focus 2: Expressing preferences
Language focus 3: The present perfect continuous
Vocabulary 1:   Shopping
Vocabulary 2:   Paraphrasing and recording
Vocabulary 3:   Towns and villages

Talking about photos
pages 88 and 89

Lead–in
Ask students where they think are the best places to go shopping for fresh food, cheap clothes and fashionable clothes in their town or area.

1–2 Focus students' attention on the photos. Ask them to work in pairs and to write down three items of vocabulary in each photo. Then get them to read the instructions. Draw their attention to the question in the box and stress that they must base their comparison around this.
Elicit some useful expressions, e.g.
In both pictures …
In the first picture … whereas in the second picture …

He/she probably …
Perhaps …
He/she might/may …
It looks + adjective

Students should time each other. Student A speaks for one minute and Student B speaks for 30 seconds. They then change roles for the second pair of photos. Remind them to use a good range of vocabulary and to paraphrase if they don't know a word. Get feedback from the class and ask various students which place they chose when they were Student B.

Vocabulary 1: Shopping   Page 88

1 Students will encounter this vocabulary in the listening on page 89. Model and check pronunciation of *receipt* (/rɪˈsiːt/), *convenience* (/kənˈviːniəns/) and *aisles* (/aɪlz/). Monolingual dictionaries can be used if necessary.

Answers					
1	out-of-town	**2**	corner	**3**	brands
4	own-brand	**5**	convenience	**6**	range
7	foodstuffs	**8**	value	**9**	aisles
10	trolley	**11**	counter	**12**	checkout
13	till	**14**	cashier	**15**	receipt

2 Students discuss the questions in pairs. Get some feedback from a few students.

Additional activity
Students cover the text, but leave the vocabulary visible. Explain that they have one minute to describe a visit to the supermarket using as much of the vocabulary from the box as possible. Student A speaks first and Student B ticks the vocabulary that they use. The student who uses the most words is the winner.

Speaking: Supermarket psychology   page 89

Students discuss the questions in pairs. Do not take feedback at this stage as they will discuss their choices after the listening.

Sentence completion
page 89

1 Students read the instructions and the Don't forget! box. Allow 45 seconds for them to read and predict the types of answers to the questions. As an example, ask what kind of word/information they might need for question 1. Play the recording twice and let students compare their answers together after the first listening. Briefly discuss any answers that caused problems.

Answers	
1	the middle
2	an outdoor market
3	children
4	fresh meat
5	(dead) animal(s)
6	(the) well-known brands
7	five times
8	bakery/bread
9	smell
10	(things) on impulse

Listening 1: Listening script 1.45

Right, well, the layout of most major supermarkets is roughly the same, and for more or less the same reasons. You'll notice that the entrance, for example, is usually situated to one side of the building. This is to ensure, of course, that shoppers walk down as many aisles as possible before they leave the store. If we had it in the middle, then they might visit only one half of the supermarket and as a result only buy half as much. The first thing you often see as you come through the entrance is the fruit and vegetable area. As well as being pleasant to the eye, this also gives customers the impression they're coming into an outdoor market. Fresh, colourful products are far more attractive than tins of convenience food so the customer is put in a good buying mood, from the start.

And next to the fruit and vegetable area is the confectionery; er, crisps, chocolates, sweets and so on. Parents often come shopping with their children and we need to ensure that they are kept happy and interested so that they don't disturb mum and dad from the business of spending money. Then at the back of the supermarket in the corner, you'll probably find the fresh meat counter. This is partly to make sure that as little room as possible is taken away from the main display areas by the staff who are serving. But it's also there so as not to distract customers when we have deliveries. They really don't want to see us bringing big carcasses of meat through the store, so, er, it's brought in through the back door. And very close to the fresh meat you can expect to see the pre-packed meat. People who are put off by the sight of blood and um – dead animals – prefer to buy their meat in the form of convenience food to prevent them having to make the connection between the product and the animal. They buy a lamb chop, but they don't think of a baby lamb in the field. The freezer goods are nearby. There's a limited amount of space so the smaller suppliers often find it difficult to get room

for their products. That's why you only tend to see the well-known brands here.

Er, moving on to the areas at the ends of the aisles – how do we decide what to put there? Well, these are key selling sites, and sales of goods at these points can be as much as five times higher than other areas. So we generally move goods to the end-of-aisle areas when we want to sell them quickly: goods which have not been selling well, and especially those which are nearing their sell-by date. Bread, too, needs to be sold quickly, but we put the bakery section in the far corner, as far away from the entrance as possible, next to other basic foodstuffs such as milk. This is so that customers have to walk past hundreds of products to reach it. Er, it's expensive to run a bakery but it increases sales of other products. The smell, too, is an important factor as it helps to create a warm, homely atmosphere in the store.

And finally, alcoholic drinks. They're often at the far end too, very near the exit. Er, by this time the shopper is beginning to enjoy the shopping experience, so he or she will buy more alcohol if it's here than if it's by the entrance. Er, the same is true for those products we put at the checkouts; er, more sweets and chocolates, usually. The kind of things people buy on impulse as they wait to pay – er, a reward they give themselves for doing the shopping.

2 Students discuss the follow-up questions in pairs. Get feedback from the class. Ask one student about the supermarket they described.

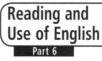 **Reading and Use of English** Part 6

Gapped text
Pages 90 and 91

Lead–in
Elicit typical questions that shop assistants ask you when you are in a clothes shop, e.g. *What size are you? Would you like to try it on? Does it fit?* Then ask students what the last item of clothes they bought was, and whether they enjoyed this particular shopping experience.

1–2 Students work in pairs to predict the reasons for hating clothes shopping, then read the text to check. Get feedback from the class.

3 Students follow the instructions. In feedback draw their attention to reference words, e.g. *1 G:* the word *now* contrasts the writer's past experience as a child with their current experience.

Answers					
1 G	2 C	3 F	4 E	5 B	6 A

Reacting to the text
Students discuss the question in groups of three. Get feedback from the class. Ask various students what thing they hate, and find out if any other students agree.

Alternative activity
For the second question ask students to write the thing they hate on a piece of paper. Collect the papers and redistribute them. Write some useful expressions on the board, e.g.
Yes, I really hate …; I find it very annoying; it really gets on my nerves; I don't mind …; it doesn't really bother me.
Students stand up and mingle and ask each other how they feel about the topic on the piece of paper.

Additional activity
Write the following on the board:
shopping online/conventional shopping
shopping with your mum/shopping with friends/ shopping alone
shopping for food/shopping for clothes or shoes
shopping in the week/shopping at the weekend
shopping in the sales/shopping the rest of the year
Students work in groups of three and discuss the advantages and disadvantages of these shopping experiences.

Language focus 1: Present perfect simple

This is a review of a grammar point that can often cause confusion. In some languages, a similar form to the present perfect simple exists but is used differently, or other tenses are used instead of the present perfect. Common mistakes are:
I have been to Italy last summer … instead of *I went to …*
It's the worst film I've never seen … instead of *… ever seen …*
I live here since I was a child … instead of *I have lived here …*

1 Students read the explanations and examples. Draw their attention to the fact that all the sentences show a link between the past and the present.

2 Students match the example sentences to the explanations in exercise 1. If you have a monolingual class, ask students to translate

sentences b and f as these are the most likely ones to cause confusion.

Answers
a 4 b 1 c 2 d 5 e 3 f 1 g 2 h 4

3a Students categorize the time expressions. Model and check the pronunciation of *since*. If students put *last summer* with the present perfect, explain that this would only be correct if it was preceded by *since*.
In some languages *yet* and *already* are the same word, so you should check understanding of these. Write the following sentences on the board:
We haven't done it ___.
We've _____ done it.
Tell students to turn to page 98 and refer them to exercise 1. Ask: *Have you done this exercise?* Point to the two sentences on the board and elicit the correct response (*We haven't done it yet*). Now refer students to exercise 1 on page 88 and ask: *Have you done this exercise?* Elicit the response *We've already done it.*

Answers	
Present perfect	**Past simple**
yet	last summer
so far today	in September
in the last few days	two weeks ago
for the last two years	before I came here
over the last week	on my 10th birthday
already	when I was younger
this month	
since I got up	

3b Students write sentences about themselves. Circulate and check their sentences.

3c Give an example. Ask a student to read out one of their sentences and ask them some follow-up questions. Circulate as students do the activity and get students to self-correct any errors related to the target language. Get some feedback from the class. Write a few of the students' errors on the board and elicit the correct forms.

Vocabulary 2: Paraphrasing and recording
Page 92

Learner training
Paraphrasing is an important skill within the *First* exam, and also in the real world. To give students

more practice on paraphrasing, you could use the system on this page with other texts, i.e. follow up reading and listening activities by writing transformation sentences which allow students to revise target language as well as practise paraphrasing. There are further paraphrasing sections in Units 10 and 13.

1a Students read the instructions and the What to expect in the exam box. Ask which sections of the exam contain elements of paraphrasing.
Students should do 1a in pairs as this is their first experience of a paraphrasing exercise. When they have finished, ask which sentence is illustrated in the picture (sentence 4).

1b Students check their answers. Remind them to refer to the line numbers to help them locate the sentences in the reading text on page 90.

Answers					
1	rid	**2**	put	**3**	for
4	end	**5**	through	**6**	taken
7	all	**8**	heart		

2 Students work in pairs to paraphrase the sentences.

Answers
Possible answers:
b I feel they are forcing me to/making me try things on …
c I start sweating.
d I go to look for my size.
e I don't care if I look scruffy/untidy …
f This is sometimes caused by/because of the shop's fluorescent lighting.

Listening 2
Part 4

Multiple choice
Page 93

Lead–in
Organize students into pairs and refer them to the two pictures. Allow them a couple of minutes to compare and contrast the pictures, then get some brief feedback from each pair.

1 Write the following categories mentioned in the listening on the board:
noise, crime, neighbours, dangers, amenities, transport, entertainment

Ask students to answer the pre-listening questions in pairs, referring to these categories. Get some feedback from the class.

2 Students read the instructions and the questions. Play the recording twice and let students compare their answers together after the first listening.

Answers													
1 B	**2** C	**3** A	**4** C	**5** A	**6** B	**7** C

Listening 2: Listening script 1.46

I = Interviewer   R = Rebecca   G = Greg

I: Rebecca, you've been living in a village for nearly five years now. What made you move to the countryside?

R: I suppose my priorities had changed with age. When I first went to London, I used to love the hustle and bustle of the place. But then I gradually became more aware of the planes roaring overhead, car horns beeping all the time, music blaring out at strange hours. I needed a break.

I: Greg, I can see you're smiling.

G: Yes. I remember when I first moved out with my family, we all found it a little too quiet. But we quickly got used to it, and now we prefer living with less noise. We also like the fact that you don't have to worry about the kids so much if they go off on their own.

R: Hmm, I'm not so sure. Some people drive like maniacs on these narrow roads. I have to keep a really close eye on my two young kids and make sure they don't wander off too far.

G: Well, we're lucky enough to have very good neighbours in the village. Everyone looks out for everyone else, and someone will soon tell you if your kids are in danger, or doing something they shouldn't be doing.

R: Yes, you can't do anything in a village without your neighbours knowing about it. But that's good, though. It's like having a big extended family.

I: What about the amenities where you live?

G: The basics are within walking distance from us; the school, the shops, even a couple of tennis courts.

R: I can't say the same, unfortunately. Being able to pop out to the shops when you need something is one of the things I miss about living in the city. We have to get the car out just to go and buy a loaf of bread. And you really do need to be able to drive to live where we do. Everyone in the village relies on their car; the bus service is just too infrequent.

G: It's better than not having one at all. We're actually trying to get the local authorities to put on at least one bus a day, particularly for the older residents who don't have a car and who sometimes need to go into town.

R: Yes, and I'm actually wondering how my two are going to find it when they become teenagers. They'll want to go into town, too. They'll probably complain of boredom and want us to go and live in the city again.

G: And who can blame them? I know at that age I would have been bored out of my mind! No cinemas, no decent shops, no cafés to sit in, no discos to go to …

I: Do you think either of you will ever go and live in the city again?

G: Naturally, I'd prefer to stay in the village and work at home rather than do a nine-to-five job in an office. I have my computer, email and the phone and a wonderful working environment. However, anything can happen and we'd be prepared to move back to London if we felt it was to our advantage.

I: Rebecca, how about you?

R: I'll be going back to work just as soon as my youngest child starts school. September of next year, in fact. Obviously I've thought about it a lot, and the fact that living where I do now will mean spending two hours driving to and from work every day. But I'd rather do that than go back to living in the city.

I: Well, thank you for both coming all that way to speak to us today. We'll have a break for music now and then …

Language focus 2: Expressing preferences

Page 93

Lead–in

Write the following sentence beginnings on the board and elicit possible endings to each sentence (examples in brackets).

I prefer eating in restaurants to … (cooking for myself).

I'd prefer to watch a DVD tonight rather than … (go to the cinema).

I'd rather not … (go out tonight).

I'd much rather … (get the train than drive).

Use a different coloured pen to highlight the differences between these expressions for talking about preferences.

1–2 Students read the examples and rules, then complete the sentences in exercise 2.

Answers

1 come back later than wait
2 paying by cash to
3 to phone him rather than
4 not get

3 Students discuss the questions in pairs. Circulate and correct any errors with the target language. Typical errors are *I would rather prefer …; I would rather to …*

Get feedback from the class. Ask various students what they said about some of the questions.

Vocabulary 3: Towns and villages

Page 94

Lead–in

Focus students' attention on the photos. Ask whether they would like to live in the villa and which of the two other places they would prefer to work in.

1a Pre-teach *pedestrian*, as this is a false friend in some languages. Students then complete the exercise. Get feedback from the class. Model and check any pronunciation issues, e.g. *building* (/ˈbɪldɪŋ/), *manufacturing* (/ˌmænjʊˈfæktʃərɪŋ/), *business* (/ˈbɪznɪs/).

Answers

2	pedestrian	3	flats	4	shopping
5	office	6	building	7	industrial
8	housing				

1b Check students' understanding of *outskirts*. Students discuss the examples in pairs.

2 If students don't know some of the words, use a sentence and ask students to guess the meaning from context, e.g.

The government need to spend some money on this area of the city, it's really <u>run-down</u>.

We stayed in a lovely <u>picturesque</u> *village in the mountains, you must go there!*

The holiday cottage was so <u>quaint</u>, *it was like something out of a fairy story.*

Students classify the adjectives in pairs, then choose adjectives to describe their area. Get some feedback from the class.

Answers

Positive: lively, bustling, pleasant, picturesque, prosperous, quaint
Negative: dull, run-down, shabby, depressing

Additional activity

Ask students to sort the words below into the correct word stress group. Encourage them to say the words out loud. This type of pronunciation exercise will also help them remember the new vocabulary.

amenities   bustling   industrial   pedestrian
picturesque   pleasant   privacy   prosperous
residential   shabby

•●●●	●●●	●●●	●●	●●●●

Answers

● ● ● ●	● ● ●	● ● ●	● ●	● ● ● ●
pedestrian industrial amenities	prosperous privacy	picturesque	shabby bustling pleasant	residential

Speaking 2
Part 1

Interview
Page 94

Students read the instructions and the Don't forget! box. Elicit some expressions for giving reasons and examples, e.g. *because of, thanks to, for example, such as, like.*

Students discuss the questions in pairs. Circulate and join in with some conversations. Get feedback from the class. Ask various students one thing they like and dislike about their neighbourhood.

Language focus 3:
Present perfect continuous   Page 95

1 Students read the rules and examples.

2 Students work in pairs to explain the differences between the sentences. Get some feedback from the class. If they are unsure about the differences, ask some concept questions, e.g. 1 *Has the speaker finished the book?* 2 *Do they shop in the supermarket on a regular basis? Where are they now?*

Answers

1a incompleteness – the book is not finished

b completed action – the book is finished

2a repetition – on a regular basis

b one occasion – they are not here now

3a focus on duration – the speaker considers *all day* to be important

b focus on completed action – the finished product rather than the duration is important to the speaker here

4a temporary – she is not staying with her on a permanent basis

b long term – this is not a temporary arrangement

3 Students work individually to complete the conversation. Circulate and help with any difficulties. Ask concept questions to help students decide on the forms, e.g. Question 2: *Are Sandra and Dave engaged now? When did they get engaged?* Question 4: *Is their engagement still a secret?*

Answers

1   've/have just heard
2   have you been
3   proposed
4   kept
5   were
6   have you made
7   've/have been saving
8   've/have both been working
9   've/have already saved
10 have (you) been doing
11 've/have been studying
12 failed

Additional activity

Have a class competition. Divide the class into teams of three. Each team uses a piece of paper as a score sheet to write down their answers. Dictate the first sentence below. Explain that they have to decide whether it is correct and if it is not, they must correct the mistake. Allow a little time for groups to confer after each sentence. Go through the answers as a class. Count the scores to find the winner.

I've tried to send this email three times this morning, I don't know what's wrong. (correct)
I'm getting really angry, this is the third time I am telling you to do your homework! (have told)
I am living in this house since I was a child. (have lived)
I've been sneezing a lot lately, maybe I have an allergy. (correct)
I've gone to the USA many times. (been)
I'm fed up. It's been raining all day. (correct)
Why is your face so red? Have you jogged? (been jogging)
I feel really satisfied. I've been writing four compositions this week. (have written)
I'm really sorry, but I haven't finished the report yet. (correct)
I've worked here since two years. (for)
My neighbours are away this week, so I've been feeding their cat. (correct)
Ahh, I've been cutting my finger! (have cut)

4 Focus students' attention on the picture. Ask if there are any reality TV shows in their country about surviving on a desert island. Find out if they like this type of programme. Try to elicit the word *castaway.*

Students read the instructions and prepare their interview questions or statements individually. You could write a few extra questions on the board to get them started, e.g.

Student A: *What else have you been eating?*
What food have you been able to grow?

Student B: *We've been cooking together.*
We've managed to catch several flightless birds.

Circulate and check they are writing the target language correctly. Students do the roleplay.

 **Writing** Part 2

Email
Pages 96 and 97

1 Students read the instructions and the What to expect in the exam box. Elicit answers and ask whether it would be appropriate to use textspeak in a letter or email.

Answers

A A formal style would be appropriate. The target reader is the director of a school. The style of the language in his email is also formal.

B An informal style would be appropriate. The target reader is a friend. The style of the language in his email is also informal.

2 Students read the task answer and answer the questions. Ask which area the students would prefer to live in.

Answers

2a Yes, it is consistently formal.

b Yes, she mentions cost, shops and proximity to the school.

3 Students find the differences between the two answers, then complete text B.

Answers

3a

A	B
less than twenty minutes	under thirty minutes
four supermarkets	five supermarkets
within easy walking distance of the school	you can cycle to the school

3b

1	plenty/lots/loads	2	thinking
3	train	4	get/travel
5	enough	6	bit/little
7	though/if	8	But
9	put	10	wait

4 Students find stylistic differences between the two texts.

Answers

4a

Openings and closings: more formal in **A** (*Dear Mr Simpson/Yours sincerely*); less formal in **B** (*Hi Rob/All the best*)

The use of nouns in **A** (*the date of your arrival/a wide choice of/because of its location*) compared to verbs in **B** (*when you're coming/plenty of … to choose from/being in the centre*)

Informal words in **B** (e.g. *Thanks/really/enormous/a lot of*); more formal/neutral equivalents in **A** (*Thank you/very/very large/a great deal of*)

Latinate verb *tolerate* in **A**; phrasal verb *put up with* in **B** (though note that *look forward to* in **A** is a phrasal verb)

4b

Dashes (*I'd definitely recommend the area – it's really lively*) and exclamation marks (*five supermarkets!*) are features of informal writing, which appear in **B**, but not in **A**.

4c

Use of contractions in **B** (*you're/it's/it'd/Justa's/there's/can't*); no contractions in **A**

Ellipsis (omission of words) in **B** (*(I) hope this is useful/(I) Can't wait to see you*); no ellipsis in **A**

5 Students read the instructions and the Don't forget! box. Ask what style the email should be. Refer students to the Useful language box and get them to work in pairs to practise making suggestions for Patrick using this language. Students write the email for homework.

Alternative activity

Students write a reply to one of the emails in exercises 1A or B on page 96.

Sample answer

Hello Patrick,

It was good to hear from you. You asked me about places to buy things so if I were you, I'd go and look at the shopping centre Amazing Prices. There are a few shops that you could try.

The best place to buy your computer equipment is Technology World, where they sell from mobiles to televisions. If you go to the computer part of the shop you'll find everything you need. There are some decent and cheap printers.

As for your clothes, go to Old Times, where you'll find old and modern clothes of all tipes. Go to Modern Clothes and you'll see some affordable and good quality clothes which are quite casual.

It's a shame I couldn't be with you, but I expect I'll see you at summer.

Best wishes
Lara
135 words

Examiner's comment

Content: The letter is short and the writer could have added some introductory information in the first paragraph. However, all the questions are answered fully.

Communicative achievement: Although the opening comment could have been extended, the conventions of an informal letter are followed. The target reader would be fully informed.

Organization: Well organized into paragraphs. Simple cohesive devices used effectively, e.g. *as for your clothes.*

Language: Simple and complex grammatical forms used with control and flexibility, and errors do not obscure meaning, e.g. *they sell from mobiles to televisions, at summer, tipes.*

There is a good range of appropriate expressions for the task, e.g. *good to hear from you, if I were you, I'd go, The best place to buy, If you go to the computer part of the shop you'll find everything you need, which are quite casual, I expect I'll see,* and the writer shows a good knowledge of vocabulary, e.g. *shopping centre, sell, decent, affordable, shame.*

Mark*: Very good pass

*Note on marking

Each of the four categories is awarded a mark out of 5. These marks are then added up to give a total score out of 20.

For the purposes of this course, the sample answers have been graded according to the following scale: **borderline**, **pass**, **good pass**, and **very good pass**.

 DVD resource: Unit 7

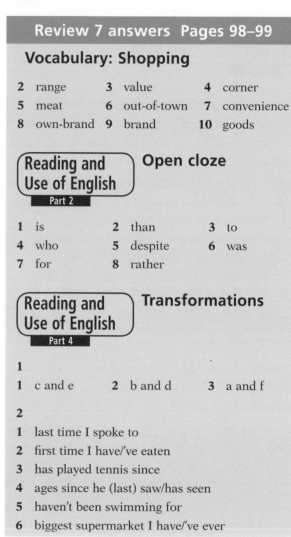

Review 7 answers Pages 98–99

Vocabulary: Shopping

2	range	3	value	4	corner
5	meat	6	out-of-town	7	convenience
8	own-brand	9	brand	10	goods

Reading and Use of English Part 2   **Open cloze**

1	is	2	than	3	to
4	who	5	despite	6	was
7	for	8	rather		

Reading and Use of English Part 4   **Transformations**

1
1	c and e	2	b and d	3	a and f

2
1 last time I spoke to
2 first time I have/'ve eaten
3 has played tennis since
4 ages since he (last) saw/has seen
5 haven't been swimming for
6 biggest supermarket I have/'ve ever

Alternative activity

In Vocabulary exercise 2, ask students to write five questions using vocabulary from exercise 1 and then instruct them to ask each other their questions.

Additional activity 1

Write the transformations from exercise 2 on page 99 onto cards. Put them in an envelope and write *Present perfect* on the front. Stick the answers on the back of the envelope. Add this to your set of revision envelopes. Bring these to a lesson towards the end of the course. Students work in pairs. They choose an envelope and work through the cards. Remind them not to write on the cards.

Additional activity 2

In pairs students brainstorm ideas for the essay question on page 99. Remind them to look at the model on page 194 and the expressions they studied on page 39.

Alternatively, they could write an article for the question below.

You have seen this announcement in an international magazine.

> **THE IDEAL PLACE TO LIVE**
>
> Would you prefer to live in a large city or a small town? Or would you rather have a house in a mountain village or by the sea?
> Write an article telling us where your ideal place to live would be and why.

We will publish the most interesting articles next month.

Write your **article** in **140–190** words.

8 Up and away

Content Overview

Themes

The unit deals with the theme of travel, including space travel, holidays and public transport. The topic of sleep is also covered.

Exam-related activities

Reading and Use of English

Part 6	Gapped text
Part 3	Word formation
Part 4	Transformations (Review)
Part 1	Multiple-choice cloze (Review)

Writing

Part 1	Essay
Part 2	Article (Review)

Listening

Part 4	Multiple choice
Part 3	Multiple matching

Speaking

Part 1	Interview
Part 2	Talking about photos

Other

Language focus:	The future
Vocabulary 1:	Sleep
Vocabulary 2:	Travel
Vocabulary 3:	Phrasal verbs
Word formation:	Adjectives

Reading and Use of English 1
Part 6

Gapped text
Page 100

Lead–in

If there has been an interesting event in the news about space travel or exploration, write the headline on the board or show a visual on the screen and ask students to tell the class what they know about it.

1 Students read the instructions. Then in pairs they discuss the two questions as they would in Part 3 of the Speaking exam. Write a few useful expressions on the board, e.g.
Which one shall we start with …
Let's talk about …
It might be …
Perhaps …

It would probably be …
They could …

2 Students read the rest of the text to check their ideas from exercise 1. Get some feedback from the class.

Answers
moving around, washing, sleeping, and a brief mention of eating (*chasing food through the air*)

3 Students work out the meaning of the phrases in bold. Remind them that guessing from context is an important skill for *First* and also in the real world. Model and check the pronunciation of *circuit*. If students have problems, ask questions to lead them to the correct definition, e.g. *What problems could you have with electrical equipment? How could you wash without using water?*

Answers	
Word or phrase	**Possible student answers**
(students may use gestures for some items)	
short-circuit	damage, or cause a problem in the wiring
wipes	damp cloths for cleaning
trickier	more difficult
chopped	cut

Dictionary definitions
short circuit *noun* [C]
a bad connection in the wires of a piece of electrical equipment, which prevents the equipment from working
short-circuit *verb* [T]
to make a piece of electrical equipment have a short circuit
wipe *noun* [C]
a small wet cloth used a single time for cleaning something
tricky *adjective*
difficult to do
chop *verb* [T]
to cut something such as food or wood into pieces

4 Students read the Don't forget! box. Ask them to look at each gap and discuss what the missing sentence might be about. Write the following on the board to get them started:
Well, here it says that … and then it mentions … so maybe the missing information is …

Students work individually to choose the sentences. Try to avoid helping them with any vocabulary.

Answers
1 E   2 B   3 G   4 A   5 F   6 D

Reacting to the text

Write the following on the board

What I'd really like/dislike is …

I think it would be amazing to …

I'd probably be a bit worried about …

Students use the expressions to discuss the questions in pairs.

Vocabulary 1: Sleep   Page 101

1 Students follow the instructions. Check their answers and demonstrate the ways of sleeping by miming someone on a train nodding off to sleep in a sitting up position. Nod your head a couple of times and then jerk awake. Ask which verb from the box you are miming. After this, mime someone falling gently asleep, and finally someone in an armchair snoozing in a relaxed manner. Elicit the word for each.

Answers
1a
1 falling   **2** nodding   **3** snoozing
1b
going to sleep: *falling asleep, nodding off*
sleeping: *snoozing*

2 Refer students to the extra activity on page 204. Check their understanding of *log* and *nap*.

Answers
1
1 get   **2** log   **3** in
4 take   **5** stay

Additional activity

Write the following questions on the board and ask students to discuss them in groups of three. Encourage them to ask follow-up questions.

Have you ever fallen asleep on any form of public transport?

Do you or any member of your family snore, sleep walk or sleep talk?

Do you ever remember your dreams?

Have you ever had a nightmare/a dream about falling/ a dream about flying/a recurring dream?

Circulate and join in with the conversations. Get some feedback from the class. Ask students who have had any kind of unusual or funny experience to tell the class.

Language focus: The future   Page 102

This is a review of ways of expressing different levels of certainty and different types of future – an area of particular confusion for students.

A Making predictions

1 Students do the exercise in pairs. Get feedback from the class. Mention the following points:

- the word order for *will* with adverbs such as *definitely*, *(almost) certainly* and *probably*: the adverbs come after *will* and before *won't*, e.g. *I will probably come to the party.* *I probably won't come to the party.*
- the difference in the level of certainty between *could* and *couldn't*. The negative form changes the meaning to 'certainty' or 'logical impossibility'.
- the form *may well not* is possible, but is not very commonly used: *may well* is normally only used in the positive.
- *likely* is an adjective and is followed by *to* + infinitive.

Answers		
a 3	**b** 1, 2 and 6	**c** 4 and 5
	Negative forms	
will probably	*probably won't/will not*	
may well*		
will	*won't/will not*	
might	*might not*	
could	*could not* (but note that the negative form changes the meaning to 'certainty' or 'logical impossibility')	
may well not exists, but *may well* is normally only used in the positive		

2 Students complete the predictions. Before they discuss them with their partner, point out that we normally give a negative opinion using *I don't think there will be …*, **not** *I think there won't be*. Write the phrase on the board if necessary to remind them. During the discussion, circulate and check they are using the target language correctly.

B Other futures

Students match the forms with the explanations. Point out that sentence 8 could go with both explanations a and b. In monolingual classes you could ask students whether the forms are similar or different in their own language. Ask strong students to translate some of the trickier forms, e.g. future perfect.

Answers
1 b   2 d   3 e   4 c   5 i   6 f   7 g   8 a   9 h

C Time linkers

Students complete the sentences individually.

Answers		
1 before	2 By	3 until
4 soon	5 when	

The present simple and present perfect simple are used after the time linkers to refer to the future.

Additional activity

Write the following on the board:

Can you send me the report as … (soon as you've finished it)

I need to clean the house before … (I go out)

If we don't hurry, the film will have started by … (the time we arrive)

You can't go out until … (you've done your homework)

I'll come round to your house when … (I've had my dinner)

Students complete the sentences in pairs (example endings in brackets). Remind them they all refer to future time.

D Further practice

1 Students work individually. Circulate and help students with any difficulties. Ask concept questions, e.g. Question 1: *Is it a prediction or a future arrangement?* Question 2: *Is it an arrangement or a decision made at the moment of speaking?*

Answers
A
1 is going to rain   2 we're going
3 we'll have to
B
4 takes off   5 I'll get up
6 we'll be driving

C

7 'm/am seeing *or* 'm/am going to see
8 will last/is going to last
9 're/are only going to sign *or* 're/are only signing
10 'll/will have finished *or* 'll/will finish

D

11 shall we meet   12 doesn't/does not start
13 'll get   14 'll probably see

2 Students discuss the questions with a partner. Circulate and check they are using the future forms correctly.

Listening 1 Part 1   **Multiple choice**
Page 103

Students read the instructions and the Don't forget! box. Allow them 45 seconds to read the questions.

Answers
1 A   2 B   3 C   4 A   5 B   6 C   7 B   8 B

Listening 1: Listening script 1.47–1.54

1 You overhear this man talking about the hotel where he is staying.

We really didn't expect this. We thought it'd be the typical economy type hotel. You know, nothing special, just a bed, a wardrobe and a shower in the room if you're lucky. Well, we were absolutely amazed by the en suite bathroom, I can tell you. It's twice the size of ours at home. And as for the view from the balcony, it's unbelievable. We really can't complain.

2 Listen to this woman talking about a job she has applied for.

… and I think that although my experience running a restaurant may not seem very relevant, it's still a people-orientated job. I am definitely a people person. I like dealing with the public. So whether it's listening to customers and giving them advice on the best places to go, or talking on the phone to tour operators and trying to get the best deal, I think I'd be well suited to the job. I have good people skills and I think that's an important strength.

3 You hear a woman talking to a tour guide.

T = Tour guide   W = Woman

T: Are you sure you had it when you left the hotel?

W: Positive. I didn't want to bring it but my husband made me put it in my bag. He said you should never leave your money or your passport in your room. And then when we were having a drink and I went to pay, it had gone. Someone must have pulled it out of my bag when I wasn't looking. It had my credit cards in it and everything.

T: It's a good job your passport wasn't in it, too. We'll have to report it straight away.

4 You overhear a man talking about a place he tried to visit on holiday.

We went there because we wanted to see the stained glass windows. They say they're among the finest in Europe and the colours are supposed to be incredible when the sun shines through them. Unfortunately, we couldn't go in because we weren't properly dressed – they won't let you in if you're wearing short trousers. And the next morning when we went back it was Easter Sunday. So of course, we couldn't get to the part where the windows are because there was a special service.

5 Listen to this conversation between a man and a teenage boy.

M = Man   B = Boy

M: Yes, your skin is quite badly burnt. How long were you out in the sun for?

B: About an hour, maybe. It was after lunch and I fell asleep on the beach.

M: Do you have any other symptoms – dizziness, a temperature?

B: No, it just really hurts.

M: Well, it doesn't sound like sunstroke. This cream should take away the sting, but if you start to feel sick or dizzy, get yourself to a doctor straight away.

B: Thanks. How much do I owe you?

M: I'll just check. One second.

6 You hear a local resident talking about tourists in her town.

I shouldn't complain really. I mean, the whole economy of this town is based on tourism and if they stopped coming, then a lot of people would be out of work and on the dole. But I do wish they'd show a little more respect. There are a lot of them who have music blaring out of their cars during the day, and then at night you get big groups coming into the centre for the pubs and clubs. And they don't seem to care that we can't sleep with them making such a racket. Most of them drunk, I shouldn't wonder.

7 You hear this boy talking to his mother.

B = Boy   M = Mother

B: Where are we going?

M: Well, we picked up a leaflet for a nature park just outside the town. They've got all sorts of wild animals and you can drive through and see them in their natural habitat. It looks very good.

B: But you said we were going to the Aqua Park.

M: We can't go in this weather. And besides, your father and I want to do something different.

B: But that's not fair. You can't just change your mind like that.

M: Don't be selfish, Steven. It's our turn today.

8 You hear a man talking about a beach he recently visited.

Now, normally I prefer a beach with fine sand, you know, so it's not painful to walk on. This one, though, had small stones – well, more like pebbles, actually – and I don't remember the brochure saying anything

about that. But anyway, we bought ourselves a pair of flip-flops each at one of the shops next to the beach, so that didn't matter too much. And then we spent most of our time there lying about in the water. It was just like being in a warm bath. I could have stayed there all day.

Vocabulary 2: Travel   Page 104

1a Students often confuse this vocabulary. Ask them to complete the exercise individually. Get feedback from the class and go over the meanings of tricky words, e.g.

journey (countable noun): the act of going from one place to another, especially in a vehicle

trip (countable noun): going somewhere and coming back, usually for a short time. Typical collocations: *business trip, school trip, shopping trip, day trip*

travel (verb): to make a journey

travel (uncountable noun): a generic term for the activity of travelling

Answers		
1 journey	2 flight	3 travel
4 cruise	5 tour	6 trip

1b Students discuss the sentences with a partner. Circulate and check they are using the vocabulary correctly. Get feedback from the class. Ask various students to comment on something interesting their partner talked about.

2 Students work individually. Get feedback from the class. Ask some concept questions if students have difficulty with any of the pairs of words, e.g. Question 2: *Which is the activity and which is the place?* Question 6: *Which of the words can be used as a noun? If something is funny what do we do? Which word means the same as 'enjoyable'?*

Answers		
1 holiday	2 campsite	3 stayed
4 enjoy	5 time	6 fun
7 excursion	8 full	9 away
10 package		

Learner training

Remind students to record the more confusing words along with the definitions in their vocabulary notebooks.

Interview

Page 104

Ask students to read the instructions and the questions and do the roleplay. Encourage them to use some of the vocabulary from exercises 1 and 2. Circulate and write down any common errors that you hear. Get feedback from the class. Write the errors on the board and elicit the correct sentences.

Additional activity

While students are discussing the sentences in exercise 1b and answering the Speaking Part 1 Interview questions, circulate and write down a few facts, e.g. *Natalie went on a long car journey from Paris to Nice. Marco went on a guided tour of Berlin last summer.* Keep these and create an error correction exercise of travel vocabulary to use in a future lesson, e.g.

Natalie went on a long car travel from Paris to Nice. Marco went on a guided excursion of Berlin last summer.

Talking about photos

Page 105

Lead–in

Show students a flashcard, for example a ski coach giving a class. Refer them to the Useful language box and elicit sentences about the picture for each of the structures, e.g.

The pupils look nervous.

He looks like a professional ski coach.

The pupil looks as if he is going to fall over.

1–2 Students read the instructions and do the task as suggested. Ask them to set the timer on their mobile phones, one minute for part A and 30 seconds for part B. Circulate, but do not interrupt students during the activity. Get feedback from the class. Mention a few things students did well, e.g. *Noriko paraphrased the word for* body guard *very well: someone who protects an important person.*

 DVD resource: Unit 8

Multiple matching

Page 106

1 Students discuss the questions in pairs.

2 Students read the instructions. Check that they understand *lack* (an absence or shortage of something). Play the recording twice and let students compare their answers together after the first listening. Get feedback from the class. Ask if students have experienced any of the problems mentioned.

Answers
1 C 2 F 3 A 4 H 5 E

Listening 2: Listening script 1.55–1.59

Speaker 1

There's a cycle path that goes right round the city, and various shorter ones within it. Now these paths are up on the pavement rather than in the road, so it's pedestrians, not motorists, that have to be careful they don't wander onto them. People have got used to the circular path and they generally keep off it when they're walking along. But it's the ones in the city centre that cause most problems, and it's here the authorities could do more to inform pedestrians, to make them aware of how it works. Every day I cycle to work and every day I get shouted at by people who still haven't caught on that it's me that has right of way, not them.

Speaker 2

Mine's a folding bike, so I get off the train, put on my helmet and head for the office. I could take the bus or the underground, but there's no pleasure in that – they both get so crowded. On the bike I feel the wind in my face and a sense that the city's mine – I can go where I want, when I want. I can even get up on the pavement and jump traffic lights or go the wrong way down one-way streets. And of course, cycling is just so healthy – I've never felt fitter. Some say it's risky too, but I find motorists tend to go more carefully when cyclists are around.

Speaker 3

A year or two ago, someone in the town hall came up with a nice idea to promote cycling in the city. On the first Sunday in every month, a number of the main streets in the centre are closed to traffic for two hours and given over to bicycles. It's gradually grown in popularity, and there's a real festival atmosphere now, with thousands of cyclists of all ages turning out every month. It's a start, and it's certainly helped to get people out on their bikes. But there's still a long way to go. We need a whole series of additional measures to make our roads more cycle-friendly.

Speaker 4

Sometimes you come across some really nasty drivers in the city. I can be cycling along, minding my own business, when some car or van comes right up close to me, almost touching my back wheel. It's really dangerous – sometimes I lose my balance and nearly fall off. It seems to be worse in the evening. I've got my bike lights, my luminous cycling jacket, my reflective cycle clips – so they can see me all right. But they seem to resent the fact that I'm there. They think they own the road and they get impatient if they have to slow down for me. I get beeped and shouted at all the time – it's very unpleasant.

Speaker 5
Cycling here is more a recreational activity than a means of transport. People don't generally use a bike to get about the city. There isn't that culture. They'll maybe rent one in one of the big central parks, or go on the cycle path that runs alongside the river. But they won't use a bike to get from A to B or to go to and from work. It's not an attractive option, really, given the quality of the air here. We're in the middle of a huge industrial area, and many pedestrians wear face masks. So people are hardly likely to expose themselves to more danger by cycling in amongst the traffic.

3 Write the following on the board;
The government should/shouldn't …
It would be a good idea if …
The local authorities need to…
If the government …
Students discuss the question in pairs; encourage them to use the expressions in their discussions.

Alternative approach
If you think your students will find this difficult, cut up slips of paper with the following ideas:
Cycle lanes within the town or city
Cycle paths in rural areas
Cycle hire as in Paris and London
No VAT on bicycles
Fun events involving bicycles
Create supervised bicycle parking areas
Organize bicycle repair workshops
Students take it in turns to pick up a card and make the suggestion using the phrases on the board. The other members of the group have to say whether they agree with the idea or not.

Vocabulary 3: Phrasal verbs   Page 106

1–2 Students work out the meanings in pairs, then practise using the phrasal verbs.

Answers
1 catch on: begin to understand
2 head for: go somewhere
3 come up with: think of
4 turn out: attend/take part in an event
5 come across: meet (by chance)
6 get about: travel around

Learner training
Remind students to record the phrasal verbs along with the definitions in their vocabulary notebooks.

Word formation: Adjectives   Page 107

1 Students work in pairs to complete the sentences. Get feedback from the class. Ask students to spell the words out loud. Correct any pronunciation issues.

Answers			
1	careful	2	healthy
3	additional	4	dangerous
5	impatient	6	unpleasant
7	attractive	8	industrial

2 Ask students to write the adjectives from exercise 1 in the correct column. They then make adjectives from words in the box in b and add them to the table in the correct column. The three rows are progressively more difficult and spelling changes are likely to be needed for the words in rows 2 and 3. Model and check the pronunciation of the adjectives.

Answers	
-ous	dangerous, poisonous, mysterious, humorous
-ful	careful, peaceful, beautiful, successful
-y	healthy, cloudy, hungry, foggy
-al	additional, industrial, original, financial, beneficial
-ent	impatient, different, apparent, obedient
-ant	unpleasant, ignorant, tolerant, hesitant
-ive	attractive, protective, decisive, descriptive

Reading and Use of English 2 Part 3   **Word formation** Page 107

Students read the text once without completing the gaps. Ask whether they think a monorail system would be a good idea in their town or city. Mention that the text contains a variety of word forms, e.g. adjectives (positive and negative), nouns (plural and singular), adverbs. Remind students that accurate spelling in this section of the Reading and Use of English paper is essential.

Answers

1	significant	**2**	numerous
3	unusual	**4**	distances
5	impressive	**6**	environmental
7	inexpensive	**8**	appearance

Writing Part 1 — Essay — Page 108

1 Ask students to cover the model answer in exercise 2. Then they should read the instructions and write notes in pairs.

2 Students read the example answer and answer the questions. If students ask the meaning of any words, encourage them to guess from context, e.g. for *stroll* ask: *Would you walk around a seaside village quickly or in a relaxed way?*

Answers

The fact that there are more opportunities to make new friends on a seaside holiday than in the countryside.

3 Students find the linking devices.

Answers

3a *Secondly, Another positive point is*
b *Without doubt, which, whereas, but, also, therefore, because, In my opinion*

4a Students read the instructions. Check for understanding.

4b Students discuss the different factors in pairs and decide on their third point.

4c Students read the instructions and the Don't forget! box, then make plans in pairs. Suggest they write down five words which they could use in their essay, e.g. *underground, passengers, avoid traffic jams, lines, fares, rapid service*.
They could also compare the means of transport they choose with other alternatives on offer in their town or area, e.g. *The underground is far more comfortable than the bus.*
Students could either complete the task for homework or you could have them do it under exam conditions in class. Remind them to refer to the Useful language boxes on pages 194 and 195.

Sample answer

The best way to travel in my area is by car, which generally has more advantages from using public transport.

Firstly, there are not trains and the busses in my area are not often. You can wait thirty minnutes to find a bus. They can be very slow and you can waist a lot of time going to a diferent place. In the car, you can travel more fastly to a variety of places.

Second point, although busses are not expensive to by tickets, they are not too clean so it is not nice to sit on them for long time. It is better to go to a place in the car because the car is more plesant.

Finally, the busses do not go to many diferent locations and you can have problems to go where you want. In the car you can decide what to visit in my area. It is not surprising that all of the people in my town use the car to go anywhere.

In my opinion, then, the car is the best way to travel in my area because it saves time, costs cheaply and you can go where you want.

Sinan Alpey
196 words

Examiner's comment
Content: Adequate coverage of 1 and 2 and candidate has added their own idea. However, the introduction is rather weak.

Communicative achievement: Register appropriate to the task. The reader would be sufficiently informed; however, the frequent inaccuracies would create a negative effect.

Organization: Clear paragraphing. Adequate use of simple linking devices, e.g. *firstly, although, finally, in my opinion.*

Language: Although the frequent errors do not obscure meaning, they do distract the reader, e.g. incorrect prepositions – *advantages from* (of), incorrect verb – *busses in my area are not often* (don't run very often), confusion with gerunds and infinitives – *problems to find* (finding), incorrect comparative – *more fastly* (faster), poor expression – *busses are not expensive to by tickets* (bus fares are not expensive), problems with quantifiers – *not too* (very) *clean, go anywhere* (everywhere), omission of indefinite article – *for* (a) *long time*, There are also many spelling mistakes which have a negative effect, e.g. *minnutes, busses, waist, diferent, by, plesant*. Some variety of structures, e.g. *The best way to travel, although, better to go to a place, diferent locations, what to visit, It is not surprising.* Some more complex collocations, e.g. *you can waist* (waste) *a lot of time, a variety of places that, saves time.* However, in general the language is simple and contains frequent inaccuracies.

Mark*: Pass

*Note on marking

Each of the four categories is awarded a mark out of 5. These marks are then added up to give a total score out of 20.

For the purposes of this course, the sample answers have been graded according to the following scale: **borderline**, **pass**, **good pass**, and **very good pass**.

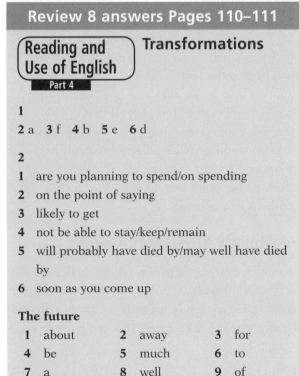

Review 8 answers Pages 110–111

Reading and Use of English Part 4 — **Transformations**

1
2 a 3 f 4 b 5 e 6 d

2
1 are you planning to spend/on spending
2 on the point of saying
3 likely to get
4 not be able to stay/keep/remain
5 will probably have died by/may well have died by
6 soon as you come up

The future

1	about	2	away	3	for
4	be	5	much	6	to
7	a	8	well	9	of
10	is	11	not	12	on

Reading and Use of English Part 1 — **Multiple-choice cloze**

1 D 2 B 3 A 4 B 5 C 6 B 7 D 8 A

Additional activity 1

Write the transformation sentences from exercise 2, page 110 onto cards. Put them in an envelope and write *The future* on the front. Stick the answers on the back. Add this to your set of revision envelopes. Bring these to a lesson towards the end of the course. Students work in pairs, choose an envelope and work through the cards. Remind them not to write on the cards.

Additional activity 2

For the Writing section on page 111 students work in pairs. They should think of a good holiday destination and write notes for the article. Refer them to the model of Seville. In the next lesson they could read each other's articles and choose a winner for the competition.

 Progress Test 4

9 Mystery and imagination

Content Overview

Themes

The unit deals with the themes of mysteries, ghosts and superstitions.

Exam-related activities

Reading and Use of English

Part 5	Multiple choice
Part 2	Open cloze
Part 7	Multiple matching
Part 1	Multiple-choice cloze (Review)
Part 3	Word formation (Review)
Part 4	Transformations (Review)

Writing

Part 2	Review

Listening

Part 4	Multiple choice
Part 2	Sentence completion

Speaking

Part 3	Collaborative task

Other

Language focus 1: Modal verbs for speculation and deduction
Language focus 2: Question tags
Language focus 3: Contrast linkers
Vocabulary 1:   Ways of looking
Vocabulary 2:   *Give*
Word formation: Adverbs

Reading and Use of English 1
Part 5

Multiple choice
Page 112

1 Ask various students the questions. Elicit recommendations for a good novel or film.

2 Students read the instructions. Explain that they should read the text for gist and not worry about tricky vocabulary yet. Discuss the question briefly as students will comment on this in more detail in Reacting to the text. Ask if anyone has been to the south-west of England and what they imagine the sea and coastline would be like, e.g. powerful, dramatic, dangerous.

3 Check students' understanding of *struck by* (impressed or surprised by). Ask students to work individually to choose the answers.

Answers

1 **C** *Laura felt the magnetic pull of the ocean beneath the black cliffs, and goose bumps rose on her arms.*

2 **B** *The tide was in and violent waves splattered the path. More than once, Laura had to leap to avoid a drenching.*

3 **D** *She almost didn't pick it up. The idea of finding a message in a bottle seemed ridiculous, like a joke or something. ... Before she picked it up, she took a good look round in case the person who'd left it there was hanging around to have a laugh.*

4 **A** *Since the bottle was shiny and new and had obviously never been in the sea, old sea dogs could be ruled out.*

5 **C** *She put down the note while she zipped up her coat and pulled her scarf tighter.*

6 **C** *What if the writer was someone in real danger? What if she was their only lifeline and she ignored them and walked away?*

Reacting to the text

Students discuss the questions in groups of three. To add an element of fun, suggest that if they have never found anything special they should invent something. When all three students in the group have spoken they can ask each other some follow-up questions and decide if they believe one another's stories or not.

Vocabulary 1: Ways of looking

In some languages there may not be an equivalent verb for these ways of looking, as an adverb is often used instead to modify the verb, so you may need to demonstrate the differences. This can be done easily by miming.

1 Students work out the meaning of the verbs in bold. If they have problems, mime them. Remind them to record this vocabulary in their notebooks.

Answers

1a

1 b   2 a   3 c

b

1 peer: look very carefully, especially because something is difficult to see

2 glimpse: see for a moment or not completely

3 glare: look at someone in a very angry way

2 Students complete the sentences with the verbs from 1a and b.

Answers

1	glanced	2	gazed	3	staring
4	glimpse	5	glared	6	peered

Language focus 1: Modal verbs for speculation and deduction   Page 114

1 Students answer the questions. Then write the following examples on the board:
I can't find my wallet. I must have left it at the hotel.
You've failed three subjects. You can't have worked very hard.
It's 3 pm and Anna's not here. She might have forgotten about the meeting.
With a different colour pen highlight the structure:
modal verb + *have* + past participle
Check students understand the differences in levels of certainty and that *can't have* is the opposite of *must have*.
Model and check pronunciation of the three sentences.

Answers

1a *might have left, might have come*
b *can't have been*
c *must have done*

2 *have* + past participle (the perfect infinitive without *to*)
3 *could, may*

2 Look at the example for situation 1 then elicit speculation for situation 2, e.g. *Paul might have been working in the garden*. Draw students' attention to the continuous form and explain that it is used when making a deduction about a prolonged action with a present result. Then students should work in pairs. Circulate and check their sentences are correct.

3 Students match the sentences with the continuations.

Answers

2 d   3 e   4 a   5 f   6 c

4 Students answer the questions, then check their answers with the Grammar reference section on page 216.

Answers

a present, continuous infinitive (*be* + present participle) without *to*
b present, infinitive without *to*
c past, perfect infinitive (*have* + past participle) without *to*
d past, (continuous) perfect infinitive without *to*
e past, perfect infinitive without *to*
f present, infinitive without *to*

Additional activity
If students need further explanation, give some more examples and ask concept questions:
1
He's wearing a suit, he might be going to an interview.
Are we sure he is going to an interview? Is the interview in the present or the past?
2
'I haven't eaten since last night.' 'You must be really hungry!'
Is it a long time since he last ate something? Is he hungry now? Are we sure?
3
The robbers might have got in through an open window.
Is this situation in the past or present? Are we sure the robbers entered through the open window?
4
He looks tired, he must have been working a lot.
Is he tired now? Are we sure he has been working a lot? Is he working now?

5 Look at the example together, then elicit possible deductions for sentence 2. Circulate while students speculate about the other sentences in pairs, and correct any errors with the target language.

 **Listening 1** Part 4   **Multiple choice**   Page 114

1 Elicit answers to the questions from various students. Ask whether they have been on a similar guided walk, but don't go into too much detail as students will get a chance to do this in question 3.

2 Pre-teach *haunt*. Allow 45 seconds for students to read the questions and underline key words. Play the recording twice and let students compare their answers together after the first listening.

Answers

1 B **2** B **3** C **4** A **5** C **6** A **7** A

Listening 1: Listening script 1.60

A = Alan Stanford   I = Interviewer

I: In the *Talkabout* studio today we have a ghost walk guide. Local man Alan Stanford takes groups of people round the town on guided tours, telling ghost stories about the historic buildings which are said to be haunted. Sounds like an interesting job, Alan.

A: Oh, it is, it's fascinating. I've been a tour guide before but mostly abroad and never here in my own home town. I wouldn't call myself an expert, but I've learnt quite a lot about our local history since I started doing this a couple of years ago. Plus, of course, I get to dress up and tell lots of ghost stories. Acting and storytelling have always been in my blood, so I'm really just doing what comes naturally to me. I have a great time.

I: And how about those who actually go on the tours? Do they get frightened?

A: Well, obviously these are ghost walks, so it wouldn't be much fun if there wasn't a bit of fear involved. Not too much, of course – we often have children in the groups, so we have to be careful. But people expect to be scared, and they'd be disappointed if they weren't, so we aim at least to give them goose bumps, and perhaps even a little fright – after which **they all laugh nervously** and enjoy the release of tension.

I: And how do you achieve that, giving them a fright?

A: Well, the mark of a good storyteller is the ability to hold an audience's attention, and that's not too hard to do when the subject is ghosts. You take the listeners into your confidence, create the right mood, make them feel safe with you. Then, just at the right moment, when they're least expecting it, you change the tone, give a shout or let out a scream. And they nearly jump out of their skin!

I: Right, yes. And does it work every time?

A: Well, it does with most audiences, people who've been thinking about the ghost walk all day, maybe all week, wondering what's going to happen. **These people usually respond extremely well.** Some of the groups we get, though, come along as part of a surprise event. People like these haven't had time to reflect on what they're coming to, they haven't been given the chance to look forward to it, and the effect isn't the same. They don't normally have such a good time, unfortunately.

I: You mentioned dressing up before. Do you do the ghost walks in character?

A: Yes, I do. And I have different costumes for different characters – there's Lord Warwick, a wealthy noble, the old sea dog Jake Redburn, John Simpkins, who's a servant … none of them real, of course – they're all fictitious. The choice of character I play often depends on the route we take and the stories to be told, or also perhaps how I'm feeling that night and the type of audience I'm expecting. As with all acting, it adds a sense of truth to the whole thing, makes it more credible. So the audience becomes engaged in the tour and responds in a more positive, sometimes more frightened way.

I: One question, I have to ask you, Alan. Do you believe in ghosts?

A: Regrettably, I have to say that I haven't seen any on the walks, or had any other paranormal experiences to impress you with. Some people in my audiences say they have, and so have some of my friends, and I wouldn't dare dispute that or suggest they're imagining things. Ghosts are real for those people who say they've seen them, and who am I to suggest they haven't? The most I can say is that I have no personal evidence they exist.

I: And of the stories that you tell on your ghost walks, do you have a favourite?

A: Well, I particularly like stories which involve smells that some buildings are said to give off when ghosts are around. I don't want to give away too much here on the programme, but the one I enjoy telling most of all is about an old woman called Sally Hardcastle, who haunts the town hall. When she appears every now and again, the place absolutely stinks. Now at first, some people thought it was a problem with the rubbish, but if you want to find out the real reason, you'll have to come along on the ghost walk.

I: Oh! We're curious now, Alan. And, if you are interested in going on a ghost walk with Alan …

3 Students work in groups of three. Circulate and listen to their discussions. Get some feedback from the class. Comment on anything interesting students said. If you happen to have an anecdote about a paranormal experience yourself, tell the class about it if you think it would be appropriate.

Word formation: Adverbs   Page 115

1–3 Students write the adverbs. Mention that adjectives like *lively, friendly, silly* have no adverb form. To get round this we normally say someone acted *in a lively/friendly/silly way* or *manner*.

Answers

1

1 nervously
2 usually, extremely
3 regrettably

Add *-ly* to the adjective (e.g. *nervously*). This also applies to adjectives ending in *-l* (e.g. *usually*) or *-e* (*extremely*). However, if the adjective ends in a consonant + *-le*, then omit the final *-e* and add *-y* (e.g. *regrettably*).

2
1 completely, solely
2 simply, gently
3 luckily, extraordinarily
4 scientifically, dramatically

3
| 1 wholly | 2 shyly | 3 fully |
| 4 publicly | 5 truly | |

4 This exercise moves closer to the exam, with examples of some of the more difficult words. Students are required to make at least two changes: (1) noun to adjective and (2) adjective to adverb (three changes in the case of *health*). Advise students to form the adjective first before moving on to form the adverb (even with number 5, where *daily* is also the adjective). Before students start, write up the order they should follow (*noun–adjective–adverb*) and refer to this if you see them making mistakes as you circulate.
Get feedback from the class. Ask students to spell the words out loud. Correct any pronunciation issues.

Answers		
4		
1 Apparently	2 accidentally	3 increasingly
4 originally	5 daily	6 repeatedly
7 carelessly	8 unhealthily	

Vocabulary 2: *Give* — Page 116

A Phrasal verbs with *give*

1–2 Students work in pairs to match the phrasal verbs to their meanings, then work out the meaning of the phrasal verbs in the sentences in exercise 2.

Answers	
1	
a give away	**b** give off
2	
1 stop doing something you do regularly	
2 allow oneself to be arrested by the police	
3 give something (physical) to several people	
4 give information to a lot of people	
5 give something to a teacher; return	
6 agree to something after initial resistance	

B Collocations with *give*

1 Check students' understanding of *broad* (wide), *piercing* (penetrating) and *sigh* (breathe out slowly and noisily to express emotion).
Remind students that collocations are words that often go together and that when they come across new ones they should record them in their vocabulary notebooks (as mentioned before, collocations in the Coursebook have been highlighted in **bold**).

Answers
1A
1 d 2 c 3 e 4 a 5 b
1B
1 e 2 d 3 f 4 a 5 b 6 c

2 Students match a general meaning to each collocation in 1B.

Answers
a 3 give great pleasure, 4 give a nasty shock
b 5 give an impressive performance, 6 give a lengthy speech
c 1 give one's best regards, 2 give full details

3 Students usually enjoy these memory activities as they are quite challenging. You could also use these to revive tired students at the end of a lesson.

Additional activity

In the last five minutes of the class, tell students they have a little test. Ask them to take out a paper and pen. Read out ten sentences, leaving out the noun from the collocation, and get students to write down the missing word, e.g. *The girl was so terrified she gave a piercing … When I saw the present I gave a broad … .*
Don't let the students confer or say the answers. Correct the answers together and then finish the class. This way they will leave with the satisfaction that they've remembered some collocations.

4 Students work in groups of three. Circulate and note down any interesting experiences they have had. Get feedback from the class. Ask various students to tell the class what they said, e.g. *Yukiko, can you tell us about the nasty shock you had last weekend?*

Reading and Use of English 2
Part 2

Open cloze
Page 117

1 You could look on the Internet for information about the superstitions of sports people from your students' country/countries. Ask them questions like:
Who always eats an ice-cream before they play an important tennis match? (Rafael Nadal)
Then let them read the examples on page 204.

2 Ask students to read the text once and to tell you why superstitions help sports people to perform better. (It makes them feel more in control and boosts their confidence.)
If students query the use of the definite article with the abstract noun *luck*, explain that this is referring to a specific piece of luck.

Answers			
1	be/make	2	which
3	not	4	to
5	than	6	yourself
7	on	8	although/though/while/whilst

3 Elicit situations where superstitious behaviour might be typical, e.g. before an important exam, on certain dates, before a job interview, wedding, etc. Write these on the board, then ask students to discuss the question as a class, referring to the situations on the board where appropriate.

Listening 2
Part 2

Sentence completion
Page 117

1 Students read the instructions and try to predict the type of information they might hear. Check their understanding of *mine* and *vanish*. Play the recording twice and let students compare their answers together after the first listening.

Answers			
1	go hiking	2	summer
3	farmers	4	German
5	October	6	eight thousand/8000
7	setting	8	maps
9	ghost	10	song

Listening 2: Listening script 1.61

Hi, I'm Sally Hurst and I've just got back from Arizona, where I spent two weeks in the Superstition Mountain Range, near Phoenix. It's an area known to many people for its luxury golf courses, and those who can afford it go there to play golf in a desert setting. But it also attracts enthusiasts of more energetic outdoor activities like rock climbing or mountain biking. And I was lucky enough to go hiking when I was there. There are miles of paths and the scenery is absolutely spectacular.

'It's a bit hot there, though, isn't it?', some of my friends have asked. Well, it depends when you go. It's early spring now, of course, and that's fine. Winter and autumn are also OK, but I certainly wouldn't advise going there in summer – whatever the reason for your visit. Temperatures can reach up to 45 degrees or more – and that's far too hot for me.

The main reason I went there was to research some of the legends and mysteries of the area for a forthcoming radio documentary. The very origin of the name, Superstition Mountains is itself a bit of a mystery. One theory says they were given their name by sixteenth-century Spanish settlers, some of whom inexplicably vanished when they went exploring there. But the more likely explanation is that it came about in the nineteenth century, when it was discovered that the local Pima Indians were frightened of the mountains. Farmers in the area attributed this fear to superstition, and they decided to give that name first to one mountain, and then the whole range.

Perhaps the most talked about mystery in the area is that of the so-called Lost Dutchman's Mine, which is supposedly somewhere in the Superstition Mountains. Far from being Dutch, the owner of the gold mine in question, Jacob Waltz, was actually German, or Deutsch in his native language. Waltz arrived in the United States in November 1839, and spent virtually all his life there prospecting for gold, firstly in North Carolina, then Georgia, California and finally Arizona. When he passed away in October 1891 he took the secret of his mine with him to his grave.

You see, apparently Waltz had found what was believed by some to be the richest gold mine in the world. But he didn't tell anyone where it was, and it's a mystery which remains unsolved to this day. According to one estimate in 1977, up to eight thousand people a year tried to locate the mine. And even today, despite the ban on mineral prospecting in 1983, many people still head for the region to see if they can find it.

Waltz left a few clues, but they weren't particularly helpful. In one of them, for example, he says, 'The rays of the setting sun shine into the entrance of my mine', but that could be just about anywhere.

I did a lot of my research for the documentary in a museum: The Superstition Mountain Museum. It's full of information on the Lost Dutchman's Mine, including a whole collection of maps which are thought to show its location – not that that's been of any use to anyone! So far, anyway.

And I saw another exhibit on the mine in a museum in nearby Goldfield. Now Goldfield was a prosperous mining town at the end of the nineteenth century, but when the gold ran out, everyone left and now it's a ghost town. It's become a popular tourist attraction as well, of course, with museums, rides and shows, but it's still quite impressive, nevertheless.

Now you may have seen a film that was made in 1949 about the Lost Dutchman's Mine entitled *Lust for Gold*, starring Glenn Ford in the role of Jacob Waltz. But here's another piece of trivia for you: in 1960, actor Walter Brennan recorded a song on the subject called *Dutchman's Gold*. Now I bet you didn't know that, did you?

Well you do now, and we're going to play it to you right after the news. To be honest, Walter Brennan talks his way through it rather than ...

2 Elicit some places with mysteries and legends. Write these on the board and ask students to discuss them in groups of three.

Language focus 2: Question tags
Page 118

1 Do the activity as a class. Elicit rules for questions tags.

Answers

The subject and the auxiliary verbs in the main clause are repeated in the question tag but the order is reversed. Also, if the verb is affirmative in the main clause, it is negative in the question tag, and vice versa.

2 Play the example sentences again and draw students' attention to the intonation. Note that the examples have been recorded separately after the listening. Then refer students to the Grammar reference on page 216.

Answers

a Sentence 1 is a real question.
b In sentence 2 the speaker expects agreement.
The difference is in the intonation:
Rising intonation (➚) = real question
Falling intonation (➘) = expecting agreement

3 Students work individually. Then play the recording for them to listen to the sentences and correct their answers where necessary.

Answers

1	do you	2	will you
3	didn't you	4	is he
5	hasn't he	6	aren't I
7	can't you	8	shall we

4 Write the first two sentences on the board, play the recording and mark the intonation together. Then play the rest of the recording and let students mark the intonation patterns.

Answers

1 You don't believe him, do you? ➚

2 You won't let me down, will you? ➚

3 You went away for the weekend, didn't you? ➚

4 He's not playing very well, is he? ➚

5 He's already passed the *First* exam, hasn't he? ➚

6 I'm right about that, aren't I? ➚

7 You can play chess, can't you? ➚

8 Let's phone Paul, shall we? ➚

5 Choral drill the intonation patterns. However, be aware that it is often easier to recognize intonation patterns than to produce them, particularly with falling intonation. The tendency is to make the intonation on all question tags rise. Don't over-insist on perfection as this may prove to be demotivating for your students.

6–7 Students follow the instructions. Circulate and check they are forming the question tags accurately. Gently correct their intonation.

Reading and Use of English 3
Part 7

Multiple matching
Page 118

1 Check student's understanding of *donor* and *gift*. Ask students to predict what happens in the stories and discuss their ideas in pairs.

2–3 Students check their predictions, then answer the questions. You could draw students' attention to the phrasal verbs *give away* and *get rid of* in C and *give out*, *hand out*, *come into* and *threw away* in D and check students remember their meaning.

Alternative approach

If you would like to make the reading more communicative you could start the activity by asking students to work in groups of four. Each student reads one of the texts and then gives an oral summary of the information to their group.

Additional activity

Find a video clip about one of the stories and write some general comprehension questions. Show the clip to students after completing the reading task, and ask them to answer the questions.

Answers
1 C *Some of the beneficiaries wanted to meet the donor to express their gratitude.*
2 A *… there was unanimous approval of the intricate sculptures from all those lucky enough to view them on display.*
3 D *… one national daily, which asked readers to get in contact if they knew who the mystery benefactor was.*
4 B *What surprised them was the huge interest shown by newspaper and radio journalists …*
5 C *There were a number of theories to explain who the donor was and why they might have given the cash away: an elderly person with no family to leave their money to, a criminal wanting to get rid of stolen money or a lottery winner trying to do some good.*
6 A *… the general view was that he or she should remain anonymous.*
7 D *I have recently been fortunate enough to come into quite a lot of money …*
8 B *… some residents expressed concern that the scarves might harm the trees and become unattractive with the effects of the weather.*
9 A *Each sculpture was carefully and suitably chosen …*
10 D *Believing it to be part of a marketing promotion, one beneficiary nearly threw the blank envelope away.*

Reacting to the text

Students discuss the questions in pairs, or if you used the alternative approach they should stay in the same groups of four.

 **Collaborative task**

Page 120

Useful language

Ask students to read the instructions for exercise 1, then do the tasks in the Useful language box. Drill intonation of the question tags.

Answers		
A		
1 on	2 in	3 for
4 on	5 out	
B		
1 is it	2 wouldn't it	3 do they
4 haven't we	5 shall we	

1–2 Students do the collaborative task in pairs. Circulate and write down any issues with the target language. Get feedback from the class. Write up some of their errors on the board and correct them together. Suggest that they record the verbs and prepositions from Useful language task 1 in their vocabulary notebooks.

3 Students discuss the Part 4 questions on page 204. Circulate, but don't interrupt the discussions. Take feedback from the class. Comment on how well different pairs performed in terms of interactive communication.

Language focus 3: Contrast linkers

Page 120

1–2 Students follow the instructions. Get feedback from the class. Highlight the rules:
Although/Even though + subject-verb clause
Despite/In spite of + gerund/noun/noun clause
Despite/In spite of + possessive adjective + (*not*) gerund
In spite of/Despite + *the fact* (*that*) + subject-verb clause

Answers	
1 but	2 Despite
3 While (*or* Although)	4 Although
5 However	6 in spite

Additional activity

Your students may need some extra practice with these contrast linkers. Make copies of the following sentences before the class.

1 *Even/Although Andrew did a lot of driving lessons, he failed the test.*

2 *In spite of/Although the pain in my knee, I decided to play the match.*

3 *Despite/Although he lived in France, he couldn't speak the language very well.*

4 *I invited my cousin to the party. He didn't want to come though/even though.*

5 *Although/Despite the fact we didn't have much money, we were still a happy family.*

6 *In spite/Despite having excellent qualifications, he didn't get the job.*

7 *She told everyone my secret despite/although my asking her not to.*

8 *This reference book is expensive. However,/Despite it is worth it.*

Give a copy to each student and ask them to choose the correct contrast linkers. Go over the rules.

Answers

1	Although	2	In spite of
3	Although	4	though
5	Despite	6	Despite
7	despite	8	However,

  DVD resource: Unit 9

Writing Part 2   **Review**
Page 121

1–3 Students work through the exercises individually. Get feedback from the class.

Answers

2

Abbey Road by The Beatles

3

a Yes.

   Good points: *it still sounds as fresh as when it was first released in 1969; Lennon and McCartney, always a guarantee of quality music; my favourites are the two written by George Harrison; the Liverpool band's use of vocal harmony on the album is outstanding, and there's a good mix of fast and slow tracks, with one or two humorous ones as well.*

   Bad points: *Ringo's contribution about the octopus is the weakest; the artwork … is tiny*

   Recommendation: *The album has songs to suit every generation, from children to grandparents, so I'd recommend it to everyone.*

b Yes.

   Paragraph 1: Introduction, reasons for buying the download

   Paragraph 2: Good points

   Paragraph 3: More good points and one bad point

   Paragraph 4: Recommendation; concluding sentence, including a bad point

c Yes.

   So, Despite, However, and, as well, but, so, Unfortunately, but

d Yes.

   Vocabulary of music: e.g. *album, band, track, drummer, cover, compose, release*

   Adjectives: e.g. *classic, scratched, fresh, gentle, outstanding, humorous*

   Structures: e.g. *This classic album … has been in our family for over forty years; … it's been played so often that it's too scratched to listen to now; it still sounds as fresh as when it was first released; he was always a better drummer than a singer, wasn't he?; The album has songs to suit every generation.*

e The style is fairly informal, with contractions (*it's, there's*), a dash (*– gentle songs of love and hope*), exclamation marks (*we still have the cover from the vinyl version!*) and the use of direct address (*he was always a better drummer than a singer, wasn't he?*).

   The style is appropriate: this is a school's English-language magazine so the readers will be other students.

4–5 Either ask students to work individually for exercise 4 and then swap their review with a partner, or ask students to work in pairs and swap their review with another pair.

Sample answer

I'd only been able to play this when I went to my friend Eli's house. So when I finally bought my own console it was the first game I bought. It involves you look after your own dogs, feed them, wash them, take them out for walks, and take them to competitions.

I like it because if you have a dog, you can learn from this game, as it gives you useful information. Your dogs are given a number of accessories and toys which you can sell in order to buy others you would prefer having. Another way to be able to buy accessories is to enter competitions, were you can win money.

There's nothing very bad to say about this game, but something that does frustrate me a little bit is that you can't go to more than 3 competitions in a day.

I think it's a game for all ages, but it will probably appeal more to young people who like animals. You can buy it in any game shop.

Elisa Pacheco
172 words

Examiner's comment

Content: Full coverage of all information required.

Communicative achievement: Lively tone suitable for this type of review. Would inform the target reader, as well as and hold their attention.

Organization: Well organized. Clear paragraphing.

Language: Minor inaccuracies with more complex language, e.g. *It involves you look (looking) after*. One spelling mistake *were* (where), which does not impede meaning. Good examples of accurate language use in often difficult areas. There is a wide range of simple and complex grammatical forms, used with control and flexibility, e.g. *I'd only been able to play, if you have a dog, you can learn from, dogs are given, in order to, prefer having, frustrate me a little bit, it will probably appeal more to young people.* Many examples of good vocabulary, e.g. *console, sell, look after, feed them, accessories, toys, appeal.*

Mark*: Very good pass

*Note on marking
Each of the four categories is awarded a mark out of 5. These marks are then added up to give a total score out of 20.
For the purposes of this course, the sample answers have been graded according to the following scale:
borderline, **pass**, **good pass**, and **very good pass**.

Review 9 answers Pages 122–123

Vocabulary: Ways of looking

1 c 2 d 3 e 4 f 5 a 6 b

Reading and Use of English Part 1 — **Multiple-choice cloze**

1 B 2 C 3 D 4 C 5 A 6 B 7 B 8 D

Reading and Use of English Part 3 — **Word formation**

1	noisily	2	traditional	3	colourful
4	evidently	5	suspicious	6	shortly
7	eventually	8	mysterious		

Reading and Use of English Part 4 — **Transformations**

1 might not be playing
2 have given you great pleasure
3 may have given
4 give away a secret would *or* give a secret away would
5 'd/had better give/hand
6 caught/got/had a brief glimpse

Ready for Listening

Listening paper

Part 1	Multiple choice
Part 2	Sentence completion
Part 3	Multiple matching
Part 4	Multiple choice

This is the third of five 'Ready for ...' units which focus on the skills areas tested in the *First* exam. The intention of this Ready for Listening unit is to train students to use the little, but valuable time they have to prepare themselves before each listening.

Part 1: Multiple Choice   Page 124

1–2 Read through the information in 1 and 2. Pay special attention to the distractors. Explain that expanding their vocabulary during the course will help them to discard distractors and choose the correct option.

Answers

2
A a blouse

Key words and expressions
It'll go really well with a skirt I bought last week.
The sleeves are a bit short, but if I wear a jacket over it ...

Distractors
Cheaper than getting a dress ...
It'll go really well with a skirt I bought last week.

3 Give students time to read the questions and encourage them to underline key words. Play the recording twice and let students compare their answers together after the first listening. Explain that they should briefly discuss what they heard if their answers are different. Correct the answers and then allow time for students to read the script on pages 230–231 for any questions they got wrong. This will help them see how distractors are used.

Answers

1 C 2 A 3 A 4 C 5 B 6 B 7 C 8 B

Listening Part 1: Listening script 2.1–2.8

1 You hear part of a sports commentary on the radio.

These two sides are very well matched. You'll remember they both met in the semi-finals last year, when the game ended in a draw. This year we've had some heavy showers in the last few days and one or two of the players are finding the playing conditions on the pitch more than a little difficult. But it's a throw-in now. Briggs takes it and passes to Duckham. Duckham tries a shot ... and it goes just wide of the post.

2 You hear a man talking on his mobile phone.

I thought at first it was some kind of virus, but now I'm wondering if it might be something more serious ... No, it's annoying. I simply can't do any work on it at the moment ... Yes, I phoned them, but they said they'd need to have it for three days before they could give me an answer ... Well, I was wondering if you wouldn't mind having a look at it for me ... Could you come round after work? ... No, that's great; the sooner the better as far as I'm concerned, as long as your boss doesn't mind.

3 Listen to this man and woman speaking.

M = Man   W = Woman

M: Lots of room for the legs, that's nice.

W: Mm, and so comfortable. It's like my favourite armchair. I could go to sleep here and now.

M: Yes, we should've had a coffee after the meal to keep us awake.

W: We'd never have got a ticket to see this if we had.

M: That's true. The queue was enormous.

W: Anyway, wake me up when it starts, won't you.

4 You hear this woman telling her friend about a restaurant.

You can't fault the food, really. Even my husband was impressed and he's always the first to complain if it's not cooked properly. No, I just felt a little uncomfortable; silver cutlery, antique furniture and everyone dressed as if it was a wedding, including the waiters. And the way they spoke to us! It was 'Sir' and 'Madam' every sentence. I suppose I'm just not used to it, that's all.

5 You hear this man talking to his friend on the phone about a day trip to London.

The play finishes at about 11... Well, I had at first thought of coming back on the train straight afterwards, but the last one's at 11.05, so I probably wouldn't make it ... Are you sure you don't mind? ... I could always stay in a hotel. There are plenty of cheap ones in that part of town ... OK, well, if you're going to put me up for the night, then you'll have to let me take you out for a meal ... No, I insist.

6 You hear a woman talking to her husband in a supermarket.

W = Woman   M = Man

W: Just look at that. It's incredible.

M: What do you mean?

W: Well, there must be about twenty different types of butter in this section. Low-fat, high-fat, Irish, Dutch, Australian – you name it, they've got it.

M: Confusing, isn't it?

W: That's not the point. I'm sure a lot of people will be disappointed there aren't twenty types of carrots and sixty different varieties of cheese. I just don't see why we need them all. And when you think of the transport costs and the fuel needed to import all this stuff and the effect this has on the environment. Oh! It makes my blood boil.

7 You hear this man talking.

We all know juvenile crime's on the increase. The police do all they can with very limited resources and then it's up to people like ourselves to sort the problem out. In this school alone we have more than twenty youngsters with a criminal record and we get virtually no support from the parents. Social services come in occasionally to give us advice on how to deal with them, but once they've gone and we close the classroom door, we're very much on our own.

8 You overhear a man talking to a woman about a flat which is for rent.

W = Woman   M = Man

W: Did you go and see that flat you were interested in?

M: Yeah, I did. It's not for me, though.

W: Why's that? Too expensive for you?

M: Well, no, I could afford it all right. It's on the edge of town near the industrial estate, and rents out there aren't as high as in the centre.

W: Hmm, that's too far out for me. I like it where I am, near the shopping centre.

M: Well, it's not as if there aren't any shops out there – there are plenty of amenities. It's just that I need space for all my computer equipment, and the lounge and the bedroom are smaller than where I'm living at the moment.

Part 2: Sentence completion   Page 125

1 Refer students to the eight statements and instruct them to work in pairs to decide if the statements are True or False. Get feedback from the class. Make sure they record the correct answers so that they can refer to these later.

Answers
1 **False**: all parts of the listening paper are heard twice.
2 **True**
3 **True**
4 **False**: the maximum number of words you need to write is normally three.

5 **False**: it is not necessary to rephrase the words you hear.

6 **False**: you do usually hear the answers in the same order as the questions.

7 **False**: if you are having difficulty with a question, move quickly onto the next. You may miss later answers if you spend too long on one answer.

8 **True**: spelling errors are accepted, but if the word is so badly spelt it is unrecognizable, then it may be marked wrong.

2 Students read the instructions and the What to expect in the exam box. Then in pairs they should predict the type of answer they might hear for each of the ten gaps. In a weaker class, check students have identified the right kind of word before going on with the listening.

Before listening, remind them to be careful to look out for distractors. Play the recording twice, and allow students to compare their answers briefly after the first listening. Correct the answers as a class.

Ask whether students would like to visit Patagonia. Find out if they know of a similar group of people anywhere else in the world.

Answers			
1	tea house	**2**	several hundred
3	isolated	**4**	farmers
5	(local) Indians	**6**	beautiful valley
7	song and dance	**8**	(groups of) teachers
9	(Welsh) flags	**10**	chocolate cake

Listening Part 2: Listening script 2.9

Argentina is a country known internationally for the tango, gaucho cowboys and premium quality beef. To many people, therefore, it comes as some surprise to discover that in certain parts of Patagonia, in the south of the country, one of the 'musts' for any tourist is a visit to a Welsh tea house, a place where you can sip tea and enjoy delicious cakes, baked according to traditional Welsh recipes. Perhaps even more surprising, though, is the fact that some of the locals can actually be heard speaking in Welsh. Exactly how many native Welsh speakers there are in the region is not known, but most estimates put the figure at several hundred, a relatively high number, given that there are just under 600 000 speakers of the language in Wales itself.

But how did these Welsh speakers come to be there? The first wave of settlers arrived from Wales in 1865. Unhappy with conditions at home, they were looking for an isolated area to set up a colony, a place where their language and identity would be preserved intact and not assimilated into the dominant culture, as had already happened in the United States. The 153 colonists who landed on the east coast of Argentina included carpenters, tailors and miners, but no real doctors and just one or two farmers. This was rather worrying, since the Chubut valley where they settled was virtually a desert, and what was needed most of all were agricultural skills.

Against all the odds, though, they survived, overcoming droughts, floods and a succession of crop failures. They were also quick to establish friendly relations with the local Indians, who helped the Welsh through the hard times and taught them some of their ways, how to ride and how to hunt. Twenty years after their arrival, some of the settlers moved up into a green fertile region of the Andes mountains, an area which they named Cwm Hyfryd, meaning 'beautiful valley'. Indeed, quite a number of places in Patagonia still bear Welsh names: Bryn Gwyn which means 'white hill', Trevelin, meaning 'milltown' and Trelew or 'Lewistown', named after Lewis Jones, one of the founders.

The Welsh have left their mark in other ways, too. Their windmills and chapels can be found throughout the region and there are a number of cultural activities, such as poetry readings, male voice choirs and the annual Welsh song and dance festival, a smaller version of the International Eisteddfod held in Wales each year. All of this helps to keep the language and traditions alive in a small corner of the world, 8000 miles from the homeland. And so too does the fact that every year, as part of a programme administered by the National Assembly for Wales, groups of teachers come to Patagonia to teach the language to the growing number of people who are interested in learning it.

And then, of course, there are the Welsh teas. For my afternoon treat, I visit Nain Ceri, reputed to be one of the best tea houses in Gaiman, where the streets and houses are adorned with Welsh flags, a reminder to visitors that they are in the self-proclaimed Patagonian-Welsh capital of Chubut. Inside, Nain Ceri is decorated with prints and paintings of Wales and the music playing is that of a traditional all-male choir. I sit next to the fireplace and my mouth begins to water as I look at the various cakes on offer. I am about to order the cream-topped apple pie to accompany my tea, when I catch sight of an irresistible-looking chocolate cake and choose that instead. I am not disappointed – it is absolutely delicious. Afterwards, I chat at length to the owner, Ceri Morgan – in Spanish, as she speaks no English and I speak no Welsh. She tells me a little more about the history of ...

Part 3: Multiple matching

Page 126

1 Students read the instructions and the What to expect in the exam box. Stress that they should

listen carefully both times before making their final decision.

2 Students read the instructions and underline key words in the statements. Play the recording twice and let them compare their answers together after the first listening. Correct answers as a class. Ask which of the jobs they think would be the most interesting.

Answers

1

Suggested underlining of key words:

A I will need a <u>specific qualification</u> to do this job.

B I currently <u>combine work</u> with <u>studying</u>.

C I <u>disagree</u> with the <u>careers</u> <u>advice</u> I have been given.

D I <u>heard</u> about this job from <u>someone in my family</u>.

E I <u>do not really mind</u> what job I do.

F I think I have the necessary <u>personal qualities</u>.

G I am <u>not clever enough</u> for the job I would like to do.

H I am studying a <u>relevant subject</u>.

2

1 B **2** H **3** D **4** A **5** F (C, E and G not used)

Listening Part 3: Listening script 2.10–2.14

Speaker 1

I've been writing for as long as I can remember, and it's something I want to continue to do for a living when I've finished university. I say 'continue' because I've already had one collection of short stories published and I've just started another. I write mostly late at night and at weekends, always after I've finished my coursework. I'm doing a maths degree, which has little to do with writing, but I believe in keeping my options open, just in case my creativity runs out.

Speaker 2

For some strange reason I want to be a tattoo artist; you know, paint people's bodies. I'm doing a course in graphic design at art college, which I've been told will be useful. The brother of a friend of mine has a studio and he lets me go and watch him work when I'm not studying at the college. It's the only way to learn, as there are no official courses and no specific qualifications for tattoo artists. At least, not as far as I know.

Speaker 3

As soon as I leave school I'm going to join the Army. I tried to do it when I was 10 but they told me to go back when I was older – so I will! You can learn a trade and do almost any job you want to, and they let you study while you're working. I'd like to work as a physical training instructor, and then maybe later try and get an engineering qualification or something like that. My granddad's an ex-soldier and he always told such good stories that I knew that was what I wanted to do. My parents just think I'm crazy.

Speaker 4

I hope one day to be a speech therapist. I'll have to get a degree in speech therapy first, and to be able to do that in a decent university I'll need to get good grades next year. It's a job which involves helping people who have difficulty communicating, and I've always known I wanted to work in one of the 'caring professions'. My uncle's a speech therapist, but I learnt all about it from a TV documentary I saw a few years ago. And that's when I thought; 'I want to do that'. Then last year I did some voluntary work while I was studying for my exams, and I was hooked.

Speaker 5

I haven't made up my mind yet, but I'd quite like to go into teaching. Naturally I've had lots of advice from teachers at school about how to go about it and how hard I'll have to work for my exams. But to be honest my decision is based not so much on my academic abilities but rather on the fact that I just feel I'd be right for the job. The teachers I look up to at school are all dynamic, outgoing people and that's precisely how I like to see myself.

Part 4: Multiple Choice   Page 127

1–3 Students work individually. Ask students to brainstorm possible problems for tall people.

Answers

3
C. Underline the whole of the first sentence.

4 Students discuss the options from exercise 3 with a partner.

Answers

A: Most of the people he works with are below average height. At one metre eighty-four, he is above the average height of one metre seventy-eight for British men.
B: We are told that he is taller than most, if not all, of the people in his studio, but we do not know if he is taller than most people in his profession.

5–6 Students complete the listening exercise, then underline the key phrases in the script and discuss the options with a partner.

Answers

5
2 B   3 A   4 A   5 B   6 B   7 C

6
2 A: We are only told that tall people come from all over the country to stay in a hotel.
   C: Not mentioned.
3 B and C are both mentioned as problems but not the biggest.
4 B: People who make comments like 'What's the weather like up there?' think they are funny. Jenny does not.
   C: Jenny says that many fellow TPC members take offence, but she is used to it now.
5 A: They stand up straighter as they grow in confidence. No one encourages them to do so.
   C: Not mentioned.
6 A: Not mentioned. Jenny says 'I've never been very good at volleyball, but I always got picked for the university team when I was a student.'
   C: Not mentioned. The word 'job' is mentioned when she says 'you can get things off the top shelf that most other people have a job to reach.'
7 A: Not mentioned. Jenny merely compares the GB and Ireland club with those in America.
   B: No. People decide for themselves if they should join.

Listening Part 4: Listening script 2.15

P = Presenter   J = Jenny Parfitt

P: Do you consider yourself to be tall, medium or short? At one metre eighty-four, I've always thought of myself as being a little on the tall side, particularly when I stand next to the people I work with here in the *Round Britain* studio. Rather curiously, most of them are below the national average height of one metre seventy-eight for men and one sixty-two for women. But when I popped in yesterday to the annual conference of the TPC – that's the Tall Person's Club of Great Britain and Ireland – I felt decidedly small. I asked one of the organizers, Jenny Parfitt, to tell me about the conference.

J: Well, this is the main event in the club's very busy social calendar. Throughout the year we put on a whole number of activities for members in their local area, like barbecues, theatre excursions, walks and so on. And this conference is the highlight of that year. It's a three-day event that gives tall people from all over the country the chance to meet in the comfort of a hotel, where they can chat, eat, dance and go sightseeing with others who are also above average height.

P: But there's also a serious side to it as well, I gather.

J: That's right, it's not all partying! We discuss a lot of important issues, too. One of the aims of the TPC is to promote the interests of tall people, to change current attitudes. We live in a heightist world, where tall people are discriminated against. Beds in hotels are usually too short for us, and we often have to sleep with our feet hanging off the end. Travelling by bus, train or plane is a major problem too – there's very little leg room and it can feel very cramped. The main difficulty, though, is finding shops that sell long enough trousers or big enough shoes. That can be a real headache.

P: I imagine too that the attitudes of other people can be a problem.

J: Yes, people do tend to stare at us when we walk into the room, treat us like circus freaks. And some actually laugh out loud, as if something funny has just happened. I think if I weren't so used to it now, I might take offence – I know many fellow TPC members do. But to be honest, I find it a little bit annoying. You get tired of it all, particularly when the fifteenth person in a day says something like 'What's the weather like up there?' And they think it's so funny.

P: Yes, not very original, is it? Does the club offer help to tall people who come across attitudes like these?

J: Yes, we regularly give advice to victims of insults and bullying at school or in the workplace. But perhaps the greatest benefit of the club is the opportunity to see that as a tall person you are not alone. When people come to their first meeting and walk into a room full of tall people, they start standing up straighter. They lose their shyness and very soon begin to feel less awkward, more comfortable about their height. It's a remarkable transformation.

P: You've mentioned some of the negative aspects of being taller than average. But surely there must be some advantages, too?

J: Oh yes, there are plenty of them. Er, for example, you can always see over everyone's head if you're watching something in a crowd or an audience, and if you're in a supermarket you can get things off the top shelf that most other people have a job to reach. And then also, you automatically become first choice for sports like basketball, volleyball or rowing. I've never been very good at volleyball, but I always got picked for the university team when I was a student.

P: Now, one thing of course we've failed to mention, Jenny, is your height. How tall are you?

J: one metre eighty-eight. And actually, I'm one of the smaller members at this conference. The tallest woman here is exactly two metres and the tallest man two metres thirty, that's an incredible seven foot six inches.

P: Goodness me!

J: Yes, impressive, isn't it? Incidentally, though, you don't need to be above a certain height to qualify as a member of the Tall Person's Club. Unlike some clubs in the USA, which can be difficult to join because of their restrictions, we are very inclusive over here. We believe that people know for themselves whether they are tall or not and it's up to them to decide if they should join.

P: Jenny, it's been fascinating talking to you …

10 Nothing but the truth

Content Overview

Themes

The unit deals with the themes of crime, punishment, truth and lies. Language structures related to these issues are also covered.

Exam-related activities

Reading and Use of English

Part 5	Multiple choice
Part 4	Transformations (Review)
Part 1	Multiple-choice cloze (Review)

Writing

Part 2	Article
Part 1	Essay

Listening

Part 4	Multiple choice
Part 3	Multiple matching

Speaking

Part 2	Talking about photos

Other

Language focus 1: *Too* and *enough*
Language focus 2: Passives
Language focus 3: Passive of reporting verbs
Vocabulary 1:   Crime and punishment
Vocabulary 2:   Paraphrasing and recording
Vocabulary 3:   Phrasal verbs

Vocabulary 1: Crime and punishment   Pages 128

1 Follow the instructions with the class. Check their understanding of *trial*. If your students have difficulty thinking of a news item, you could project an image or write up the headline from a recent crime which has been in the news.

A   Crimes and criminals

1–2 Elicit the crimes shown in the photos (vandalism and shoplifting). Ask students to do exercises 1 and 2 as suggested. During feedback, highlight the difference between *rob* and *steal*:
rob someone or somewhere, e.g. *The gang robbed the bank. My mother was robbed.*
steal something, e.g. *The pickpocket stole my wallet.*
Model and check the pronunciation of *burglary* (/ˈbɜːɡləri/), *fraud*(/frɔːd/), *piracy*(/ˈpaɪrəsi/) and *mugging*(/ˈmʌɡɪŋ/).

B   Punishment

1 Students work in groups of three. If they ask the meaning of any of the words, try and get another student to give them a definition. Some groups may come up with a different order for types of punishment. If so, ask them to justify their reasons and check they fully understand the terms.

2 Students work in groups of three. Remind them to refer to the Useful language box. Get feedback from the class and find out whether different groups agree on the punishments.

Additional activity

Ask your students to write a summary of a crime which is in the news. They should bring this to class and exchange it with their partner and discuss the seriousness of the crimes. If you have access to a virtual forum you could set the activity up online.

Listening 1
Part 4

Multiple choice

Page 129

1 Students work in pairs to discuss crime novels and films. You could also include TV crime series in the discussion.

2 Students read the instructions and the questions. Encourage them to underline key words. Check their understanding of *genre* (a type of writing). Play the recording twice and let students compare their answers after the first listening.

Answers

1 C **2** A **3** B **4** B **5** A **6** C **7** B

Listening 1: Listening script 2.16

I: Interviewer   J: Justin Blakelock

I: With us today is local crime writer, Justin Blakelock. Justin, perhaps I should begin by asking you why you decided to write crime fiction rather than any other genre?

J: Whenever I'm asked that question, people think I'm going to say it's because I've always loved reading crime novels. Well, I have, but I'm actually much more of a science fiction fan than anything else, and that's the kind of thing I was writing when I first started out as an author. But then my editor – an ex-policewoman curiously enough – saw elements of crime writing in my work and she gently pushed me in that direction.

I: And was it her idea to set your novels here in Brighton?

J: No, that was mine. Firstly, because I love the place so much and, despite the crime theme, I do try to show it in a positive light. But also, even though I'm writing fiction, I want my stories to be as real and accurate as possible. And because I grew up in this area, because I know it so well, it makes sense for me to set them here. There are too many novels that lack credibility because they're set in fictional places, or they're set in real places which are not accurately described.

I: You show two versions of Brighton in your books, don't you?

J: That's right. To the visitor, Brighton seems a very peaceful city. It has this gentle, calm exterior – the very solid seafront buildings and pleasant shopping streets. But like many other cities it has its darker, more criminal places – the rundown buildings and areas that the tourist rarely sees. And that's also true of many of the characters I create. At first, they seem to be very gentle, very pleasant people, but there's something darker, more criminal hiding below the surface.

I: And how about your protagonist, Detective Inspector George Trent? He's a little more straightforward, isn't he?

J: Yes, yes he is. He does have the occasional moment when he surprises everyone – if not, he'd be too dull. But essentially, what you see is what you get with George. He's very scruffy, slightly overweight, and completely disorganized. He doesn't worry about things like dressing up or combing his hair – he thinks he's good enough as he is, he's very comfortable with the way he looks. And that's really what makes him such a likeable character, I think.

I: Yes, he's not attractive, but he's very human, isn't he? Now, Justin, you have a very popular website. Can you tell us about that?

J: Yes, sure. Well, the original idea behind the site was to get my name out there more and promote my books. But it gradually evolved into a blog – usually articles aimed at crime writers who were just getting started. And then other established authors began reading and commenting on my posts, and now it's effectively become a forum, a kind of debating club.

I: Can you give us an example of the kind of advice you give?

J: Well, I've just posted a list of things you should remember to include in a crime novel. So for example, make sure your detectives have enough paperwork to keep them busy. Real detectives have loads to do, so your fictional ones should be doing their fair share too. To be honest, it's the kind of thing writers ought to pick up themselves by watching what goes on in a police station. There's absolutely no substitute for that. But it's good to compare notes and for every ten pieces of advice I give, you can read twenty more in the comments from other writers who've done their own research. It's a support service, a secondary source.

I: And a very useful one. Now Justin, your last book, *Western Road*, is currently being made into a film. You must be delighted.

J: Yes, I am. More or less. The American producers wanted to move the action to Chicago, but I made it a condition that it had to be filmed in Brighton with British actors. I only wish I'd insisted on having more control over the script. It moves too fast for my liking. But that's the film world for you – what can you do?

I: Not much, I guess. Justin, thank you for coming in. Good luck with …

---

3 Students work in pairs to discuss the question. You could also add the following question:
Has your city, or a place you know well, ever been used as the setting for a crime novel or film? What was it about?

Language focus 1:
Too and *enough*

Pages 129

1 Students do a and b individually.

Answers

1a

a nouns **b** adjectives and adverbs

c before **d** after

1b the infinitive with *to*

Additional activity

If your students need more practice, ask them to complete the following sentences with *too, too many, too much* and *enough*. If possible make one copy per student before the lesson or to use as a quick revision activity in the next lesson.

1 *Football players earn … , it's completely unacceptable.*
2 *I didn't write quickly … , so I couldn't finish the exam.*
3 *It's … hot in here, can you open the window?*
4 *There's … pollution in my city.*
5 *There are … cars on the roads these days.*
6 *I haven't got … time, can I finish this later?*
7 *It's … cold to go out today.*
8 *The teacher explained the grammar … quickly for me to understand.*
9 *I'm not tall … to reach the top shelf.*
10 *There aren't … glasses on the table.*

Answers

1	too much	2	enough	3	too
4	too much	5	too many	6	enough
7	too	8	too	9	enough
10	enough				

2 Students complete the sentences individually. Remind them they must use between two and five words. Circulate and help students if they have difficulties. Ask concept questions, e.g. sentence 2: *What's the opposite of small? Do we put* enough *before or after an adjective?*

Answers

1 too quietly for me to
2 not tall enough to
3 aren't/are not enough eggs for
4 there were too many

3 Students write their own sentences. Circulate and check students' sentences are correct.

Reading and Use of English
Part 5

Multiple choice
Page 130

1 Students discuss the questions in pairs. You could write the following on the board to help them with the first question: *romantic partners, children, work colleagues, business world, neighbours, strangers.*

2 Students read the article to compare their ideas. Encourage them to guess any difficult vocabulary from the context. Get feedback from the class.

3 Pre-teach *monotonous* (boring) and *surveillance equipment* (equipment for watching and listening to people in secret) before students complete the task.

Answers

1 D   2 C   3 A   4 D   5 B   6 A

Reacting to the text

Ask students to discuss the questions in pairs. Get some feedback by asking various students to summarize what their partner said.

Vocabulary 2: Paraphrasing and recording
Page 132

1 Students complete the sentences. Circulate and help students if they have difficulties. Ask questions like the following:

Sentence 1: *Which verb can we use to say something is your fault?*

Sentence 4: *How can we make the noun* hour *into an adjective?*

Sentence 6: *What adjective can we use to say it's possible to obtain something?*

Answers

1	blame	2	far	3	good
4	hourly	5	run	6	available
7	own	8	former		

2 Students paraphrase the sentences.

Answers

Possible answers:
b Concentrated faces make the place feel busy.
c We always follow the law very closely in our work.

d It is not only women who are patient.

e People are more prepared to talk about their feelings to a woman.

f Clients do not want to take part.

g She smiles a little.

Language focus 2: Passives   Pages 133

1 Students look at the passive sentences and answer the questions.

Additional activity

Write some more examples of the passive on the board to check students understand the usage and form, e.g.

Many homes are burgled every day. (present simple)

The robbers are being held in the police station overnight. (present continuous)

Some pupils have been caught shoplifting. (present perfect)

All violent criminals should be punished severely. (modal verb + infinitive without *to*)

The driver complained about being breathalysed. (preposition + -*ing* form)

Elicit the time and tense for each sentence. Use a different colour pen to highlight the structure: *to be* + past participle.

Pay special attention to the passive after modal verbs, and the use of the gerund after certain verbs and prepositions.

Answers

Answers

1a

1 *will not be accepted*

2 *could be done*

3 *not to be overheard*

4 *is called away*

1b to be, past

1c

2 the clients   3 her staff

1 The agent is obvious (the court officials) so does not need to be mentioned.

4 The agent is not known by the writer, or is not important in this context.

2 As students do the exercise, remind them to identify which tense is needed for each gap by looking at the time references in bold. Then they can form the passive. They should also refer to the Grammar reference on page 217. After checking

the answers, draw students' attention to the visual and ask if they know of any news stories where an unusual person has managed to stand up to criminals.

Answers

A be categorized

B will be/are going to be installed, has/have been criticized

C were increased, are/have been found, have been contacted, to be made

D were fined, was told, were/had been warned, would be taken, was not turned

E was being pushed, be attacked, being treated, was sent

3 Students work in groups of three to discuss the questions. Write some useful expressions on the board and ask students to use them in their discussions.

The problem is becoming more and more ...

The main problem is ...

What do you think about ... ?

In my opinion ...

Do you agree with ... ?

I strongly disagree with ...

Circulate and join in with the discussions. Get feedback from the class by asking students to tell the class about antisocial behaviour in their neighbourhood, e.g. *Galina, can you tell us what you said about young people behaving badly in your town?*

Writing   **Article**
Part 2   Pages 134

1 Check the students' understanding of *astonishingly* (very surprisingly), then ask students to do the exercise as suggested.

Answers

1 Personally   2 Astonishingly
3 Sadly   4 Unfortunately/Sadly
5 Curiously   6 Worryingly
7 Interestingly   8 Happily

Additional activity

Students work in pairs. Student A chooses a sentence and reads it out and Student B has to make a comment, for example:

A: *Personally, I think that any form of physical punishment is unacceptable.*
B: *Oh yes, I totally agree. My mum never smacked me, she just told me off and explained why I shouldn't behave badly.*

Then Student B reads out another sentence and they continue in the same way. Tell them not to use sentences 2 and 8 as these don't refer to general opinions.

2–3 Check students' understanding of *litter* (rubbish dropped on the ground). Ask them to cover the model answer in exercise 3, then read the instructions and discuss their ideas in pairs. They can then compare their ideas with the model answer.

4–5 Students analyse the model answer, as suggested.

Answers

4

a   *A load of rubbish* (this expression can also be used to express disagreement or criticize something)

b   *I'm sure the people of Brenton don't drop crisp packets and drink cans on the floor in their own home.*

c   *So why do so many think it's acceptable to do so on the streets of our town?*
But surely they, more than anyone, want a town they can be proud of, don't they?

d   *Incredibly, Clearly, Unfortunately, surely*

e   *So, And, But* (Normally, these are used as conjunctions to link two ideas in the same sentence. Here they are used informally at the beginning of a sentence to link the ideas which follow with those in the previous sentence.)

f   *But surely they, more than anyone, want a town they can be proud of, don't they?*

5

Paragraph 1: A criticism of some of Brenton's residents and their tendency to drop litter.
Paragraph 2: The serious nature of the problem in Brenton, and the impression left on tourists.
Paragraph 3: Suggested solutions.
Paragraph 4: A criticism of the council and a reason why they should take action.

6 Students read the instructions and the Don't forget! box, then brainstorm ideas in pairs before writing the article.

Sample answer

<u>Graffiti everywhere!</u>

Walls, schools, blocks of flats and offices – everywhere in my neighorhood is covered of graffiti. It's as an illness which has caught the buildings.

Is it art? No, it is mostly untidy writing of young people who don't have nothing better to spend their time. It makes the town to look ugly and seem if somebody drop a can of paint on the area. When the young people would do it in their own house, their parents would get crazy. So it is difficult to understand why do they do it in the street.

So what can be done to cure this illness? Obviously, the best thing is catch the people who do this kind of thing and make them to clean the building. In addition, if I were the council, I would make a special place, where it is allowed to paint the wall all what you want. Then the people will do graffiti there and not on the buildings.

Perhaps they could also do a class of graffiti in order to become better. Then we could admire their work rather than see it like a problem.

Klaus Fischer
190 words

Examiner's comment
Content: Full coverage of the questions.

Communicative achievement: The catchy style in which the article is written would hold the reader's attention. The reader would be fully informed; however, the writer has been penalized due to frequent inaccuracies.

Organization: The article is clearly divided into appropriate sections. The writer has used rhetorical questions and simple linking devices effectively, e.g. *obviously, in addition, perhaps*.

Language: Although the frequent errors do not obscure meaning, they do distract the reader. Some examples of inaccuracies are incorrect prepositions – *covered of* (in) *graffiti*, problems with use of passive – *which has caught the buildings* (which the buildings have caught), *where it is allowed* (people were allowed*)* to paint the wall all what you want (as much as they wanted), incorrect quantifiers – *don't have nothing* (anything), problems with bare infinitive – *It makes the town to look ugly* (town look), problems with prepositions and incorrect tenses – *seem* (as) *if somebody drop* (had dropped), *like* (as) *a problem,* incorrect conditionals – *When* (if) *the young people would do* (did) *it,* problems with indirect questions – *understand why do they do* (why they do). Despite frequent inaccuracies, some complex language is included, e.g. *what can be done to cure, if I were the council, I would, make a special place, rather than.*

The writer also shows a good knowledge of vocabulary, e.g. *walls, blocks of flats, neighborhood, illness, untidy, drop a can of paint, cure this illness, admire.*

Mark*: Good pass

*Note on marking
Each of the four categories is awarded a mark out of 5. These marks are then added up to give a total score out of 20.
For the purposes of this course, the sample answers have been graded according to the following scale: **borderline**, **pass**, **good pass**, and **very good pass**.

Additional activity
Bring in flash cards or project some images of graffiti on the screen. Ask students to comment on the message and reasons for each one. Discuss whether all graffiti should be banned or whether it is a form of art. You could look for a video clip about graffiti and prepare a comprehension activity. Obviously the cultural setting in which you are teaching should be taken into consideration before using any authentic material.

Talking about photos
Page 136

Lead–in
Brainstorm reasons why parents tell their children off, e.g. for not doing homework, poor school grades, unacceptable treatment of siblings, not doing household chores, overuse of Internet, noise, music, TV, undesirable friends, staying out late, going to bed or getting up late, etc.

1–2 Students read the instructions. Elicit some useful expressions and write these on the board for them to use while they do the activity. Encourage them to use the language of deduction from Unit 9 and the following expressions:
I get the impression …

I expect …
He/She probably …
She looks …
He may have …
I think he must have …

Circulate and write down a few errors. Get some feedback from the class and ask whether students think it's good to have strict parents. Write the errors on the board and correct them together.

 DVD resource: Unit 10

 **Multiple matching**
Pages 136

1 Remind students that we say *tell a lie* and not *say a lie*. Ask them to read the text on page 204. You could draw a time line on the board and elicit the types of lies children tell at different stages of their life.

Answers
to avoid punishment, to spare a friend's feelings, to keep secrets, to increase a child's power and sense of control

2 Students discuss the questions in pairs. Get them started by giving an example of a lie you told as a child.

3 Students read the instructions. Check their understanding of *hurt* and *hurry*. Play the recording twice and let students compare their answers together after the first listening.

Answers
1 E   2 A   3 H   4 G   5 C   (B, D and F not used)

Listening 2: Listening script 2.17–2.21

Speaker 1
I was supposed to check all the windows were closed before we left the house for my swimming class, but I was rushing to get ready and I forgot. When we were in the car, my dad asked me if I'd remembered to do it. I didn't want to be late, so I lied and said I had. That morning we were burgled – lost all our TVs and computers. As soon as I heard what had happened, I **owned up** to my dad about lying – I felt so guilty, I had to tell him. Plus it was pretty obvious they'd got in through an open window – there was no sign of a forced entry anywhere.

Speaker 2
When I was about five or six, I took a pair of scissors out of a kitchen drawer and cut off a big chunk of my hair in front of my friends. I'm not sure why – maybe I

was just **showing off**, trying to make myself look big. I kept being asked the same question: 'Have you cut some of your hair off?' My mum, my dad, the hairdresser … And I kept saying 'no'. I said it so many times, I almost believed it in the end. I thought I'd **got away with** it, but my mum told me recently she'd always known what had happened.

Speaker 3

I once typed out a note to my teacher and forged my mum's signature, so I could **get out of** doing sport. I think I said I had a stomach ache or something. My mum **found out** and went mad. Like an idiot I'd created a file with the name 'sick note' on our main computer and she spotted it a week or so later. Why I didn't delete it, I have no idea – it was a stupid mistake. My mum was really upset. She said I'd used her to lie to my teacher, which was true, of course. I didn't have to do sport that day, though.

Speaker 4

My mum gave me a hundred pounds in cash to pay for a school trip to France. When I went to give the money to the French teacher, I couldn't find it anywhere. I knew my mum would be angry with me, so I **made up** something about being mugged on the way to school. She phoned the head and they called the police. They realized fairly quickly I was lying, because the second time I described what had happened I got confused and it came out all wrong – not all the details were the same. I've never been in trouble with so many people in one day.

Speaker 5

I remember when my neighbour **came over** a year or so ago. She knocked on my door and said she'd **run out of** flour and asked if she could borrow some. It was a Sunday afternoon and the shop on the corner was closed and she wanted to bake a sponge cake for her kids. Well, I did have some, and under normal circumstances, I'd have been more than happy to lend it to a neighbour in need. But she'd never done me any favours, and in fact, she'd been positively unfriendly to me on occasions. So I said I was sorry, but no I didn't have any flour, and if she hurried she might catch the shop down in the town before it closed.

4 Write the following useful expressions on the board:

I remember I lied once because I forgot to …

When I was really small I pretended …

Once I took …

I'll never forget the time I lost …

When I was a teenager I often used to lie about …

Students then discuss the question in groups of three. Get feedback from the class. Ask a few students to tell the class about some of their partners' lies.

Vocabulary 3: Phrasal verbs   Page 137

1 Students work in pairs to guess the meanings of the phrasal verbs. Get feedback from the class by eliciting possible definitions for each phrasal verb.

Answers	
show off:	behave in a way that is intended to attract people's attention and make them admire you
get away with:	manage to do something bad without being punished or criticized for it
get out of:	avoid doing something that you should do
find out:	discover a fact or piece of information
make up:	invent an explanation for something, especially in order to avoid being punished
come over:	visit someone in the place where they are, especially their house
run out of:	use all of something so that you do not have any left

2 Students record the phrasal verbs as suggested.

3–4 Circulate and check students are writing accurate sentences with enough information to indicate which phrasal verb is missing.

Alternative activity

Students work in pairs. Instead of doing exercise 3, they write three questions using the phrasal verbs. Then they join with another pair and ask each other the questions.

Language focus 3: Passive of reporting verbs   Page 137

1 Go through the information with the class. Write the example sentences on the board and highlight the forms in a different colour pen. Elicit suggestions for how to change the second sentence.

Answers
is believed he made up the story about being mugged

Additional activity

If your students need more practice, write the following sentences on the board, including the prompts in the brackets, and ask students to complete them.

The suspect is thought … in Oxford. (be)
The gang are believed … in the north of England. (hide)
Two prisoners are said … from the high-security jail. (escape)
It is estimated that thirty football hooligans … (arrest)

Answers

The suspect is thought to be in Oxford.
The gang are believed to be hiding in the north of England.
Two prisoners are said to have escaped from the high-security jail.
It is estimated that thirty football hooligans have been arrested.

2 Students complete the sentences. Circulate and help students with any difficulties.

Answers	
1	believed to indicate
2	are said to be trying
3	is considered to be
4	are thought to use
5	is known to have lied

3 Students discuss the question in groups of three. You could write the following useful expressions on the board to help them.

I think there's some truth in this one …
I don't think there's any truth in this one …
I can tell when my brother/sister/mum/dad is lying, because …
My mum says that when I lie …
It's so obvious when … lie because they usually …

Review 10 Answers Pages 138–139

Phrasal verbs

1

1	ran	2	get	3	sort	4	find
5	fell	6	give				

2

1	making	2	owned	3	taken		
4	giving, put	5	bringing	6	Cheer		

Reading and Use of English Part 4 — Transformations

1 be kept free of
2 is given a warm
3 was paid (at) an hourly or was paid at the hourly
4 being left on their
5 did not/didn't deserve to be
6 not to blame for

Reading and Use of English Part 1 — Multiple-choice cloze

1 D 2 A 3 B 4 C 5 C 6 A 7 C 8 D

Additional activity 1

Exercises 1 and 2 could be adapted to make a short quiz.

Additional activity 2

Write the transformations from page 138 onto cards. Put them in an envelope and write *Passives* on the front. Stick the answers on the back. Add this to your set of revision envelopes. Bring these to a lesson towards the end of the course. Students work in pairs, they choose an envelope and work through the cards. Remind them not to write on the cards.

 Progress Test 5

Content Overview

Themes

The unit deals with the themes of weather, extreme conditions, natural disasters and concerns about the environment.

Exam-related activities

Reading and Use of English

Part 7	Multiple matching
Part 6	Gapped text
Part 2	Open cloze
Part 4	Transformations (Review)

Writing

Part 1	Essay
Part 2	Email (Review)
Part 2	Review (Review)

Listening

Part 2	Sentence completion
Part 1	Multiple choice

Speaking

Part 3	Collaborative task

Other

Language focus 1: *So, neither* and *nor*
Language focus 2: Conditionals
Vocabulary 1:   Weather
Vocabulary 2:   *Put*

Vocabulary 1: Weather   Page 140

Lead–in

If there has been a news story about severe meteorological conditions somewhere in the world, write the place on the board and elicit information about the event and related vocabulary.

1 If you have a mixed nationality group, ask students to sit with someone from another country. Students describe their typical weather in pairs. Suggest that they refer to the photos of the type of weather typical in their country. You could also ask which season they like/dislike most.

2 In each group of adjectives, students will probably know at least one or two, so they should be able to do the exercise without any help. Model and check the pronunciation of *glorious* (/ˈglɔːriəs/) and *rough* (/rʌf/). Get feedback from the class. Write any words they don't know on the board, then give

example sentences so that students can guess the meaning from context, e.g.
The sky was a bit overcast, so we decided not to go to the beach.
There was a severe storm last night, so we thought it would be safer to stay at home.
It was only fine rain, so we didn't get very wet.
Lots of trees were blown down by the gale-force winds.

Answers					
1	storm	**2**	rain	**3**	winds
4	sunshine	**5**	sea	**6**	clouds
7	showers				

3 Students follow the suggestions.

Alternative activity

Play word tennis. Students work in groups of three. One is the umpire and the others are the players. The players close their books. The umpire says a noun from exercise 2 and the players have to say related adjectives as quickly as possible. Either student can say a word first. When they run out of words the last student to have spoken wins the point, and the umpire says a new word, e.g.
Umpire: *wind*
Player A: *strong*
Player B: *gale-force*
Player A: *light*

4 Students complete the gap-fill.

Answers	
2	strong/gale-force winds
3	snow showers
4	angry-looking/thick clouds
5	Heavy/Torrential rain
6	calm sea

Additional activity

After you have corrected exercise 4, ask one student to read out the first sentence again. Then continue a short conversation, e.g.
Student: *There's a lovely clear sky tonight so we might see a shooting star.*
Teacher: *Yes, it's true. Do you remember the last time we saw one when we were on holiday in Hawaii?*
(The student will probably look confused, so you may need to insist.)

Don't you remember, we were in that amazing beach cafe at midnight.
Student: *Oh, yes.*
You: *Then all those dolphins appeared and everyone went swimming with them …*
When students have grasped the idea, get them to do the same in pairs. Each time they finish a mini-conversation they should go on to the next sentence.

5 Students work in pairs to describe the photos and answer the questions.

Sentence completion
Page 141

1 If you have a mixed nationality group, ask students from different countries the questions.

2 Focus students' attention on the pictures. Elicit *swallow*, *crow* and *sheep*. Students read the instructions. Encourage them to predict the type of information they might hear for each gap. Play the recording twice and let students compare their answers together after the first listening.

Answers			
1	twenty-five/25 years	2	farmers
3	*Weather Signs*	4	high/higher
5	frosty	6	donkeys
7	hills	8	(the) grass
9	red sky	10	heavy rain

Listening 1: Listening script 2.22

Hello, my name's Michael Gallagher, and I've come to talk to you about one of my great passions: the weather. Now for the past forty years I've worked as a postman in an area which includes some of the more remote parts of County Donegal. And for more than twenty-five of those years I've been using traditional methods to make predictions about the weather.

Now, as a postman, I've had the privilege of meeting many people from the surrounding towns and villages, particularly farmers, who've taught me a great deal about how to interpret what goes on in the natural world – the behaviour of the animals, birds, insects and plants that are all around us. These people have had to struggle with the elements to make a living from the land, and over the centuries they've built up a vast store of knowledge and folklore to help them read the signs which are present in nature, signs which can help us predict the weather.

You can read more about these in my book, which is called *Traditional Weather Signs*, but I'll give you a few examples now of what's in it. Let's start with birds. Birds are very sensitive to changes in the weather, and we can learn a lot from them. For example, swallows flying low are a sign that rain is on its way, and so are crows if they're flying in groups. But swallows flying high tell us that the weather's going to get better.

Cats, too, can help us predict the weather, particularly if they're sitting by the fire. A cat washing its face there is a sure sign of wet weather. But if it's sitting with its back to the fire, then you know that frosty weather is coming. Farm animals are good indicators, too. Cows, horses, goats, sheep – you just have to watch the way they behave. Cows, for instance, they don't stay in the middle of a field if they sense a storm approaching, and neither do horses or donkeys. If you see them grazing with their backs to a hedge, you know the weather's going to turn bad.

Now some of you will know me from my longer-range forecasts, which are reported in the media from time to time. Last year, for example, I got it right when I said we were going to have a warm summer in Ireland. Now I knew that, because the sheep on the low ground started heading back to the hills in late spring to graze, and that's always an indication that the harsh winter and spring are over and good weather is on the way.

And then I predicted that cold snap we had two winters ago, and I got that from a combination of events. The sheep were hungry, so they started coming off the mountains at the beginning of December to look for food. Then there was the fact that grass started growing as late as October on the lowland, and also the way the sun was shining on the mountains – it was giving off an orange glow.

The sun, the moon, the stars – they've all been used to make predictions for centuries in rural Ireland. Many of us are familiar with the saying 'red sky at night, shepherd's delight', meaning that the weather will be fine tomorrow if the sky is red at the end of today. But there's a whole lot more that can be predicted from what's up there above us. And you can read more about that in my book.

Now I'm sure some of you would like to know what the weather's going to be like in the week ahead. Well, where I live we can expect some very heavy rain for the next three or four days. I noticed the frogs were coming out of the mud this morning and they weren't their usual bright green colour. They were much darker. Now that's a bad sign. As for this part of the world …

3 Ask various students the questions. Get them to translate any expressions about the weather to see if there is an equivalent saying in English. You could also ask whether they know of any other examples of animals revealing instincts for natural phenomenon, e.g. elephants have been known to climb to the hills before a tsunami.

Language focus 1: *So, neither* and *nor*　　　Page 141

1 Read the sentences with the class and elicit answers to the questions. You may need to give some further explanation. Write the following sentences on the board and highlight the rules.
I don't like swimming and neither does my dad. (We both dislike swimming.)
'I'm going to the cinema later.' 'So am I.' (We are both going to the cinema.)
'I didn't do the homework.' 'Neither did I.' (Neither of us did the homework.)
My sister has been to New York, but I haven't. (We have had different experiences.)

Answers

Neither and *so* are used when something is true for all people referred to in the sentence.
Neither is used with reference to grammatical negatives and *so* with reference to affirmatives.
Use the same auxiliary verb (e.g. *do, have, will, would*) that appears in the main clause (or the verb *to be* if that is the main verb used), e.g. *I'll read the book and so will Rita/but Rita won't.*
Use *do, does* or *did* if no auxiliary verb appears in the main clause, e.g. *I went home and so did John/ but John didn't.*

2 Point out to students that the auxiliary in the reply must be the same as in the statement, but that the form may be different. Do the first question together to illustrate this (*I **am*** and ***are** we*).

Answers

1 c　2 e　3 f　4 g　5 a　6 h　7 b　8 d

Reading and Use of English 1
Part 7

Multiple matching
Page 142

1 If you have a mixed nationality group, ask students to sit with someone from another country. Check their understanding of the vocabulary. Get students who know the words to give a definition to the class. Model and check pronunciation. Start by talking about a personal experience. Then students should work in groups of three. This will increase the probability of one of them having experienced the natural phenomenon.

2 Students work in groups of three. Elicit some film vocabulary from the class, and write suggestions on the board to guide their discussions, e.g. *plot, main characters, special effects, scene, the ending.*

3 Students read the instructions and the Don't forget! box. Allow them time to underline the key words before they read the article. Check their understanding of *absorbing* (something that holds your attention).

Answers

1 C　*I couldn't put the novel down when I was reading it, and the film adaptation gripped me in the same way.*

2 A　*… what impressed me most about this film was the quality of the lead performances.*

3 B　*It's obvious from the start who will fall victim to a twister, and there are no surprises in the central love story, either.*

4 D　*… the final scene might not be what you're expecting. It certainly didn't turn out the way I thought it would.*

5 A　*… it was the positive opinions I'd seen online … that persuaded me to buy the DVD.*

6 C　*The special effects are so well done, my first impression was that I was watching a real storm. And if I hadn't seen the special features on the DVD afterwards, I'd probably still think they hadn't employed any visual tricks.*

7 E　*I always find it works better for me if I watch it during a storm or when it's snowing outside.*

8 B　*… unlike in numerous other films of this genre which slowly build up to a dramatic climax, they appear from the very beginning.*

9 E　*… it's all good fun, and as long as you see it as that and don't look for any deeper message, you should enjoy the film.*

10 D　*…creating a number of unforgettable, if slightly disagreeable moments.*

Alternative approach

If you would like to make the reading more communicative, you could start the activity by asking students to work in groups of five. Each student reads one of the reviews and then gives an oral summary of the information to their group. Then they should do the reading task as suggested.

Reacting to the text

Students discuss the questions in groups of three. Check their understanding of *appealing* (attractive and interesting).

Language focus 2: Conditionals

Page 144

1–2 Students match the films to the conditional sentences, then identify the verb forms. You may need to give some further examples. Write the following sentences on the board and highlight the verb forms in a different colour pen.

Ice melts when you heat it.
If I arrive late for work, my boss will be angry.
If I had more money, I'd buy a new house.
If I had driven more carefully, I wouldn't have had an accident.
If you had taken the medication, you would be better now.

You should also mention that in zero conditional sentences other present forms are possible, e.g.
If you live in a large city, you are probably suffering from stress.
In first conditional sentences, other future forms and imperatives are possible in the main clause, e.g.
If you see Helen, tell her about the meeting.
If you behave badly, I'm not going to let you go to the party.

Answers
1 and 2
Zero conditional   *The Day after Tomorrow*   present simple, present simple
First conditional   *Twister*   present simple, *will* + infinitive without *to*
Second conditional   *The Day after Tomorrow*   past simple, *would* + infinitive without *to*
Third conditional   *Twister*   past perfect, *would* + perfect infinitive (*have* + past participle) without *to*
Mixed conditional   *The Perfect Storm*   past perfect, *would* + infinitive without *to*

3–4 Students do the exercises in pairs. If your students need further practice, ask them to complete these sentences.
In general, if students study hard, ...

If you revise all these phrasal verbs, ...
If you had concentrated more in class, ...
I wouldn't feel so tired this morning if ...

Answers
3
Zero conditional   *whenever*
First conditional   *a possible*
Second conditional   *future*
Third conditional   *past*
Mixed conditional   *present*
4
The different modal verbs, *will*, *should* and *might*, express different levels of certainty on the part of the speaker.
a *will* expresses certainty: the speaker feels certain they will be home by six o'clock.
b *should* expresses probability: he/she thinks they are likely to be home by six o'clock.
c *might* expresses uncertainty or possibility: he/she is not certain, but thinks it is possible they will be home by six o'clock.

5 Students work individually. In feedback, check their understanding of the conjunctions.

Answers		
a long	**b** providing	**c** condition
d unless		

6 Students correct the mistakes individually. Get feedback from the class. If students have made mistakes, write up some of the sentences and highlight the structures in a different colour pen.

Answers
1 If you'd asked me ...
2 ... if I find out ...
3 ... if she hadn't phoned ...
4 If I drink ...
5 ... I'll never go ...

7 Students do the activity on pages 202 and 204. Circulate and check students are following the instructions correctly.

Conditionals: Expressing regret

Students do the exercise in pairs. Circulate and correct any errors.

Answers

Possible answers:
1. If I hadn't gone skiing, I wouldn't have broken my arm.
2. If I hadn't committed a foul, the referee wouldn't have sent me off.
3. If I hadn't been using my mobile phone, I wouldn't have crashed into a tree.
4. If I hadn't gone out of the room, the cat wouldn't have eaten the fish.
5. If I'd worked harder, I would have got a better grade.

Note: In each of the above sentences, *might* can replace *would* in order to express possibility rather than certainty. The negative auxiliaries *hadn't* and *wouldn't* are usually stressed but in the affirmative they are usually unstressed.

 DVD resource: Unit 11

Vocabulary 2: *Put*   Page 145

1 Students do exercises a and b individually. If they need help, write the missing words for 1a on the board in the wrong order.

Answers

1a

1	at	2	down	3	together
4	with	5	up		

1b
1. put at risk: endanger
2. put down: stop reading
3. put together: assemble
4. put up with: tolerate
5. put your feet up: relax

2 The sentence beginnings contain enough information for students to work out the answers from the context. Check their understanding of *groom* (the man getting married at a wedding). Get feedback from the class. Ask which sentence is illustrated in the visual (Sentence 8).

Answers

1 g   2 a   3 d   4 e   5 h   6 b   7 f   8 c   9 i

3–4 Students work individually.

Answers

3

a	put up	b	put off	c	put on

4

1	pressure	2	effort	3	money
4	blame				

Additional activity

Students discuss the following questions in pairs (you can project them on a whiteboard or OHT, or prepare individual copies before the class). Circulate and check they are responding to the questions correctly.

Have you ever put on a play or musical?
How can you avoid putting on weight?
What television channel do you usually put on?
Has your government put up taxes recently?
Do you often put up friends or relatives?
Do you ever put off doing what you should do today until another time?
What could put you off your meal in a restaurant?

 **Collaborative task**
Page 146

Ask students to read the instructions for the collaborative task, then turn to the Useful language box. Check their understanding of the vocabulary items. Ask students who know the words to give a definition to the class. Alternatively, you could take images from the Internet and create a visual to check the vocabulary.

1–2 Before starting, allow students some time to refer to the language on page 128. Model and check the pronunciation of *biofuel* (/ˈbaɪəʊfjuːəl/) and *exhaust* (/ɪɡˈzɔːst/). As this is a topic where students will have quite lot to talk about, you could give them more time than they would have in the Speaking exam.

Answers

Household waste: bottle bank, plastic containers
Dirty streets: dropping litter, cigarette butts
River and sea pollution: oil slick, dumping waste
Traffic pollution: biofuel cars, exhaust fumes
Climate change: global warming, greenhouse effect

Alternative activity

In a future lesson students could play word tennis with this vocabulary (see page 117 of this book)

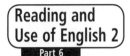

Gapped text
Page 146

1–2 Refer students to the photo and discuss it as a class. Ask students what the meaning of the word *trash* is and elicit that it is another word for *rubbish*. Ask students to discuss the questions, and elicit answers from various students, putting any new vocabulary on the board.

3 Students complete the activity individually. Remind them to look at the information before and after the gaps. They can check their answers in pairs before you check answers as a class.

Answers

1 E 2 A 3 G 4 C 5 F 6 B

4 Elicit suggestions from the class. Some ideas might include choosing products carefully to avoid buying those which have a lot of plastic packaging; buying loose meat and vegetables in bags instead of pre-packed in plastic trays from the supermarket; reusing plastic pots at home instead of buying plastic storage products; buying products made from other materials (e.g. glass bottles).

Open cloze
Page 148

1 Students discuss the question in pairs.

2 Students read the text to check their ideas. Get feedback from the class. Ask whether they think World Carfree Day is a good idea.

3 Allow time for students to look back at page 44 of the Coursebook, as instructed in the What to expect in the exam box. Ask students to do the task, then circulate and guide students to the right word if they are having difficulties, e.g.
Question 2: *This is an expression to show the reason we do something.*
Question 3: *This is a conditional sentence.*
Question 4: *This is a phrasal verb, it means 'to participate'.*

Answers

1	This/The	2	order	3	if
4	part	5	such	6	However
7	has	8	without		

4 Students discuss the questions in pairs. You could write the following words on the board and encourage students to refer to these when talking about their family's dependence on the car: *work, holidays, weekends, school, shopping, social events.*

Essay
Page 148

Students read the instructions and the How to go about it box. Working in pairs, they should brainstorm ideas and write a plan for the essay. Encourage them to demonstrate their knowledge of vocabulary. They could also refer to the model of an opinion essay and Useful language box on page 195.

Sample answer

Without doubt, the environment is in danger and all people have a challenge to do something about it. However, even small things that individuals do can make a difference.

First of all, people can try to reduce pollution by taking public transport or by using less energy. Exhaust fumes from cars are a big threat to the atmosphere, so this is one way that an individual can make a contribution to helping the environment.

Secondly, we should try to recycle as much as we can at home in order to cut down on household waste. For example, if everybody brought their old bottles to a bottle bank instead of dumping them, there would have been less waste in the natural landscape.

Finally, individuals need to work together as a team. We should encourage each other to recycle more and conserve energy, and educate in our schools about the importance of taking care of our planet.

In conclusion, I disagree with the statement and I believe that individuals can definitely make a difference. If everybody tries a little bit, the result will be effective.

Fehér László
183 words

Examiner's comment

Content: Very good realization of the task.

Communicative achievement: Consistently appropriate format and register. The essay would have a positive effect on the reader, who would be fully informed.

Organization: The article is well-organized with suitable paragraphs and the writer uses linking expressions effectively.

Language: High level of accuracy. The writer uses a wide range of simple and complex grammatical forms with control and flexibility. Shows a very good knowledge of vocabulary related to the environment, e.g. *exhaust fumes, threat, atmosphere, recycle, household waste, bottle bank dumping, waste, landscape, taking care of*.

Mark*: Very good pass

*Note on marking

Each of the four categories is awarded a mark out of 5. These marks are then added up to give a total score out of 20.

For the purposes of this course, the sample answers have been graded according to the following scale: **borderline**, **pass**, **good pass**, and **very good pass**.

Listening 2
Part 1

Multiple choice
Page 149

This listening recycles vocabulary from the whole unit.

Students read the instructions and the What to expect in the exam box. Elicit that the third conditional is used as a distractor. Play the recording twice and let students compare their answers together after the first listening.

Answers
1 C   2 A   3 C   4 B   5 C   6 B   7 A   8 A

Listening 2: Listening icon 2.23–2.30

1 You hear a man talking about a new fire station that has just been built.

I really can't understand why they put it all the way out there. They maintained that if they'd built it in the heart of the city, there would have been problems getting out to fires in the rural areas. Too far and too much traffic, they said. But that's exactly why it would have made more sense to build it in the centre instead of on the edge. You know, it takes a fire engine nearly twenty minutes to get from that suburb to the other side of the city.

2 You hear a man talking about litter.

If I was a member of the Council, I'd make sure something was done about the mess on the streets. It's an absolute disgrace. Local people need more help to keep them clean, and that help has to come from the authorities. There aren't enough litter bins, for one thing, so the pavements outside my premises are covered with paper, drink cans and cigarette butts. Before I open up in the morning I have to spend about ten minutes sweeping it all up. I wouldn't sell anything if I didn't.

3 You hear an environmentalist speaking on the radio about a recent project.

You have to remember that some species of plants were facing extinction in the area. People would come out to the countryside for a picnic, see all these beautiful flowers and pick them, without realizing the effect this was having. If we hadn't made this a conservation area and limited the number of people coming in, then we'd have no flowers at all, and people would be really upset. As it is, we can congratulate ourselves on the action we took and look forward to a brighter future for this patch of countryside.

4 You overhear this woman talking to her friend about her holiday.

M = Man   W = Woman

M: So what was it like?

W: Marvellous. Just what we were looking for.

M: And what was that?

W: Well, if we'd gone to one of the other islands, we'd have had to put up with busy roads and crowded beaches.

M: So weren't there many tourists where you went?

W: Oh plenty. More than we expected really. But it didn't seem to matter, because with the vehicle restrictions there was almost a total lack of exhaust fumes, no congestion and very little noise. And because the island's so small, you could walk everywhere, anyway.

5 You hear a conversation between two people.

M = Man   W = Woman

M: I think we should all get together and decide what we're going to do. I can't put up with it any more.

W: Neither can we. The noise of that boy's music makes the whole house shake. My husband says it's just like being in an earthquake, only worse.

M: Of course it's the parents' fault, but it's no good talking to them. They're no better than he is.

W: And his teachers can't control him, either. Apparently, he's as rude to them as he is to all of us.

M: So, let's have a meeting of all the residents in the street and we'll decide how to deal with him.

6 You are listening to the radio when you hear the following being read.

Violent storms swept across the south coast today, causing widespread damage to property. Torrential rain and gale-force winds lashed seaside towns and several people had to be evacuated from their flooded homes by rescue services. One man in Bognor narrowly escaped death as the car he was driving was crushed by a falling tree, which had been struck by lightning.

7 You overhear this conversation between a man and his neighbour.

W = Woman   M = Man

W: What's the problem, John?

M: Well, we lost a lot of our plants last night.

W: It wasn't our cat, was it?

M: No, the wind. Pulled up all the roses, it did. Blew down a few bushes, too.

W: I'm sorry to hear that.

M: Oh, not to worry. I'd be grateful if you'd give me a hand to clear up the mess, though.

W: I'd be pleased to.

8 You hear a man talking about a recent environmental disaster.

Something's got to be done. These massive petrol tankers should just not be allowed to sail so close to our shores. The oil slick has already killed thousands of birds and the beaches are a disaster area. Demonstrating is all very well, but it's not going to clean up the mess, is it? We can't leave it in the hands of the politicians, so we've just got to get down to the coast and get our hands dirty with the rest of the volunteers. You coming?

Review 11 Answers Pages 150–151

Vocabulary

A Weather

1

1 light rain/winds/showers
2 heavy rain/storm/showers
3 strong winds

2

1 c   2 f   3 h   4 a   5 d   6 b   7 e   8 g

B *Put*

1	up	2	on	3	off	4	on
5	up	6	off				

Conditional sentences

1 stays, will/'ll probably
2 had/'d known, could have prepared
3 wouldn't do, paid
4 had/'d taken, would not/wouldn't be
5 will/'ll send, start
6 would/'d have done, had not/hadn't helped
7 usually works, feed
8 would/'d go, had

Reading and Use of English — Part 4

Transformations

1 if I hadn't/had not spoken
2 I would not/wouldn't have written
3 not help you unless you
4 as long as you give/hand/send
5 is being put at
6 is not/isn't calm enough for

Additional activity 1

Exercises 1, 2 and 3 could be adapted to make a short quiz.

Additional activity 2

Write transformation sentences 1–5 from page 151 onto cards. Put them in an envelope and write *Conditionals* on the front. Stick the answers on the back. Add this to your set of revision envelopes. Bring these to a lesson towards the end of the course. Students work in pairs, they choose an envelope and work through the cards. Remind them not to write on the cards.

Alternative activity

Instead of Writing activity 2, ask students to invent a film in pairs and write a review. This will avoid the potential problem of plagiarism.
They should fill in the following information:
Title
Genre
Actors
Setting
Plot

12 Looking after yourself

Content Overview

Themes

The unit deals with the themes of food, drink, ailments and injuries.

Exam-related activities

Reading and Use of English

Part 7	Multiple matching
Part 2	Open cloze
Part 3	Word formation (Review)
Part 4	Transformations (Review)
Part 1	Multiple-choice cloze (Review)

Writing

Part 2	Report

Listening

Part 3	Multiple matching
Part 4	Multiple choice

Speaking

Part 2	Talking about photos

Other

Language focus 1:	Countable and uncountable nouns A
Language focus 2:	Countable and uncountable nouns B
Language focus 3:	Reported speech
Language focus 4:	Reporting verbs
Language focus 5:	Reported questions
Vocabulary 1:	Food and drink
Vocabulary 2:	Health matters
Word formation:	Nouns 2

Vocabulary 1: Food and drink   Page 152

Lead–in

Ask students to discuss the following questions in pairs:

How healthy is the food from your country?
What is your favourite and least favourite food?

1 Students work in pairs. If they have any problems guessing the vocabulary from context you could mime the verbs to help them guess.

Answers

1. fussy eater: someone who only eats the food they particularly like and refuses to eat anything else.
2. eat up: eat all of something
   leave food on your plate: not eat all of your meal
3. chew: bite the food in your mouth into small pieces
   swallow: make food or drink go from your mouth, through your throat and into your stomach
   bolt down: eat food very quickly
4. sip: swallow a drink slowly a bit at a time
   gulp down: swallow a drink very quickly
5. soft drink: cold, non-alcoholic drink
   still drink: drink without gas bubbles
   fizzy drink: drink with gas bubbles
6. drink straight from a bottle or a can: drink something without pouring it out first
   drink from a glass: drink something having first poured it into a glass

2 Model and check the pronunciation of *fussy, gulp, swallow* and *chew*. Elicit some answers to questions 2 and 4 from the class and write any frequency adverbs they use on the board. Elicit any additional frequency adverbs they know, e.g. *rarely, seldom, hardly ever, occasionally, sometimes, usually, now and again, from time to time, tend to.* Encourage students to use them when they are discussing the questions.

Circulate and correct any pronunciation issues. Get feedback from the class. You could ask whether they consume a lot of fizzy drinks and junk food, and what the effects of this are.

Additional activity

In the next lesson, give students the definitions from exercise 1 and ask them to write the words. Alternatively, make sets of cards and get students to match the definitions with the words.

Language focus 1: Countable and uncountable nouns A   Page 152

1 Focus students' attention on the pictures. Ask them whether the nouns *chocolate* and *cake* are countable, uncountable or both. Then get students to describe the quantities of each one shown in the pictures. Elicit the following possibilities and write them on the board:

a chocolate/some chocolate/some chocolates/a bar of chocolate/a box of chocolates

a cake/cake/some cake/a slice of cake/a piece of cake

If *bar* is a false friend in your student's language, mention that we say *a bar of chocolate*, but not *a bar of bread*.

Students make a table in their notebooks and write the nouns from the box in the correct category (countable, uncountable, or both). Suggest that they add more nouns as they come up in the Coursebook.

Answers

milk **U**   diet **C**   chicken **U, C** (for a whole one)
health **U**   chip **C**   chocolate **U, C**
meal **C** (**U** = animal feed)
pepper **C** (vegetable), **U** (spice)   spaghetti **U**
cake **U, C**

2 Check students' understanding of the quantity words; draw or mime any tricky ones. In class feedback, model and drill pronunciation:

a piece of cake /əpiːsəv keɪk/; *a slice of toast* /əslaɪsəv toʊst/; *a plate of spaghetti* /əpleɪtəv spəˈɡeti/; *a teaspoon of sugar* /əˈtiːspuːn əvˈ ʃʊɡər/.

Answers

1   cheese/toast/cake/chocolate
2   cheese/toast/cake
3   spaghetti* (also plateful)
4   sugar/salt
5   salt
6   chocolate
7   jam
8   milk
* note that spaghetti is used with a singular verb in English

Multiple matching
Page 153

1 Students discuss the questions in groups of three.

2 Students read the instructions and the Don't forget! box. Allow them time to underline key words. Play the recording twice and let students

compare their answers together after the first listening.

Answers

1 B   **2** E   **3** H   **4** F   **5** C   (A, D and G not used)

Listening 1: Listening script 2.31–2.35

Speaker 1

I tried crash diets, such as one where you just eat cabbage soup, and another where you drink nothing but lemonade with some salt and pepper for about seven days without any food. They worked temporarily, but after a while I put the weight back on. Then I was introduced to these diet pills and my weight went down to 65 kilos. But I wasn't earning a great deal of money and I simply couldn't afford to keep it up. That's when I decided to save my money and join a gym.

Speaker 2

I used to eat a lot of junk food. It was quick, inexpensive and it satisfied my hunger immediately. The problem was, I ate very little fresh food, and this had a serious effect on my health. I became overweight and suffered all sorts of illnesses. The doctor strongly advised me to rethink my attitude to food. If not, he said, the consequences could be very serious. Well, you can't ignore advice like that, can you? So I started to eat more healthily. And now if I get hungry between meals, I have a little cheese or some nuts, just to keep me going.

Speaker 3

I'm under no real pressure to lose weight, but I take care over what I eat, simply because it makes me feel better. When I want to treat myself, I have a piece of cake or a few biscuits. I read a lot about dieting, and most nutritionists seem to agree that as long as you eat sweet things after a meal, then there's no problem. So, for example, I only ever eat chocolates after lunch or dinner. And never too many of course – just one or two.

Speaker 4

I like eating and I'm not at all interested in dieting. But I do go to see a nutritionist, who helps me maintain a sensible, balanced diet: plenty of fresh fruit and vegetables, er, meat and fish, carbohydrates such as rice and pasta, several glasses of water a day – and no snacks between meals. She told me to give up cheese, but I ignored her. I enjoy good food and I don't want to deprive myself of the things I love.

Speaker 5

A large number of people follow diets, but very few of them are happier as a result. We are constantly under attack from advertising and the media, who tell us that 'thin is beautiful'. I used to believe this and think that I wouldn't find a boyfriend unless I was really skinny, that I had to weigh under 60 kilos for boys to like me. But of course, now I realize there's more to it than that. Just being yourself is what counts and I don't pay much attention to what others think or say.

3 Elicit answers to the question from round the class. You could prepare some visuals of very thin and oversized models to stimulate the discussion. Obviously you should consider the cultural context of your students before doing this.

Language focus 2: Countable and uncountable nouns B   Page 153

1 Focus student's attention on the picture and the question. Elicit that we use *a few* with countable nouns and *a little* with uncountable nouns, so by saying *Just a few* she is saying that she wants a few glasses of water.

Answers

Just a few: followed by a countable noun in the plural = a few glasses (of water)

Just a little: followed by an uncountable noun = a little (water)

By saying *Just a few* she really means she wants *a lot*.

2 This exercise serves as a test-teach-test approach to the language. Students do the gap-fill in pairs. Remind them that the words can be used more than once and that more than one word may be possible in some spaces.

3 Students correct their answers while listening.

Answers

Speaker 1

a some   **b** any   **c** deal

Speaker 2

d lot   **e** little   **f** little
g some/several

Speaker 3

h piece   **i** few   **j** no/little   **k** many

Speaker 4

l plenty   **m** several/many   **n** no

Speaker 5

o number   **p** few   **q** much/any

Additional activity

You may need to give some further explanation. Draw a table on the board with these headings:
Words used with countable nouns
Words used with uncountable nouns

Words used with countable and uncountable nouns
Ask students to put the following words into the correct categories.

some a/an	*all*	*no*
a lot of	*lots a few*	*many*
plenty of	*each*	*several*
little	*a large number of*	*a little*
much	*a great deal of*	*a large amount of*
any	*every*	*few*
most		

Answers

Words used with countable nouns: *a/an, few, a few, many, a large number of, each, every, several*
Words used with uncountable nouns: *little, a little, much, a great deal of, a large amount of*
Words used with countable and uncountable nouns: *some, any, no, a lot of, lots of, all, plenty of, most*

Ask students the difference in meaning between these pairs of sentences:
I have a little money./I have little money.
I have a few friends./I have few friends.

The first sentence in each pair has a positive meaning (some or more than expected) and the second sentence has a negative meaning (not as much/many as desired).
Check students' understanding of *plenty* as they sometimes confuse this with *a lot*. Ask which sentence is correct:
There were plenty of people on the beach. (Incorrect)
I've got plenty of time, so I can help you. (Correct, meaning 'more than enough')

Reading and Use of English 1
Part 7

Multiple matching
Page 154

1 Students work in pairs. During feedback, ask students whether they know any good vegetarian restaurants in their town or city, and get them to tell the class about the type of dishes served.

2 Students predict the content of the article, then read it quickly to check. If students ask the meaning of *peelings* or *waste,* refer them to the picture. Ask what would normally happen to the peelings and why this is a waste.
Explain that predicting the content of any text will help them understand it better, and that reading through quickly for gist will aid their general

comprehension and enable them to answer the questions more easily when they read it a second time.

3 Students complete the exercise individually. Encourage them to guess difficult words from the context.

Answers	
1 B	*... his curry is banana-skins curry, the skins filling in for what would normally be meat.*
2 D	*... we also plan to set up a webcam to livestream what we do in the kitchen ...*
3 C	*Certainly the figures on waste are a cause for concern.*
4 A	*And the reason we don't notice it is because that's the way we all cook – they simply cook like us, and, indeed, we cook like them.*
5 E	*At a time when we are having to tighten our belts, we could all do with cutting down on the throwaway ...*
6 B	*... if he uses one part of a vegetable or fruit, he'll use the rest of it elsewhere, as long as it isn't harmful to health.*
7 A	*... nearly all of the chefs waste food. Not consciously, but still they do it.*
8 D	*... he'll teach kids ... He is also targeting slightly older cooks.*
9 A	*I used to watch and think: 'I could make a dish out of what you are throwing away alone.' So that's what he started doing.*
10 C	*'I believe in spreading what knowledge I have of my type of low-waste cooking, I don't want to lecture people,' Jordan says. 'But I do want to try and show people there's another way.'*

Reacting to the text

Students discuss the questions in pairs. Get feedback from the class and write any interesting ideas on the board. Add the following, and elicit comments from the class:
frequency of shopping trips, sell-by dates, freezing left over food, exact quantities, food storage

Language focus 3: Reported speech
Page 156

1 Write the example on the board and elicit the rule. Highlight the key words in a different colour

pen. Explain that the tense usually steps back from the present simple in direct speech to the past simple in reported speech, but can remain unchanged if the reported statement is still true.

Answers
The present simple changes to the past simple. The present simple is also possible in the reported version, as the statement *'he doesn't want to lecture people'* is still true.

2 Students complete the reported speech in pairs. Remind them that all the statements take a step back into the past except for one. Look at the example together and draw their attention to the change in the time expression.

Answers	
b	She said she *had* seen him twice *that* day.
c	He told me she *had been* living *there* for years.
d	He said he *had spoken* to her *the previous* week.
e	He told me he *had been* working *the day before*.
f	They said they *had asked* her several times.

3–5 Students work in pairs.

Answers	
3	
Direct speech	**Reported speech**
b present perfect simple	→ past perfect simple
c present perfect continuous	→ past perfect continuous
d past simple	→ past perfect simple
e past continuous	→ past perfect continuous
f past perfect simple	→ past perfect simple

4	
Direct speech	**Reported speech**
will	→ would
may	→ might
can	→ could
must	→ had to

Would, might, could, should and *ought to* do not change in reported speech.

5	
Direct speech	**Reported speech**
two days ago	→ two days before/ earlier/previously

next month	→ the following month/ the next month
tonight	→ that night/evening
this morning	→ that morning
now	→ then

6a Write some examples of direct speech on the board and ask students who they think said each sentence, e.g.
'The robbers stole two thousand pounds.' (Newsreader)
'You will need to bring your dictionaries next Monday.' (Teacher to students)
'I've had lots of meetings this week.' (Work colleague)
'I can't help you now, I'm doing the washing up.' (Mother/father to their child)
Elicit the reported speech for each sentence. Then students should write their own examples of direct speech individually. Tell them not to use questions as you will be looking at the rules for these later on. Circulate and check they are doing the task correctly.

6b Students look at the sentences in pairs and form the reported versions.

Reading and Use of English 2
Part 2

Open cloze
Page 156

1 If you have a mixed nationality group, ask students to work with a student from another country.

2 Remind students to read the text once for the general meaning before completing the gaps. Circulate and help students if they have difficulties. Ask questions to help them, e.g.
Question 1: *Is the noun 'attention' countable or uncountable? What's the opposite of 'a lot of attention'?*
Question 2: *How can we emphasize the word 'not' so that the expression means 'in no way' or 'not in the least'?*

Answers			
2			
1 little	**2** all	**3** than	**4** at
5 which	**6** one/each	**7** to	**8** no

3 Ask various students the questions. Elicit other situations in which using a mobile could be considered rude.

Speaking
Part 2

Talking about photos
Page 157

Students are given a chance to do Part 2 with the exam time limit in Ready for Speaking and in Unit 14. If you haven't already used strict timing, introduce it here.

1–2 Students read the instructions. Ask them to look back to pages 7 and 105 and to write down five expressions used for speculation, giving preferences and making deductions. Explain that they should try to use these during the speaking task.
In feedback, comment on how well they used the expressions, and then ask which place they chose when they were Student B.

Language focus 4: Reporting verbs
Page 157

This section reviews and extends students' ability to report what people have said. Students are encouraged to categorize verbs depending on the grammatical patterns that follow them. As this is an area which often causes problems you will need to recycle the language in future lessons.

1 Write the example sentences on the board and highlight the patterns in a different colour pen. Check students know that *tell* is used with a direct object and *say* is used without a direct object, as this is a typical error.

2 Check students' understanding of the verbs. If necessary give example sentences and ask students to guess the reporting verb, e.g.
I'm going to kill you! (threaten).
You shouldn't touch that, it's dangerous. (warn).
Ask students to make two columns in their book and fill in the verbs from exercise 2 under the headings:
Verb + object + infinitive with *to* and
Verb + infinitive with *to*

Answers

advise	offer
(verb + object + infinitive with to)	(verb + infinitive with to)
order	refuse
urge	threaten
persuade	ask
warn	*promise
tell	
remind	
ask	
encourage	
recommend (and same patterns as *suggest*)	

* can also take an object, e.g. *He promised me that he would …*

3 Students write the reported speech individually.

Answers

1 refused to clean her room
2 reminded him to take his sandwiches
3 threatened to call the police if I didn't turn my music down
4 warned/advised her not to take the car out (as/because/since the roads were very icy)
5 ordered/told him to get out of his office immediately
6 urged/encouraged/persuaded me to report the theft to the police

4 Write the sentences on the board and highlight the patterns with a different colour pen. Draw students' attention to the structure in the second sentence:
*The doctor recommended **he do** more exercise.*
Elicit an answer to the question.

Answers

The infinitive with *to* is not used after *suggest*.

5 Look at the first problem together on page 202. Elicit advice using each of the structures and write suggestions on the board, e.g.
You shouldn't eat cheese in the evening.
If I were you, I'd have a relaxing bath before going to bed.
Why don't you buy a new pillow?
Try counting sheep!

For the second parts, refer to the examples on the board and elicit sentences using reporting verbs. Students then continue to give and respond to advice following the prompts on page 202 and 204. If your students are strong, ask them to do this orally. If it is a weaker class, allow them time to write sentences and then report them to another pair.

Vocabulary 2: Health matters   Page 158

1 Ask students to look at the vocabulary in the two boxes. Point to parts of your body in a different order and elicit the words. Students do exercises A and B individually. They should be able to guess the answers from the context. Get some feedback from the class. If some students are still unsure of any vocabulary, encourage other students to give them definitions. Model and drill the pronunciation of any difficult words.

Answers

A
1	heart attack	2	tooth decay
3	stomach ache	4	blood pressure
5	ear infection		

B
1	black eye	2	sore throat
3	stiff neck	4	runny nose
5	sprained ankle		

2 Students memorize the collocations as suggested.

Additional activity
In the next lesson do the following warmer. Write the collocations from 1A and B on cards and cut them in half. In pairs students put the two halves together and write five sentences using the vocabulary.

3 Students work individually. Get feedback from the class, getting students to explain the differences between the two words in each question.

Answers

1	bandage	2	a plaster
3	prescription	4	plaster
5	injection		

4 Students work in groups of three. Encourage them to interact by showing surprise and asking follow-up questions. Write the following on the board:

Really?

Oh dear!

That must have been awful!

Did you?

Circulate and show surprise or concern for students' accidents and ailments. Get feedback from the class and ask students if their partners told them anything surprising.

Listening 2
Part 4

Multiple choice
Page 158

1 Students discuss the question in pairs.

2 Students read the instructions, then underline key words in the questions. Play the recording twice and let students compare their answers together after the first listening.

Answers
1 C 2 B 3 A 4 B 5 A 6 C 7 A

Listening 2: Listening script 2.36

I = Interviewer   N = Naomi Price

I: On *Health Matters* today we have personal trainer Naomi Price. Naomi, what exactly does a personal trainer do?

N: Well, in my case I try to improve people's quality of life and overall health, by helping them develop their fitness, strength and posture – and working on their diet, as well. These are the general goals, but of course, each client has their own specific, individual goals, so before we do anything, I carry out a needs analysis in order to establish exactly what it is a person wants to achieve. This includes asking them about their diet, their injury history and any medical complaints or conditions they have, such as high blood pressure. Then basically, I design exercise routines and give advice on nutrition in response to the information they give me.

I: And what reasons do clients have for coming to see you?

N: Oh, there's a wide range. I get a lot of clients, especially older ones, who simply want to lose a bit of weight or lower their cholesterol levels. I also have a large number of younger clients who've been injured while doing sport and want to get back to full fitness – that's my area of expertise, it's what I specialize in. I also help one or two people train for marathons and triathlons, but mostly it's people who just want to improve their all-round fitness and as a result, their general self-confidence.

I: And I imagine it's important to build up a good relationship with your clients.

N: Yes, it is. I'm not one of those fitness instructors you sometimes see in films shouting orders at people to do fifty press-ups or run ten times round the park. Certainly, clients have to be dedicated and prepared to work hard when they're with me, but I also want them to enjoy exercising as well. So it's important, I think, for a trainer to bring an element of fun into the sessions, and I always make sure my clients have a good laugh when they come to me.

I: Now your workplace is your garage, isn't it, Naomi?

N: Well, yes, what used to be my garage. I don't park my car there any more – it's full of equipment. There's a rowing machine, two treadmills, two exercise bikes and loads of weights and things. I've also got a massage table, but that's in my lounge, where it's warmer. And then with some people, I go to the park or a nearby wood to run or simply to add a bit of variety to the classes. Clients appreciate that – they've told me that other local trainers they've been with always hold their sessions inside.

I: You haven't always been your own boss have you?

N: No, I used to work in a gym. The good thing about that was I learnt a lot from watching the other gym instructors and their interaction with the clients – both good and bad examples. I also got experience of working with a lot of different clients, but the trouble was, I rarely had the chance to build up long lasting relationships with them. The client list was different every month – someone would join the gym in April, say, and by June they'd be gone.

I: And is that why you left?

N: It wasn't the only reason. I was getting tired of working on Saturdays, for one thing – I'd only had two or three Saturdays free in over a year. But it was the whole sales thing that I was least happy about. When they told me I had to persuade people to buy things with the gym's logo on it, that's when I made the decision to resign. I just didn't feel comfortable pushing T-shirts and baseball caps, as well as things like protein supplements people maybe didn't need. It's not my style.

I: Are you pleased you became self-employed?

N: Oh, yes, I've got so much more freedom, and so far, touch wood, things are going really well. I thought I might have to put adverts in the local newspaper to get business but those clients I brought with me from the gym tell all their family and friends about me and those people tell all their friends … and so it goes on. The power of word of mouth.

I: Let's hope your success continues, Naomi. Thank you for coming in to the studio.

3 Students discuss the questions in groups of three. Write the following questions on the board and ask students to discuss these after talking about the ones in the Coursebook.

Have you ever had a sports injury?

Which is more important, doing exercise or eating healthily?

What are the sports facilities like in your neighbourhood?

Word formation: Nouns 2   Page 159

1–3a Students work individually. Correct each exercise before moving onto the next. Take feedback from the class and write the answers on the board to ensure spelling is accurate. Model and check pronunciation of any difficult words. Encourage students to use their vocabulary notebook to record any new word along with its other forms, e.g. *prove* (verb) *proof* (noun).

Answers

1

| 1 analysis | 2 injury | 3 complaints |
| 4 pressure | 5 advice | 6 response |

2
1 saying, meeting, building, advertising
2 pressure, departure, pleasure, signature
3 arrival, refusal, survival, approval
4 warmth, depth, truth, growth
5 flight, sight, weight, height
6 friendship, membership, championship, partnership

3a
2 loss, solution   3 success   4 choice
5 knowledge   6 speech   7 proof
8 belief, belief

Additional activity

Recycle the words from previous exercises as short races during future lessons. Divide the class into groups of three. Write five words on the board and explain that they have three minutes to write as many other forms of the word as possible. Emphasize that they must be spelt accurately. The group with the most correct words is the winner.

3b Students discuss the statements in groups of three.

Language focus 5: Reported questions   Page 160

1 Students discuss the questions in pairs. Then write the examples on the board and highlight

the changes. You may need to give a few more examples:

Where are you going? (He asked where I was going.)
Do you enjoy watching football? (He asked if I enjoyed football.)

Answers

1b
- auxiliary verbs *do, does, did* – disappear
- verb tenses – 'step back' a tense
- word order – the same in reported questions as for statements (subject + verb)
- yes/no questions – use *if/whether*
- punctuation – question marks are not used

2 Students work individually. They can check answers in pairs before you check answers as a class.

Answers

1 how long she had been a doctor
2 what had made her decide to enter the medical profession
3 how many patients she saw each day on average
4 if/whether her friends often asked her for medical advice
5 if/whether she was planning to retire soon

Writing Part 2   Report   Page 160

✎ If you have students who are interested in preparing for the *First for Schools* version of the exam, turn to pages 136 and 137 at the end of this unit for Short Story preparation and exercises (photocopiable).

1 Ask students to cover the model answer, then get them to read the instructions and brainstorm ideas. They could use a table like the one below to organize the report.

Sport	Best places	Reasons
running		
swimming		
cycling		

2 Students read the model answer and compare the information with the places in their table.

3a Mention that relative pronouns like *which* and relative adverbs like *where* are also linking words. Students work individually.

Answers		
1 well	**2** here	**3** but
4 where	**5** This	**6** as
7 However	**8** which	

3b This section on creating links is aimed at stronger students. It is not always easy to achieve smooth linking in reports, as by nature they are rather disjointed.

Answers
1 In the paragraph on running, the writer refers to the promenade. The paragraph on cycling then begins with *Cycling is forbidden on the promenade, but …*
2 The writer finishes the paragraph on cycling by mentioning the views of the sea. The paragraph on swimming then begins with *Swimming in the sea is not recommended, as …*

4 Students work individually. Emphasize the importance of following the rubric carefully in any writing task, and making sure everything you write is relevant to the question. You may lose marks in the exam if you do not complete all parts of the question, or if you give details that are not relevant.

Answers
Cycling
… your students can burn a few calories after class.
… with more superb views of the town and the sea.
Swimming
… there is a lake just outside the town, which is pleasant to swim in and less crowded than the town's swimming pool.
Conclusion
… your students will be able to do sport and enjoy beautiful scenery at the same time.

5 Students read the instructions as well as the Don't forget! and the Useful language boxes. The latter also serves to give content ideas. Suggest a few other areas which could be included such as the speciality of the house, staff, décor and

music. Students could organize their ideas using the table below. Remind them that they can invent information if they wish.

Restaurant	Location	Reasons

Additional activity

When students have planned their reports, do a mingling activity. Explain that they should choose one of the restaurants and then stand up and chat to different students and try to convince them to come out on Saturday night for a meal. Whoever persuades the most students to come with them is the winner. Write the following on the board to get them started:
A: *Would you like to come out for a meal on Saturday night?*
B: *Well I'm already going out, but I could change my plans, where are you going?*
A: *To the Green Frog in London Road …*

Sample answer
Report
The aim of this report is to tell you the best places to eat cheaply in my area and say why. I will also say why, in addition to the reasons of cost I think the students will enjoy eating in these places.
Where can you eat cheaply
If I were you, I'd go to the shopping centre out of town. Here are many restaurants from different countries like Italian, Mexico, Chinese, Spanish and also Greece. In addition you eat very well and it is not espensive, you can do shopping or see a film in the cinema which is there. The students will enjoy to see a film after they eat.
Furthermore, I recommend you the area next the sea. Here are many good restaurants for eating fish and the prices are affordable. The best restaurant is 'Ocean Blue' where everything is blue, example chairs, tables, walls etc. The fish is catched local and is delicious. Also, the atmosphere is pleasant, friendly and lively.
Conclusions
To sum up, the students can eat tasty, delicious and cheap food in the shopping centre and next the sea.
Regina
186 words

Examiner's comment

Content: Full coverage of the information requested.

Communicative achievement: Although the report is slightly too informal, the tone is still polite and informative. The reader would be well informed.

Organization: The report is clearly divided into appropriate sections. Conventional linking devices are used adequately, e.g. *in addition, Furthermore, To sum up.*

Language: A number of errors, but none of which obscures meaning, omission of *there – Here* (there) *are many restaurants*, confusion with gerunds and infinitives – *enjoy to see*, omission of prepositions – *next* (to) *the sea,* (for) *example chairs*, inaccurate past participle – *catched*, incorrect word form – *local* (locally), and one spelling mistake – *espensive*. There is an adequate range of appropriate expressions for this type of task, e.g. *The aim of this report, Where can you, If I were you, I recommend.* The writer also shows a fairly good knowledge of vocabulary, e.g. *affordable, pleasant, friendly, lively, tasty, delicious, shopping centre.*

Mark*: Good pass

*Note on marking
Each of the four categories is awarded a mark out of 5. These marks are then added up to give a total score out of 20.
For the purposes of this course, the sample answers have been graded according to the following scale: **borderline**, **pass**, **good pass**, and **very good pass**.

Review 12 Answers Pages 162–163

Reading and Use of English Part 3 — Word formation

1 wholly	2 illnesses
3 choice	4 poverty
5 refusal	6 rising
7 unfortunately	8 discourage

Reading and Use of English Part 4 — Transformations

1 have/'ve lost (some) weight since
2 advised Matt not to go
3 knowledge of English amazes
4 if/whether she knew how
5 offered to give Dawn
6 would not be (very) many

Collocation revision: Units 1–12

1	clothes	2	musician
3	(tele)phone	4	film
5	job/work	6	hair
7	town/neighbourhood/area		
8	trip	9	give
10	sentence	11	wind(s)
12	drink		

Reading and Use of English Part 1 — Multiple-choice cloze

1 C 2 B 3 A 4 C 5 D 6 D 7 A 8 C

Additional activity
After doing the collocations revision exercise, divide the students into pairs and allocate them one unit each. Ask them to write five gapped sentences using collocations from their unit and to put the answers on the back of the page. Circulate and check the sentences are correct and that it will be possible to guess the missing words. Make sure they write the unit number at the top of the page. Students then swap their sentences and look at the corresponding unit in order to complete the gaps. Ask them to write their answers on a separate paper. They should continue swapping papers until they have done all the exercises.

 DVD resource: Unit 12

Progress Test 6

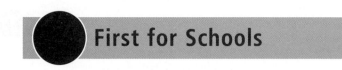

First for Schools

Writing *Part 2* **Short story**

> This photocopiable is intended for those students who are preparing for the *First for Schools* exam. It replaces the Writing section on reports on pages 160 and 161 of the Coursebook.

1 Read the following Part 2 instructions and the plan made by a student.

You have decided to enter a short-story competition. The competition rules say that the story must begin with the following words:

There is one meal I will never forget for as long as I live.

Your story must include:

• a phone call
• a television

Write your **story** in **140–190** words.

> **Plan**
> • Begin with words from question
> • 'Anniversary meal' – going out together for six months
> • I arrived late – my girlfriend was angry
> • Television in restaurant – football match – more angry
> • Her friend phoned her – talked for long time
> • Big argument – split up

2 Read the student's answer below, ignoring the gaps, and answer the following question.
What changes did the writer decide to make to his plan in exercise 1?

> There is one meal I will never forget for as long as I live. My girlfriend, Tess, and I had been going out together for six months, **(1)** _and_ we decided to celebrate our anniversary in our favourite restaurant.
> Tess was understandably upset **(2)** _____ I turned up half an hour late. I'd set off early from home **(3)** _____ on my way to the restaurant I realized I'd left my wallet behind and had to go back to get it. **(4)** _____, just as we were deciding what to order, the waiter turned the television on, **(5)** _____ he wanted to watch a football match. **(6)** _____ I'm not a big football fan, I found it difficult to take my eyes off the enormous screen on the wall in front of me. Tess was beginning to get very annoyed, **(7)** _____ we changed seats to stop me watching the football. **(8)** _____, the situation just got worse. A friend phoned me on my mobile, and I couldn't get rid of him, **(9)** _____ though I kept telling him I was with my girlfriend.
> **(10)** _____ that time, Tess was furious with me. Suddenly, she got up from the table and rushed out of the restaurant. Not surprisingly, I never saw her again.

136

© Macmillan Publishers Limited 2013. This page may be photocopied and used within the class.

PHOTOCOPIABLE

3 Complete the gaps in the student's answer in exercise 2 with the following linking words. The first one has been done for you.

although	~~and~~	because	but	by
even	however	so	then	when

4 Find examples in the answer in exercise 2 of the following features:
   a different past tenses
   b good vocabulary and structures

5 Either write your own answer to the question in exercise 1, using a different plan, or write an answer to the following question:

You have decided to enter a short-story competition. The competition rules say that the story must begin with the following words:

I will never forget the day I decided to get fit.

Your story must include:
- a gym
- an accident

Write your **story** in **140–190** words.

> **Don't forget!**
>
> Your story should include:
> - a variety of past tenses
> - a wide range of vocabulary
> - time linkers, e.g. *as soon as, afterwards, while*

Short story

Teacher's notes

1 Students read the instructions and the plan. Ask them to cover the model answer. In pairs they should invent a story using the ideas in the plan. Get some feedback from the class, and ask one pair to describe the basic plot of their story.

2–3 Students do the exercises individually.

Answers
2 In the plan the girl's friend phoned her – talked for long time Big argument – split up In the story the writer's friend phoned him. His girlfriend rushed out of the restaurant. **3**

1	and	**2**	when	**3**	but
4	Then	**5**	because	**6**	Although
7	so	**8**	However	**9**	even
10	By				

4 Students work in pairs to find and underline the features in the story. Ask why each of the tenses is used.

Answers
4 **a** Past perfect simple: *I'd set off, I'd left* Past perfect continuous: *My girlfriend and I had been going out* Past continuous: *we were deciding, Tess was beginning* Past simple: e.g. *we decided, I turned up, I realized* **b** Suggested answers: *Tess was <u>understandably upset</u> when I <u>turned up</u> half an hour late, I'd <u>set off</u> early, I found it difficult to <u>take my eyes off</u> the <u>enormous</u> screen, we <u>changed seats</u> to <u>stop me watching</u> the football, I couldn't <u>get rid of</u> him, I <u>kept telling</u> him, <u>rushed out of</u> the restaurant, <u>not surprisingly</u>.*

5 Students read the instructions and the Don't forget! box. If you decide to use the new essay question, get them to brainstorm ideas and write a plan in pairs. Suggest they look at the Grammar reference section for Unit 4 on page 212, and also the word bank for Unit 2 on page 206, as this contains sports vocabulary.

Learner training
When you mark the stories, take one error from each student's work and make a worksheet. Underline the error and add your correction symbol after the sentence. You may need to semi-correct some sentences so that they only have one mistake. When you hand back their work, give them the worksheet and ask them to correct the sentences.

Ready for Speaking

Speaking exam

Part 1	Interview
Part 2	Talking about photos
Part 3	Collaborative task
Part 4	Further discussion

In this unit students go through the various parts of the Speaking exam, finding out exactly what happens at each stage, how long each stage lasts, and looking at useful strategies and language.

The classroom management should correspond with the instructions given in the Coursebook in order to make the practice activities as authentic as possible. As the aim of this unit is to inform students and give them help and practice, it is probably better not to correct them during the activities. However, you could write down some common errors and look at these in the feedback later.

Students can watch a recording of the Speaking exam which is analysed in this Ready for Speaking unit on the Ready for First Practice Online website.

Introduction   Page 164

Students read the introduction, with their books closed. Ask the following questions:
How many parts are there in the Speaking exam? (four)
How long does the exam last? (about 14 minutes)
How many students usually do the exam together? (two)
If you take the exam in a group of three, how long will it last? (about 21 minutes)
What does the interlocutor do? (conduct the exam and ask the questions)
What does the assessor do? (listen and assess your performance)
Do both the interlocutor and the assessor give you a mark? (Yes)

1 Students work in pairs.

Answers

Part 1 b	Part 2 d	Part 3 a	Part 4 c

2 Students discuss the questions in pairs. After this, Student A should turn to the answer key on page 269 (or you can make the key from the Teacher's Book available to them), and Student B should leave the book open on page 164. In this way they can look at the questions and check the answers at the same time. For homework, you could ask them to write ten tips on how to do well in the Speaking exam using some of the expressions below.

It's essential/important to …
You should always …
Don't forget to …
You need to …
Try to …
One mistake that some candidates make is to …
You don't have to …
Don't worry if …
You shouldn't …
You mustn't …

Answers

Part 1

a No. Certainly, students should avoid trying to give over-complicated answers which cause them to become confused and so make unnecessary mistakes. However, very short one-word answers are usually inadequate and do not give the examiners a sufficient sample of language to assess. Students should therefore answer questions with appropriate detail.

b No. Long, pre-prepared answers will be interrupted by the interlocutor. As well as sounding unnatural they are often inappropriate to the question asked. Students may practise for this part of the test, but they should not try to prepare and learn long answers.

c Yes. Students will be nervous at the beginning but this part of the test is designed to relax them by asking questions on areas which are familiar to them.

Part 2

a No. Students are not required to describe the photographs in detail. They should compare them and then do the task which is given to them by the interlocutor and reproduced as a direct question above the photographs.

139

b Yes, as long as the student has tried to address both parts of the question. It is better to fill the minute and be interrupted than to run out of things to say before the allotted time finishes.

c Clearly the student should focus on the instructions that the examiner gives, though exam nerves often cause students to miss part of the instructions and it is perfectly acceptable for students to ask for them to be repeated. However, this is not really necessary as the second part of the interlocutor's instructions is printed in the form of a question above the photographs.

Part 3

a Good that the student had a lot to say. However, it seems that he/she may not have been respecting the rules of turn-taking, an important aspect of interactive communication. If students are paired with quiet, more reticent candidates, they should invite them to take part in the discussion by asking questions such as 'What do you think?' or 'What would you do?' Attempts to dominate the conversation will be penalized.

b No. As with Part 2, students should use the full amount of time allotted. The purpose is not to complete the task in the shortest time possible: rather, students should be aiming to provide enough relevant and appropriate contributions for the examiners to assess their English accurately.

c Yes. This student and his/her partner have clearly made full use of the time available. Students are not penalized if they fail to reach a decision, as long as it is clear that they are at least trying to do so.

Part 4

a Yes. Candidates should certainly be speaking more than the examiner! The implication here also seems to be that the candidates have been responding to each others' comments, something which is actively encouraged in Part 4.

b No. It is not only what you say but how you say it which is important throughout the exam. 'Nonsense, you must be mad' sounds rude and is not the best way to disagree with someone in a discussion such as this. Alternative expressions of agreeing and disagreeing are given on page 36 in Unit 3.

c No. Students should respond to questions appropriately and not try to divert the discussion to their favourite topic of conversation.

Part 1: Interview Page 165

1 Students work individually. Circulate and check their questions are correct.

2 Students read the instructions and the Don't forget! box. Set a two-minute time limit, to make the task more authentic. Explain that Part 1 is designed to help them relax and that if they make mistakes they will still have a chance to show their ability in the other sections of the Speaking exam.

3 Students listen and answer the questions. Get feedback from the class. Point out that the two candidates are quite strong, though they do make some speaking errors.

Additional activity
Write the following errors from the interview on the board and ask students to correct them in pairs.
I like films where happen many thing.
I'll work in a big company, as accountant.
I want to go to the university and study business studies first.
Answers
I like films where many things happen/a lot happens.
I'd like to work in a big company, as an accountant.
I want to go to university and study business studies first.

Answers
2 Christina has obviously come with a prepared speech. The interlocutor asks where she is from and, having answered the question, she begins to talk about her family.
3 Paolo should develop his answers more, without pausing too much. He does improve by the end of Part 1, when he answers more confidently.

Speaking Part 1: Listening script 2.37
I = Interlocutor   C = Christina   P = Paolo
I: Good morning. My name is Kate Benton and this is my colleague Paul Flint. And your names are?
C: Christina.
P: My name is Paolo.

I: Can I have your marksheets, please? Thank you. Where are you from, Paolo?

P: From a small town near Ravenna. In Italy.

I: And you Christina?

C: I'm from Corinth, in Greece. I have lived there all my life. I live there with my three sisters and my parents. I'm in my last year at school. My mother works in …

I: Thank you, Christina. First we'd like to know something about you. Paolo, what kind of sports are you interested in?

P: Er, I play football, tennis, and I go swimming.

I: How often do you play football?

P: Once a week. Yeah, every Saturday. In a team.

I: And you Christina, do you have any hobbies?

C: Well, not really hobbies, but in my free time I like to go to the cinema, read, going out with my friends, er, things like that.

I: What sort of films do you like to watch?

C: Oh, I like action films. I like films where happen many things. I don't like romantic or historical films. They are very slow sometimes, they are not very interesting for me.

I: Paolo, do you work or are you a student?

P: I work in my uncle's computer business.

I: And how important is English for your work?

P: Well, yes, it's very important. I have to read a lot of things about computers in English. Everything is … well … most things are written in English nowadays.

I: Christina, what do you hope to do in the next few years?

C: Well, I want to go to the university and study business studies first. Then, if it is possible, I'll work in a big company, as accountant or something like that. Maybe, in the future I can use my English and find a job in another country. That would be very exciting.

I: What kind of job do you hope to be doing in ten years' time, Paolo.

P: Well, ten years is a long time, so I'm not sure what will happen. First, I want to help my uncle expanding his business and then perhaps in the future, I could set up my own business.

I: Thank you.

Part 2: Talking about photos   Page 166

Refer students to the Useful language box. One worry that students sometimes have is that they will go blank in the exam. These fillers will give them the chance to gather their thoughts and help them feel more confident.

1 Students read the Don't forget! box and the instructions. Remind them that student A must speak for one minute and that they should

paraphrase if they don't know a specific word. Draw their attention to the boxed question above the photos. Set a timer during the activity so that students get a clear idea of how long they need to speak for. Circulate, but do not interrupt students. Take feedback from the class and make some general comments about what various students did well, e.g. *Well done, some of you paraphrased … really well. All of you used linking devices, that's great!* etc.

2 Students listen to Christina and Paolo and answer the questions. Then they can compare their answers with the key on page 273.

Answers

1 Christina compares the photographs very well, using language such as *both pictures* and *whereas*. She addresses the second part of the task well, with a reasonable range of language (*get out of the towns and cities where they live, in the open air, they can be lazy, peaceful*) and she successfully corrects herself when she says *in a camping* and *in the nature*.
Paolo does not actually compare the photographs at the beginning, though when addressing the second part of the task he does say that the people in both pictures are enjoying being with others. His range of language is good, particularly when speculating: *they must be enjoying themselves, it looks as if they are in the class, they might be listening to some music*, and he successfully corrects himself when he says *they are doing progress*.
Both candidates use fillers.

2 Christina gives a much more complete answer than Paolo, who makes no attempt to fill the 30 seconds he is given for this part.

Speaking Part 2: Listening script 2.38

I: In this part of the test, I'm going to give each of you two photographs. I'd like you to talk about your photographs on your own for about a minute, and also to answer a question about your partner's photographs. Christina, it's your turn first. Here are your photographs. They show people on holiday in different places. I'd like you to compare the photographs and say why you think the people have chosen to go on holiday to these different places. All right?

C: Yes, well, er, in the first picture I can see a small beach, a pretty beach, with several people and in the

141

background a small town or village with mountains behind, and, er, in … whereas in the other picture there are only four people, a family, and they are probably in a camping, a campsite. Er, what else … yes, and er, in both pictures the people are having a relaxing time but are doing different things. In the first picture they are taking the sun or swimming in the sea, whereas in this one they are just … well, sitting down. Er, what else … yes, and, well … people go to these types of places because they want to get out of the towns or the cities where they live. They want to, er, change their routine … er, be in, er … the open air. Yes. And, er, some people prefer to go to the beach, like in this picture, where they can be lazy all day. And other people prefer to be in the nature, in the, the countryside, where it's very quiet … and peaceful, and they can do lots of things like maybe go walking or cycling, and the children can play and have lots of fun … er …

I: Thank you. Paolo, which of these places would you prefer to go to on holiday?

P: Er, I would rather go camping. I don't like going to the beach on holiday. There are too many people.

I: Thank you. Now, Paolo, here are your photographs. They show people doing exercise in different places. I'd like you to compare the photographs, and say what you think the people are enjoying about doing exercise in these different places. All right?

P: OK. In the first picture I can see two men who are jogging, in a park or a forest maybe. Er, one man is middle-aged and the other is younger. They must be enjoying themselves because they are both smiling, perhaps because of something one of them has just said. In the other picture it looks as if they are in a class doing some step exercises. The woman at the front is probably a teacher, in the yellow top. I can see a speaker on the wall, so they might be listening to some music while they are doing their exercise. What are they enjoying? Er … in the first picture they are enjoying being together. Jogging is not good fun on your own – it is much better to do with a friend, having a chat. And they are outside all the time, and that's enjoyable. In the other picture, too, in the gym, they are probably enjoying being with other people, and they might make new friends there. They are probably enjoying having a teacher as well – if the teacher is good, they can feel like they are doing progress … making progress.

I: Thank you. Christina, which of these places would you prefer to do exercise in?

C: Well, I think it is much better to be in a class with other people, like in this photo. Jogging is not very interesting for me, even if I do it with a friend. You run and that's it. But in this type of class you do many things – it is, er, it is more variety – yes, and you can meet new people and make new friends, like Paolo said. Definitely I would prefer to do exercise in a gym.

I: Thank you.

Part 3: Collaborative task   Page 167

1 Students read the instructions and the Useful language box. If your students have done a Part 3 task before, treat this as if it were the exam and ask them to spend fifteen seconds thinking and then to start speaking. However, if this is their first experience you should give them longer to think of ideas. Remind them to interact well. Set a timer for two minutes.

2 Students read the instructions. Allow time for them to refer to the expressions on page 120 of Unit 9. Set a timer for one minute. In class feedback, ask which options they chose in Part 2.

3 Students listen to Christina and Paolo and answer the questions. They may need to look at the script for question 1. Elicit answers from the class.

Answers
1 Christina asks Paolo questions to encourage him to speak.

Which one shall we start with?
It could be good fun, don't you think?
Now, what do you think about the concerts?
Do you agree?
I think nearly everyone will like this, don't you?

2 They both agree on the medieval fair. Christina's second choice is the dressing-up activity and Paolo's is the computer exhibition. At the end they are about to compromise by choosing the theatrical representations, as long as they are humorous.

Note the following words and expressions used by Paolo and Christina:

First task
I think it would appeal to all different types of people.
… it would also attract people of all ages.
It could be good fun.
I think it would bring in lots of families with young children.
This would be ideal for people who work near the museum.
I think they'd probably be more suitable for adults.
… nearly everyone would find them enjoyable …

Second task
I think Paolo made a good point earlier that …
… we both agreed that …
As I said before …
… we did both agree before that …

Speaking Part 3: Listening script 2.39

I = Interlocutor   C = Christina   P = Paolo

I: Now, I'd like you to talk about something together for about two minutes. I'd like you to imagine that the History Museum in your town would like to introduce some new features to attract more visitors. Here are some of the ideas which have been suggested and a question for you to discuss. First you have some time to look at the task. Now, talk to each other about what types of people these different ideas would appeal to.

C: Which one shall we start with?

P: Let's talk about the computer exhibition first. I think it would appeal to all different types of people, because computers are so important today. Young people especially would be interested to see what they were like twenty or thirty years ago, before they were born.

C: Yes, and older people, like our parents or even our grandparents would be interested to remember what computers were like when they were younger. OK, let's move on to the medieval fair. I think it would also attract people of all ages. It could be good fun, don't you think?

P: Yes, I do. Er ... visitors could take part in different activities and games and eat medieval food. And if the organizers dressed up in costumes, then that would make history very colourful and realistic. I think it would bring in lots of families with young children.

C: Yes, I agree. Now, what do you think about the concerts? This would be ideal for people who work near the museum. They could come during their lunch break and have a relaxing moment.

P: That's true, but I don't think many people would be able to go, especially if the museum is in this city – everyone is busy all day. But retired people would probably appreciate it and have more time to enjoy it.

C: Yes, I suppose you're right. It would be very pleasant for them. Now, let's move on to the theatrical representations. I think it depends if they are serious or funny. If they are serious and formal, then I think they'd probably be more suitable for adults, or people who go to the theatre a lot. But if they are funny, if they make people laugh, then I think nearly everyone would find them enjoyable, including the children. Do you agree?

P: Yes, definitely. I think if the museum wants to attract more visitors, then they have to make sure that they appeal to as many different types of people as possible.

C: Exactly. And I think this will be true for the dressing up in costumes. I think nearly everyone will like this, don't you?

P: Well, I'm not so sure. Er ... it wouldn't appeal to me for example. I don't like dressing up or attracting attention to myself. Families with children would enjoy doing this and taking photos of each other, but I don't think couples or people on their own would be very interested.

I: Thank you. Now you have about a minute to decide which two ideas would be most successful in attracting new visitors.

C: Right. Well, I think Paolo made a good point earlier that the museum must appeal to as many different types of people as possible. And I think we both agreed that the medieval fair would attract people of all ages, so, Paolo, do you agree that that might be one of the best two choices?

P: Yes, I do. I think it is – it doesn't matter if you are on your own, in a couple, with friends, in a family – everyone would enjoy it and I am sure it would bring in many ... many visitors to the museum. I think this is also true for the computer exhibition, but you don't agree, I think.

C: No, I'm sorry. I know you like computers, but I would be bored! People have enough of computers at work. As I said before, I think nearly everyone will like the dressing up – not you, maybe, but if the museum wants to attract more visitors, it needs to have more fun activities, not more exhibitions.

P: OK, so we don't agree on that. But, we did both agree before that if the theatrical representations were funny and not serious, then that would be very successful.

C: Yes, that's true. I think that ...

I: Thank you.

Part 4: Further discussion   Page 167

1 Students read the instructions and the Don't forget! box. Student A asks the first three questions and Student B the remaining questions. Remind them to interact with each other.

2 Students listen to Christina and Paolo and answer the questions. Look at the answers together and ask whether they used any of the same expressions.

Ask how Christina paraphrases the word for a museum showcase (*like boxes, in glass boxes or cupboards*) and how Paolo paraphrases domestic appliances (*domestic machines we use for cooking or other jobs*). Remind them that paraphrasing is an important technique which they should employ when they don't know an item of vocabulary.

Answers
1a When answering the first two questions they do not interact at all, failing to respond to what each other says. Rather than a discussion, there is a series of short monologues.
b They interact much better in the second half of Part 4.

2 In the second half Christina helps the interaction by asking questions to involve Paolo: *What do you think, Paolo? Don't you agree?* and *Do you really think a robot could do all of our ironing for us?* and Paolo responds accordingly.

Speaking Part 4: Listening script 2.40

I = Interlocutor   C = Christina   P = Paolo

I: Christina, what do you think makes a good museum?

C: Well … in general I think the museums are a little boring. You only look at objects which are in … er, how do you say? Er, like boxes? Er … glass boxes, er, cupboards? Er, there is nothing to do. But, er, I think if you could touch things in an exhibition, or do fun things like dressing up, that would make it more interesting … more enjoyable experience.

I: Uh huh. Paolo?

P: I think ideas like the medieval fair are good because they help you to have a better idea of life in the past. The last year I went to a museum where people in costumes explained how different things were used. Er, even they cooked with some old saucepans and things. Er … perhaps they weren't real, but it doesn't matter. The important is that you can imagine how people lived before.

I: How could the teaching of history in schools be improved?

C: Well, er, I'm not really sure, er … in school we sit and listen the teachers … listen to the teachers, and write what they say. In Greece there are so many ancient monuments that, er, perhaps we could visit them more and not just read and write about them all the time.

I: What do you think, Paolo?

P: Er, when I was in school we just listened to the teachers. I think history was the worst subject for many people. I think we need better teachers who are good at making a subject more interesting for pupils. I don't know, I think it depends on the teacher.

I: What was the most important moment in the history of the twentieth century?

C: Well, I haven't really thought about it before, but, er, perhaps it was … yes … I think it was when the first man landed on the Moon. I have seen pictures of this, and I think it must have been something quite incredible at that time. Now, travelling to space is quite normal, but that moment was very different. What do you think, Paolo?

P: Well, I think the landing on the Moon was important, but travel in space would not be possible if we did not have computers. The invention of the computer, for me, was the most important moment. It changed the way we live …

C: You only say that because you like computers!

P: No, but everything we do needs computers nowadays. Er … industries, banks, companies, hospitals – everything depends on computers. Er, and if the computers break down, then people cannot do their jobs properly. We cannot survive without computers.

C: Maybe, but I think there are more important things that happened in the last century. Things with people and not machines. For example, when people started to think more about the environment. The planet is in bad condition, and if organizations like Greenpeace didn't exist, then, er, it would be much worse. Don't you agree?

P: Yes, you're right, but even organizations like Greenpeace need computers to do their work!

I: Paolo, what items from our lives today will be in the history museums of the future?

P: Well, in addition to computers … er, possibly, some domestic ap-, ap-, domestic applications? No, it doesn't matter … er, domestic machines that we use for cooking or other jobs, things like the cooker, the vacuum cleaner or the iron. Many of these things will be replaced by robots which do not need people to operate them.

C: Do you really think a robot could do all of our ironing for us?

P: Sure. We already have robot vacuum cleaners to clean our floors, so why not robot irons?

C: Well, I think one thing in the museums of the future will be the money. I think the credit cards and smartphones will be the only things we use. Already, some people never pay for things with cash. Er, … in only a few years I think they will stop making the money.

I: Thank you. That is the end of the test.

13 Animal magic

Content Overview

Themes

The themes in this unit are the arts and animals.

Exam-related activities

Reading and Use of English

Part 6	Gapped text
Part 3	Word formation (Review)
Part 4	Transformations (Review)

Writing

Part 2	Email
Part 2	Article (Review)

Listening

Part 4	Multiple choice
Part 2	Sentence completion

Speaking

Part 3	Collaborative task
Part 4	Further discussion

Other

Language focus 1: Hypothetical situations
Language focus 2: Prepositions and gerunds
Vocabulary 1:   The Arts
Vocabulary 2:   Paraphrasing and recording
Vocabulary 3:   Animals
Vocabulary 4:   Verbs followed by prepositions.
Word formation: suffixes -ible and -able

Vocabulary 1: The Arts   Pages 168

Lead–in

Ask students whether they have been to an exhibition recently. Get them to describe the exhibition and say whether or not they would recommend it.

1 Students do the exercise in pairs. In feedback, explain the difference between *classical* and *classic*, and *priceless* and *pricey*, as these are a common area of confusion.
classical = traditional, by well-known and widely recognized composers or authors
classic = typical, or judged over a period of time to be of the highest quality
priceless = such a high value that a price cannot be calculated
pricey = expensive

Answers					
1	classical	2	opera	3	stone
4	gallery	5	painting	6	novel

2 Write the categories on the board and elicit vocabulary for each one. Model and practise the pronunciation of any tricky words, e.g. *musician* (/mjuˈzɪʃn/), *violinist* (/vaɪəˈlɪnɪst/), *choreographer* (/kɒriˈɒɡrəfə/), *sculptor* (/ˈskʌlptə/).

Answers
Possible answers: music: musician, composer, conductor, orchestra, pianist, violinist literature: novelist, writer, author, publisher art: artist, painter, art collector opera: opera singer, tenor, soprano, cast, director ballet: ballet dancer, ballerina, choreographer sculpture: sculptor

Reading and Use of English
Part 6

Gapped text
Page 168 and 169

1 Elicit answers from various students. Ask whether they know who the artist is (Damien Hirst).

2 Ask students to follow the instructions. Encourage them to guess difficult vocabulary from context. Explain that the *First* exam is getting closer and they need to rely on their intuition.

Answers
1 C   2 F   3 A   4 G   5 D   6 B

Reacting to the text
Students discuss the questions in pairs. Write the following additional questions on the board.
Do you or anyone you know own an original piece of art? Why it is special?

Additional activity
Make a visual showing a variety of art types. Project this on the screen and ask students to discuss which types they like most and least.

Vocabulary 2: Paraphrasing and recording
Page 170

1 Remind students not to refer to the text until they have attempted all the questions. When they correct their answers, encourage them to spend some time looking at the expressions in their original context.

Answers			
1	changed	2	fetched
3	raises	4	doubt
5	freely	6	branched, taken
7	sensation	8	come

2 Ask students to follow the instructions.

Answers
Possible answers:
1 Animal rights activists were strongly opposed to his *Amazing Revelations*.
2 In 1994, people paid a lot of attention to *Away from the Flock*.
3 People say he painted only five himself.
4 This is not the first time artists have got others to do some of the work for them.
5 People will remember him most because of his art.

Language focus 1: Hypothetical situations
Page 171

A Wishes

1 Write the example sentence on the board and elicit the meaning. Ask the following concept questions:
Is the speaker an artist? (No)
Would the speaker like to be an artist? (Yes)

2 Students complete the rules in pairs. You may need to give a few more examples of the three types of sentence.
Write the following sentences on the board and highlight the key words in a different colour pen. Remind them that *if only* can also be used instead of *wish*, but is slightly more emphatic.
*I wish my city **wasn't** so expensive.*
*I wish you **would tidy** your room.*
*I wish I **had left** my passport in the hotel safe.*
If you have a monolingual class you could ask

students to translate the sentences and compare any differences in grammar.

Answers	
a	the past simple
b	*would*
c	the past perfect

3–5 Ask students to work through the exercises individually. Remind them to refer to the rules in exercise 2 and the Grammar reference. Circulate and check students are completing the exercises correctly. If they have difficulties go through the activities as a whole class.

Answers
3
a I wish I ~~would~~ **could** give up smoking.
b *I wish she could come to my party on Saturday.* The speaker <u>knows</u> that she cannot come. *I hope she can come to my party on Saturday.* The speaker <u>does not know</u> if she can come or not.
4

1	could	2	didn't	3	hadn't bought
4	would	5	you'd listened		

5

1	were	2	would stop	3	had/'d gone
4	had	5	would/'d make		

B *It's time* and *would rather*

1 Elicit answers from the class. Write the correct answers on the board and check that students have grasped the rule. Highlight the structure in a different colour pen.

Answers	
1 didn't	2 went

2 Students read the instructions. Write the sentence beginnings on the board. Elicit complaints they might make to the first three people, e.g.
I wish you wouldn't worry about me so much. (mother)
It's time you grew up and stopped being so annoying. (younger brother/sister)
I'd rather you didn't text me when I'm with my boyfriend. (best friend)

Circulate and check the sentences are correct. Get feedback from the class. Find out which pair had the most similar complaints. Ask various students to read out one of their sentences.

Additional activity

Develop the sentences into a string of mini roleplays. Student A reads out their first sentence and Student B has to respond, A then continues the exchange. Give an example.

A: *I wish you wouldn't worry about me so much.*

B: *I'm sorry, but you're only 17 and I always imagine something has happened to you when you aren't back by midnight.*

A: *I know, but I always tell you where I'm going and Steve brings me home.*

B: *Yes, but he drives so fast. I wish he would drive more safely.*

Circulate and write down some errors. When they have finished write the errors on the board and correct them together.

Listening 1
Part 4

Multiple choice
Page 172

1 Students discuss the questions in pairs. Refer them to the pictures if they don't know any of the vocabulary. If they ask you for key language (e.g. *cage*, *tank*, *feed*) you could write the words on the board.

2 Students read the instructions and underline key words. Check their understanding of *tame* and *harm*. Play the recording twice and let students compare their answers together after the first listening.

Answers
1 C **2** A **3** B **4** B **5** A **6** C **7** B

3 Students discuss the questions in pairs. Write the following additional questions on the board for fast finishers:

Is it right to keep a dog in a city flat?

Which animals have a special relationship with people?

How can animals be used to help disabled people?

Listening 1: Listening script 2.41

P = Presenter   S = Sally Jefferson

P: Ants, spiders, snakes and rats may not sound like ideal house companions, but as Sally Jefferson can confirm, an increasing number of animal lovers in the Radio Carston area have taken to keeping them as pets. Sally is the owner of Animal Crackers, a large pet shop in the centre of Carston. Sally, why the move away from cats and dogs?

S: Well, primarily, I think the trend reflects changing lifestyles. Cats and dogs need a lot of looking after, whereas insects and spiders, for example, are very low-maintenance – they more or less take care of themselves. And that's perfect for busy working couples who are out of the home most of the day and can't afford to spend a great deal of time on the more traditional kinds of pets. And, er, and then of course, there's the so-called educational pet, ants in particular.

P: Yes, I was surprised to hear that you sell a lot of them in your shop.

S: That's right, leaf-cutter ants mostly. You can create your own colony in an ant farm – that's a glass box like a big fish tank filled with clean sand or soil. You can watch them in their nest, digging tunnels and cutting leaves, all collaborating to achieve a common goal. It's a great lesson in the benefits of teamwork, especially for children. And for that reason a lot of parents come in and buy them.

P: And do the kids like them?

S: Yes, most do – after all, ants are fascinating creatures to watch close up. But of course, they're not furry or cuddly, and children can't interact with them in the same way that they can with a cat or a dog. If you pick them up or try to play with them, they can give you quite a nasty bite. So inevitably some children start to grow tired of them, pay less attention to them.

P: Right. And how about spiders? You were telling me before the programme that you sell tarantulas – can they be handled?

S: It's not advisable, but in this case it's more because of the risk involved to the tarantula than to the owner. They do bite, of course, and as we've seen in films, sometimes with fatal results. But a bite from the species we sell is rather like being stung by a bee. No, the main problem is that they are fragile creatures and if they run around when they're on your hand or arm, there's a danger they'll fall off and hurt themselves very badly. So best not to get them out of their cage too often.

P: No, indeed. Now let's move on to another type of pet that seems to be in fashion these days – snakes. Do they need a lot of care and attention?

S: That really depends on the species you buy – different species have different requirements. What's common to the corn snakes and ball pythons that we sell is that they can sometimes go for months without eating. So, if you're going on holiday you don't have to worry about finding someone to feed them while you're away. However, it's important to realize that many snakes have a lifespan of more than twenty years – so

---

you need to be aware that you are making a long-term commitment when you buy one.

P: And what sort of things do they eat?

S: Mice, mainly, and perhaps rats or even rabbits for some of the larger species. It's better to give them pre-killed animals, which can be bought frozen at reasonably little cost from pet stores. Besides being more humane for the mice and rats and so on, it's also safer for the snakes. A rat can seriously wound a snake when it's acting in self-defence.

P: Interesting that you mention rats, because of course, they too are kept as pets nowadays, aren't they?

S: That's right. They make very good pets and they don't bite quite as readily as most people think. You need to bear in mind, though, that they like being with other rats, so they really need to be kept in pairs or even groups, and in a large cage, too. Technically, of course, they're nocturnal animals but they're very flexible creatures – they will adapt to their owners' schedules and are happy to come out and play when people are around during the day.

P: You don't feed them to the snakes, do you, Sally?

S: No, don't worry, we never do that …

Word formation: Suffixes
-ible and *-able*   Page 173

1 In this exercise students see the word forms in an authentic context. Students answer the question. As you go through the answers, ask whether the words in bold are adjectives or adverbs.

Answers		
a tarantulas	**b** rats	**c** ants
d pre-killed animals		

2 Students complete the words with a suffix or prefix. This exercise helps students see word formation as a mechanical process. First they decide the type of word: adjective, adverb or noun. Then, where necessary they add a suffix, prefix or both.

Answers
1 unpredictable
2 impossibility
3 incredibly, comfortably
4 responsibility, valuables
5 inaccessible
6 considerably

3 Students discuss the questions in pairs, using the phrases given. For the second part of the question you could add some extra times. If there has been a public holiday or interesting local event recently, add this, e.g. music festival, Bastille day, Valentine's day.

Additional activity

Recycle the words from this exercise as a short race during a future lesson. Divide the class into groups of three. Write five words on the board and explain that they have three minutes to write as many other forms of the word as possible. Emphasize that they must be spelt accurately. The group with the most correct words is the winner.

Language focus 2: Prepositions and gerunds

1 Ask students what the rule is when a verb follows a preposition. They then do the exercise as suggested.

Answers		
a without	**b** like	**c** about

2 Students read the rules. Write the two example sentences on the board and highlight the position of the gerund. Then students should do the exercise individually.

Answers			
1 to	**2** off	**3** over	**4** up
5 of			

3 Students read the information. Ask if they know any other linking words that function as prepositions, and write these on the board, e.g. *after, apart from, as a result of, as well as*. Then allow time for students to look at the Grammar reference section. While they are doing the transformation exercise, circulate and help with any difficulties. During feedback, draw their attention to the difference in grammar between *although/ even though* (+ clause), and *despite/in spite of* (+ gerund) in questions 1 and 2, as this is a common area of confusion. If you have a monolingual class, you could ask students to translate some of the sentences to see if the structures are similar or different in their language.

Answers

1	knowing how unhealthy
2	of getting rid of
3	instead of driving
4	result of his flight being

Additional activity

Remembering prepositions is not an easy task. You will need to recycle them frequently. Write short exercises like the one in the Coursebook. Use personalization to make them more memorable, e.g. *Andrei is looking forward ___ going back to Moscow at Christmas.*

Vocabulary 3: Animals   Page 174

1a Check students' understanding of the vocabulary in the box. Get students who know the words to give a definition, e.g. *a bat is an animal that flies at night, a peacock is a bird with a beautiful tail.* Draw students' attention to the picture of a mule and the first sentence. Check they understand *stubborn.* Then ask which of the expressions they think the picture of the owl illustrates. As you get feedback, drill the pronunciation of the weak forms, e.g. /əz blaɪnd əz ə bæt/.

Answers

2	bat	3	bee	4	fox
5	lion	6	peacock	7	mouse
8	lamb	9	ox	10	owl

1b You could give another example of someone from your own family, e.g. *My husband is as quiet as a mouse in the mornings. He gets ready for work without waking anyone up. I don't know how he manages.* Encourage students to respond to each other, e.g. *Really, you are lucky. My husband makes lots of noise in the mornings.*

2 Students complete the animal expressions. Ask students if they have similar expressions to those in exercises 1 and 2 in their own language.

Answers

1	fly	2	horse	3	fish
4	cat, dog	5	bear	6	frog

3 Students could use monolingual dictionaries to look up any words they don't know. During

feedback, check their understanding of the more difficult vocabulary by asking various students to give a definition.

Answers

a	bird	**b**	fish	**c**	cat	**d**	horse

4 Students discuss the questions in pairs. Get some feedback from the class. Ask students to justify their choice of animal for each question, and find out if other students agree.

 **Collaborative task**   Page 175

1 Students read the instructions, the What to expect in the exam box and the Useful language box. Emphasize that the timing in the Speaking exam is strict and that they should make sure they complete the tasks effectively within the time limits. Use a timer during this activity.

2 Students read the instructions and do the task. Use a timer. Get some class feedback and ask whether they covered the main points within the time limits. Get various pairs to justify their choice of job in Part 2.

 **Further discussion**   Page 175

This further discussion section focuses on work rather than animals, because the most obvious questions to ask about animals are dealt with in other parts of this unit (pet shop listening, animals in space listening and the post listening questions). Emphasize that the topic of work is very important in the Speaking exam. Encourage students to interact with each other. Use a timer. Circulate, but do not interrupt students. Get feedback from the class and try to make some general comments about what various students did well.

 **Sentence completion**   Page 176

1 Elicit answers from various students.

2 Students read the instructions. Encourage them to predict the type of information they will hear for each gap. Play the recording twice and let students compare their answers together after the first listening.

Answers

1 monkeys
2 ten thousand/10 000
3 (one-)minute('s) silence
4 stamps
5 (human) hand
6 New Mexico
7 flashing light
8 sixteen/16
9 half an orange
10 fingerprint

Listening 2: Listening script 2.42

Dogs, cats, chimps, monkeys – even frogs and fish; they've all been up into space at some time in the last fifty years or more. The first living creature in space, of course, was Laika, the dog, who was launched aboard Sputnik 2 on 3 November 1957 by the Soviet Union. Laika, unfortunately, died just a few hours into the flight, and the first animals to actually survive a space mission were two monkeys called Able and Baker. That was in May 1959, when they were fired 300 miles into space from Cape Canaveral in Florida. The pair were weightless for nine minutes and monitored for their heart beat, muscular reaction, body temperature and breathing. They travelled at incredible speeds – up to ten thousand miles an hour – before coming down safely in the South Atlantic near Puerto Rico, 1500 miles away.

Not surprisingly, the use of animals for space research has been unpopular with animal welfare groups ever since it began. Back in 1957, for example, every day that Laika was in space, the National Canine Defence League in Britain asked all dog lovers to observe a one-minute silence. Space scientists have been accused of being cruel to animals and strongly criticized for carrying out their experiments on defenceless creatures. In the meantime, many of the animals themselves have become celebrities. Laika's space flight attracted a huge amount of attention from the world's press, and the dog's image appeared on stamps in a number of countries, including Romania, Poland and Albania. And in 2008, over fifty years after her historic flight, a monument was erected in honour of Laika in Moscow. It features a dog standing on the combination of a rocket and a human hand.

Another animal to achieve celebrity status was Ham, a three-year-old chimp who was sent into orbit in January 1961 to find out whether humans would be able to survive in space. Originally from Cameroon in Africa, Ham was bought by the United States Air Force and sent to New Mexico, where he was trained for the tasks he would carry out during his space flight. For unlike previous animal astronauts, Ham would be more than just a passive passenger. He was taught, for example, to pull a lever in response to a flashing light; if he did so within five seconds of seeing the light flash, he would receive a reward of food. The purpose was to see how well tasks could be performed in space. During the mission, Ham was weightless for over six minutes. His capsule suffered a drop in oxygen levels but he was safe inside his space suit and sixteen minutes after launching from Cape Canaveral, he splashed down in the Atlantic with nothing more than a bruised nose. When the rescue helicopters eventually got to him, he was rewarded with an apple and half an orange. He had beaten the first man into space, the Russian Yuri Gagarin, by over two months. Afterwards, Ham retired to the US National Zoo in Washington DC, where he was well looked after and enjoyed a celebrity lifestyle. His picture appeared on the cover of *Life* magazine and he even received fan mail, some of which he replied to by sending admirers his fingerprint. In 1980, a very overweight Ham moved to North Carolina Zoo, where he died three years later.

3 Model the activity by eliciting answers to the questions from stronger students, and then responding using expressions for agreeing and disagreeing. Write any useful expressions on the board to help students develop their opinions, e.g.
I'm totally against …
They should only be used if …
In some circumstances I think …
Well yes, but it depends on …
I suppose you're right …
I agree (up to a point) …
Students discuss the questions in groups of three. Circulate and record a few common errors. During class feedback, write these on the board and elicit the corrections.

Vocabulary 4: Verbs followed by prepositions.

Page 176

1–2 Students complete the exercises individually.

Answers

1
of, for

2

1	for, c	2	for, e	3	for, a
4	for, h	5	for, i	6	from, b
7	from, d	8	on, j	9	on, f
10	on, g				

3 For activity b give students an example by reading out a sentence ending and getting them to guess the sentence beginning, e.g. (My parents prevented me from) ... *going to the disco, because they said I was too young.*

Learner training
Encourage students to record the verbs along with the prepositions in their vocabulary notebooks.

4 Encourage students to respond to their partner's comments. Write the following expressions on the board to help them:
Really?
Oh dear, what a shame.
You must have felt terrible/embarrassed/angry/ annoyed/proud.
That's strange, because exactly the same thing happened to me.
During feedback ask students to tell the class about something interesting their partner said.

 DVD resource: Unit 13

 **Email**
Page 177

This activity serves as a checklist of the marking criteria for *First* writing answers. The writing section on reviews in Unit 9 also considered features of effective writing, and the criteria are studied again in the Ready for Writing section on page 193. This is one of the few times a faulty 'model' is shown. The other occasions are Unit 5 (essay) and Unit 14 (application letter). The main aim in this unit is to focus on the importance of content: answering all the points in the question and ensuring the content doesn't go off the point. Students need to understand that good, accurate English does not guarantee a high mark. It is important that they realize that while a brief general opening paragraph is appropriate, the majority of their letter should be devoted to dealing with the specific task outlined. The effect on the target reader is a further issue here: David is not very encouraging, so the reader would be left with a negative impression of the writer's country.

1 Ask students to copy the table below. Make sure they leave enough space to make comments and give examples. By doing this, students will be encouraged to analyse the email in more detail.

Range of language	
Style of the language	
Use of paragraphs and linking words	
Accuracy	
Relevance	
Effect on the target reader	

Circulate and check they are doing the task correctly. Get some feedback from the class. Ask whether they noticed the weaknesses in the example email. Students could refer to the answer key at the back of the book, if they have the answer key version, or they can refer to the key below.

Answers

Range of language: the range of language is sufficiently varied and appropriate for this task, e.g. ... *to get away from the city ... the path that goes along the coast ... it can get a bit windy ... there are some good views from the cliffs.*

Style of the language: Appropriately and consistently informal, e.g. *You must be mad ... It was great ... Lots of people ... I'd find it a bit boring ... if you like that kind of thing.*

Use of paragraphs and linking words: The answer is clearly organized into paragraphs, although the closing comments are limited to a single word, *Bye*. There is a good range of linking devices, e.g. *I got a summer job after that so I could pay for my holiday to Greece, where I spent most of the time sunbathing ... Anyway ... Firstly/ Secondly ... Personally ...*

Accuracy: Very accurate.

Relevance: The opening paragraph, whilst relevant, is overlong. The majority of the letter should be devoted to giving information about walking areas. In addition, the answer does not address the issue of wildlife mentioned in the question and this would be penalized in the exam.

Effect on the target reader: The target reader would not be sufficiently informed about areas where she could go walking and see interesting wildlife. The tone of the letter is also rather dismissive of walking and this would have a negative effect.

Sample answer

Hi Anna

Good to hear from you. I've finished my exams a week ago and I also went walking as I like nature aswell. I now quite a lot of places where you can go walking but I will only give you a couple of places.

Personally, I think that a lovely walking area is a path just outside the village of Alameda. The path is a bit rocky but not too steep. It's got some stunning views and you might catch sight of a vulture or two. Keep an eye out for eagles aswell.

Another walk is a coastal path in the south of Spain. People come here to observe dolphins and flamingos. It's a gentle circular walk which takes you round a nature reserve famous for its plants and colourful birds.

I hope this is usefull. Good luck in your exams.

Best wishes
Lara
146 words

Examiner's comment

Content: Full coverage of the information requested.

Communicative achievement: Suitably friendly informative tone. Reader would be fully informed.

Organization: The letter is clearly organized with suitable paragraphs and simple linking devices are used effectively.

Language: Minimal errors do not impede understanding, e.g. incorrect use of *ago* with present perfect. There are two spelling mistakes – *now* instead of *know*, and *usefull*. Has used more complex collocations accurately. Good range of appropriate expressions for this type of task – *Good to hear from, Good luck in your exams, Best wishes*. Use of more complex collocations, including *Keep an eye out for, catch sight of*. The writer also shows an excellent knowledge of vocabulary, e.g. *path, rocky, steep, stunning views, vulture, eagles, dolphins, flamingos, gentle circular walk, nature reserve*.

Mark*: Very good pass

***Note on marking**

Each of the four categories is awarded a mark out of 5. These marks are then added up to give a total score out of 20.

For the purposes of this course, the sample answers have been graded according to the following scale: **borderline**, **pass**, **good pass**, and **very good pass**.

2 Students read the instructions and the Useful language box. Allow time for them to write notes about the countryside in their area. Ask various students which aspects they have included. Students write the email for homework. Before you mark their work, make a photocopy of the writing criteria table. You can put five or six on one side of A4 paper to save photocopies. Cut these up and staple them to the emails. Give students a mark for each of the criteria.

Review 13 Answers Pages 178–179

Reading and Use of English
Part 3

Word formation

1	peacefully	2	remarkable
3	originally	4	responsibility
5	appearance	6	proof
7	unreliable	8	statements

Vocabulary

A The Arts

1	portrait	2	sculptures
3	novel	4	open-air
5	priceless	6	playwright
7	composer	8	exhibition

B Animals

1 Lion

C Prepositions

1 to, to, for
2 on, for, without
3 for, to, to
4 for, of, for

Reading and Use of English
Part 4

Transformations

1 I lived closer to
2 wish I had not/hadn't told
3 rather you did not/didn't wear
4 to playing the guitar well
5 prevented us (from) having
6 insisted on seeing

Additional activity 1: Transformations

Write transformation sentences 1, 2, 3 from page 179 onto cards. Put them in an envelope and write *wish* and *would rather* on the front. Stick the answers on the back. You could add few more transformations of your own. Add this to your set of revision envelopes. Bring these to a lesson towards the end of the course. Students work in pairs, they choose an envelope and work through the cards. Remind them not to write on the cards.

Additional activity 2: Writing Part 2

In the Writing Part 2 section of the review you could give students a third option, as follows.

You have a part-time job in a pet shop. The manager has asked you to write a reply to this email from a customer.

> I would like to buy a pet as a companion for my elderly mother, who lives alone. She is reasonably active but a dog would be too much for her. Could you make two suggestions and say why they might be suitable?
> Thank you in advance
> Yours sincerely
> Rosemary Pendle

Write your **email** in **140–190** words.

Additional activity 3: *First for Schools* Writing Part 2

If you have students who are interested in taking the *First for Schools* version of the exam, give them the following short-story question instead of the article question on page 179.

You have decided to enter a short-story competition. The competition rules say that the story must begin with the following words:

I will never forget the day I decided to get fit.

Your story must include:
• a gym
• an accident

Write your **story** in **140–190** words.

Content Overview

Themes

Mind your language is a play on words. This expression can be used as a warning to someone who is swearing (using bad language). This unit deals with the theme of learning languages.

Exam-related activities

Reading and Use of English

Part 5	Multiple choice
Part 2	Open cloze
Part 1	Multiple-choice cloze (Review)
Part 4	Transformations (Review)
Part 3	Word formation (Review)

Writing

Part 2	Article
Part 2	Letter of application

Listening

Part 3	Multiple matching
Part 1	Multiple choice

Speaking

Part 2	Talking about photos

Other

Language focus 1: Compound adjectives
Language focus 2: Expressing purpose
Language focus 3: Ability
Vocabulary 1:   Phrasal verbs with *turn*
Vocabulary 2:   *Make* and *do*
Word formation: Suffixes *-ful* and *-less*

Lead–in

Focus students' attention on the photos. Ask them in what ways English is important to the different people.

Listening 1
Part 3

Multiple matching
Page 180

1 Students work in pairs. Ask if anyone has had an embarrassing experience as a result of not speaking English perfectly.

2 Allow students thirty seconds to read the questions before they listen and answer.

Listening 1: Listening script 2.43–2.47

Speaker 1
I never had time to go to the German classes my company arranged for us at work, so I used to put CDs on in the car on the way in every morning and just let the language wash over me. I was completely immersed in it for the whole journey. Then I'd play the same section on the way home and that was enough to ensure I learnt what I'd listened to in the morning. When I go to Germany on sales trips now I have very few problems understanding people. Business seems to be improving too.

Speaker 2
I went to Spain, twice, when I was studying languages at university; once on holiday and the next year to work in a bar. The holiday was a disaster in terms of language learning. I spent most of the time with my English friends and hardly learnt a thing. When I went back there to work, though, I spoke Spanish all day and my speaking and understanding really improved. That experience working abroad helped me pass my final exams just as much as studying, I'm convinced. Oh, and I'm getting married this year to my Spanish girlfriend.

Speaker 3
I spent three years teaching English in Poland with my boyfriend back in the late nineties. It took us both quite a long time to learn any Polish in the beginning, partly because of laziness, but mostly because we were working long hours teaching and speaking English all day. Things got better, though, once we eventually got to know a few Polish people and we had more chance to speak the language. We weren't quite confident enough to go and see films in Polish at the cinema, but we certainly felt more integrated.

Speaker 4
When I left university I desperately wanted to work abroad, but all three French-owned companies I applied to turned me down at the interview stage. I'd only ever learnt grammar when I studied French at school. I had no difficulty at all with that, but when I actually had to speak the language in the interview it was a real problem and I'm sure the interviewers couldn't understand a word of what I was saying. So I signed up for a two-month general language course in Paris and thanks to that, when I came back, I got the first job I applied for.

Speaker 5
Here in Wales everyone can speak English, but it's compulsory for all students to learn Welsh up to the age of sixteen. My mum and dad both came to Wales from England, so I only ever spoke in English till I started school. But all my lessons there were in Welsh – right from day one – and I picked it up really quickly. So then I had the two languages – English with my parents and Welsh with my friends. I sometimes spoke Welsh at home, too, with my brother. It was great, 'cause we could talk about things in front of my mum and dad and they had no idea what we were saying – it was really useful sometimes!

3 If you are a language learner yourself, you could summarize your own experience. Encourage students to respond to their partner's sentence.

Vocabulary 1:
Phrasal verbs with *turn*   Page 181

1 Elicit answers to the question from the class.

Answers
reject

2 Students work individually. The sentences contain enough contextual clues for students to guess the meaning of the phrasal verbs.

Answers
1 d 2 f 3 b 4 e 5 g 6 a 7 h 8 c

3 Students work individually, then check their answers in pairs. Check answers as a class.

Answers		
a turn out	b turn up	c turn up
d turn over	e turn off	f turn off
g turn back	h turn into	

Additional activity 1
Students work in pairs. They take it in turns to cover up the sentence endings and try to complete the sentences orally from memory.

Additional activity 2
Write the following on the board and get students to discuss the questions in groups of three.
Have you ever:
turned up really late for an important event?
turned off at the wrong road and got completely lost?
been on a journey where you've had to turn back because of the weather or some other problem?
been in a situation which turned into a nightmare?

Language focus 1:
Compound adjectives   Page 181

1 Read the information together and elicit the answer to the question. Then ask students to read the Grammar reference on page 221. After this, write up some more examples and highlight the use of past participles, present participles, singular

nouns with a plural number and compound adjectives without a participle, e.g.
air-conditioned classroom
a ten-kilometre walk
time-saving device
top-of-the-range car
Mention that we can also add *-ed* to a noun to make a compound adjective, e.g. *open-mouthed, long-legged, red-headed.*

Answers
The nouns are singular even though the number is plural.

2–3 Students complete the exercises individually. Circulate and help students who are having difficulty. Refer them to the example which corresponds to the question, e.g. question 1: a five-minute walk/a four-hour flight; question 2: English-speaking country/Spanish-speaking tour guides, etc.

Answers	
2	
1 five-minute	
2 English-speaking	
3 blonde-haired, blue-eyed	
4 Italian-born	
5 well-behaved	
3	
1 free	2 time
3 tempered	4 brand/label
5 down	6 haul/distance
7 force	8 air

4 Give some examples, e.g. *I've got a 92-year-old aunt. She's really amazing, she still lives alone and manages to cook for herself. I hope I'm like her when I reach the same age.*
Ask students to write the sentences and then to tell their partner about them.

Additional activity
Make a set of cards, using the pairs of words below cut up into adjectives and nouns. Use them as a revision activity in the next lesson. Students match the compound adjectives with the nouns, e.g. *a home-made cake.*

a home-made	*cake*
an air-conditioned	*classroom*
a tree-lined	*avenue*
a French-born	*sculptor*
a fully-grown	*shark*
a made-up	*story*
a laid-back	*hippy*
a money-making	*enterprise*
sweet-smelling	*soap*
a long-lasting	*relationship*
a world-famous	*politician*
a fifty-dollar	*note*

Then ask them to write five sentences using the compound adjectives.

Reading and Use of English 1
Part 5

Multiple choice Page 182

1 Elicit answers to the question from the class. Some disadvantages might be:
- starting to speak later than other children
- mixing the languages – verbally and when writing
- embarrassment when speaking to your parents in front of non-bilingual peers.

Ask whether they know anyone who is bilingual and how this has affected their life.

2 Students complete the exercise individually. Set a limit of eleven minutes. Explain that this is the approximate amount of time they will have in the exam. They should guess any difficult vocabulary from context.

Answers
1 C 2 D 3 C 4 D 5 B 6 A

Reacting to the text
Students discuss the questions in groups of three. Add a few more questions:
Do you have more than one language in your country?
How important is it to keep minority languages alive?
How effective is language teaching in high schools in your country?

Vocabulary 2: *Make* and *do* Page 183

In some languages *make* and *do* are the same verb, so students often make mistakes with these.

1 Students complete the sentences.

Answers	
1	do, make
2	have/'ve made, doing/to do
3	make, do
4	making, to make
5	do, do
6	to make, make
7	doing, do, do
8	to do, to do, to make

2 Students discuss the sentences in pairs.

Additional activity
Books closed. At the end of the lesson give students a short test. Read out the following sentences and ask them to choose the correct verb, *make* or *do*. When you correct the sentences get students to write the collocations next to the verb, e.g. *make a big effort, do an exercise.*

1 *You need to … a big effort over the next couple of weeks before the first exam.*
2 *There's still time to … a little more progress.*
3 *… all the exercises in the Workbook.*
4 *… sure you arrive early for the exam.*
5 *Just try and … your best.*
6 *If you … a mistake in the Speaking exam try to correct yourself.*
7 *Don't spend too long trying to … up your mind about the answer to a question.*
8 *I really hope you … well in the exam!*

Answers

1	make	2	make	3	Do
4	Make	5	do	6	make
7	make	8	do		

Language focus 2: Expressing purpose Page 184

A *In order to, so as to* and *so that*

1 Students read the explanation. Write the example sentences on the board and highlight the patterns in a different colour pen.

2 Students work in pairs, and then check their predictions of the rules in the Grammar reference.

Answers

so that + present simple/*can/will* = future
so that + *could/would* = past

3 Students complete the sentences in pairs. Circulate and check they are writing the structures correctly.

Answers

Possible answers:
1 ... we can email her every day.
2 ... to get a place near the stage.
3 ... as to increase my chances of getting a job.
4 ... I wouldn't have to do gym at school.
5 ... to be nearer her parents.
6 ... not to wake anyone up.
7 ... I can go out afterwards.

4 Students discuss possible reasons in pairs. Circulate and correct any errors with the target language.

B *In case*

1 Students read the rules. Write the example sentences on the board and highlight the structures in a different coloured pen.

2 Students work in pairs. Circulate and check they are completing the sentences correctly.

Answers

Possible answers:
1 ... you have problems with the other one.
2 ... it broke down again.
3 ... you are burgled or there's a fire.
4 ... I have to do overtime.
5 ... I saw something good for my dad's birthday present.
6 ... the alarm goes off by accident.

Roleplay: Expressing purpose

1 Students read the instructions. Circulate and help students with any difficult vocabulary they want to include in their list.

2 Before students do the roleplay, elicit some expressions for giving and refusing advice from the class, and write some suggestions on the board, e.g.
I really think you should take ...
I insist ...

You'll definitely need ...
I won't need ...
Don't be ridiculous ...
I'll never use ...
That's really not necessary ...
OK, I suppose you're right ...
Circulate and record any errors with the target language. Write these on the board after the activity and elicit corrections.

 Writing 1 Part 2 — **Article**
Page 185

Students read the instructions and the How to go about it box. Then they should brainstorm ideas for the article in pairs. Elicit phrases for making suggestions and write useful expressions on the board, e.g.
It's a good idea to ...
You should always ...
Why don't you ...
Don't forget to ...
Remember to ...
It's important to ...
Students write the article for homework.

 **Speaking** Part 2 — **Talking about photos**
Page 185

1–2 Students read the instructions and the What to expect in the exam box, then do the tasks. Use a timer. Ask students whether they feel they are fully prepared for the *First* exam. Suggest that they meet with their partner the week before the exam and practise some of the speaking activities from the Coursebook.

 DVD resource: Unit 14

 **Listening 2** Part 1 — **Multiple choice**
Page 186

Students read the instructions. Remind them to make use of any time to read the question and the options. Play the recording twice.

Answers

1 C   2 B   3 B   4 C   5 A   6 C   7 A   8 B

Listening 2: Listening script 2.48–2.55

1 You hear a man talking about the language school he owns.

We've benefited enormously from being so close to a number of large companies. We're right on their doorstep, so they can either have classes on their premises or else send their workers round to us – usually before or after office hours, but sometimes even during their lunch break. We don't exactly offer the cheapest courses in town, and there are other schools in the area whose teachers are more qualified, more experienced than ours. But we try to make up for that with youthful enthusiasm and, as I say, the key to our survival – and growth – has been the fact that we're so conveniently situated.

2 You overhear a young woman talking to a friend about going abroad.

M = Man   W = Woman

M: Are you nervous about going to France?

W: Excited mostly, but yeah, a bit nervous too I suppose.

M: You don't speak much French, do you?

W: No, but that's not the problem. I know enough to get by and it'll be fun trying it out on people in the shops and asking for directions and so on. It's more about not knowing how long it'll take me to get a job. It needs to be fairly soon, otherwise I'll run out of money.

M: Ah, you'll be all right. If you can't survive, then I don't know who can.

3 You hear a man giving part of a speech.

I'd like to say how flattered I feel to have been invited to open this magnificent sports centre. And I'm particularly proud of the fact that you voted unanimously for my name to be given to the centre. If I think back to all my sporting successes, the medals I've won and records I've broken, none of them ever gave me as much pleasure as this moment today. As a child growing up in this area, I never dreamed I would one day be standing here …

4 You hear a woman talking to her friend about going rock climbing.

M = Man   W = Woman

M: Looking forward to going rock climbing, Sally?

W: Well, to tell you the truth, I haven't made my mind up about it. Everyone tells me it's great fun, especially when you realize that you're quite safe, with all the ropes and everything. But what if you get stuck and can't go on? That's what worries me. I can't see I'm going to enjoy myself, clinging to a rock for survival, waiting for someone to come and pull me off. Still, I won't know if I don't try, will I?

5 You hear a man talking on the radio.

What I like about it is that you're doing things that nobody else has done before, discovering things about yourself as well as the world you live in. I've been to places I never knew existed until I got there, and I've travelled enormous distances without seeing another living soul. It's not whether it's the highest, the hottest

or the coldest that matters to me, but being the first person to set foot there … and surviving to tell the tale.

6 You hear a woman talking to a friend about her husband's work situation.

Of course, I wasn't happy about him losing his job. We had a few **sleepless** nights, I can tell you, what with the mortgage to pay and two hungry kids to feed. But no one was to blame for what happened, and **thankfully**, it all worked out in the end. I'm just glad it's all over now. I don't know how we'd have managed to survive if he hadn't been taken on at the power station.

7 You overhear a man talking to his wife about a friend.

W = Woman   M = Man

W: Dave's been very **successful**, hasn't he? He's done well for himself.

M: Yes, well, it's hardly surprising, is it?

W: Why do you say that?

M: Well, it was the same thing at school. Fortune always smiled on him – he seemed to pass exams **effortlessly** and now he's making money in the same way. He makes a few good decisions, invests in the right companies and bingo! Suddenly he's a millionaire. Still, it couldn't happen to a nicer guy. No one deserves it more than him.

8 Listen to this woman talking to her son on the phone.

Yes, well, we're very pleased you actually managed to phone us. At least you've succeeded in doing something right. You may have noticed, however, that it is now two o'clock in the morning … Yes, but you said you would be home by twelve. If you aren't capable of keeping promises then you shouldn't make them … No, we can't come and pick you up. You're old enough to be able to solve your own problems now.

Additional activity

Ask students to underline any phrasal verbs in the script and to write a synonym next to these.

make up for – compensate

get by – survive

run out of – use all of something

grow up – gradually become an adult

make up your mind – make a decision

work out – to end in a satisfactory way

take on – to be given employment

pick up – take someone in a vehicle

Word formation: Suffixes *-ful* and *-less*   Page 186

1 Students complete the sentences.

Answers		
a sleepless	**b** thankfully	**c** successful
d effortlessly		

2–3 Write the following words on the board and elicit the adjectives and adverbs.

care (careful/careless/carefully)

sleep (sleepy/sleepless/sleepily)

success (successful/unsuccessful/successfully/unsuccessfully)

Students then do exercises 2 and 3 as suggested.

Answers

2

Noun	Positive adjective	Negative adjective
home	–	homeless
power	powerful	powerless
skill	skilful (Am* skillful)	unskilled
pain	painful	painless
point	–	pointless
delight	delightful	–
end	–	endless
harm	harmful	harmless
peace	peaceful	–
stress	stressful	unstressful
thought	thoughtful	thoughtless

* In the exam, candidates should be consistent in their use of either American or British English spelling.

3

1	skilfully/skillfully	2	carelessness
3	thoughtful	4	uneventful
5	painless	6	cheerfulness
7	pointless	8	homelessness
9	peacefully	10	harmless

Language focus 3: Ability   Page 187

1 Focus students' attention on the caption in the picture. Ask why it is strange. Elicit that *wasn't able to* is too formal and that *couldn't* would be more appropriate when speaking to a dog! Students then do exercise 1 individually.

Answers

1	to phone	2	doing	3	keeping
4	come	5	to solve		

2 Students work individually. When they have checked their answers in the Grammar reference, you could go over the following rules as these tend to be the areas which students have greatest difficulty with.

- When we talk about ability to do something on one occasion in the past, *could* is not possible except when it is used with verbs of the senses: *see, smell, hear, feel, sense, taste.*
- When we talk about inability to do something on one occasion in the past, *couldn't* is possible.

Answers

a be able to: there is no infinitive form of *can*.

b been able to: there is no past participle of *can*.

c was able to/managed to: for ability on one occasion in the past, *could* is not possible.

d unable: this word is an adjective, not a verb, so does not change its form.

e incapable: the negative prefix for this adjective is *in-*, not *un-*.

3 Students work individually. Circulate and help them with any difficulties. Ask questions which will lead them to the correct answers, e.g.

1 *Do we need to use a preposition with* capable? (yes)
What verb form do we use after a preposition? (gerund)
2 *Which preposition do we use after* succeed? (in)
3 *Is* despite *a preposition?* (Yes)
What verb do we use instead of can *if we need the gerund?* (be able to)

Answers

1 is capable of going
2 did not/didn't succeed in convincing
3 being unable to play
4 had been able to
5 incapable of turning
6 did not/didn't manage to buy

4 Circulate and record any errors with the target language. After the activity write the errors on the board and elicit the correct structures.

 **Reading and Use of English 2**   Part 2

Open cloze   Page 188

1 Students complete the open cloze activity.

Answers

1	who	2	being	3	and
4	to	5	without	6	out
7	was	8	well		

2 You could tell the class a survival story about yourself or someone you know. Then ask if anyone else has another survival story.

Writing 2 — Part 2 — Letter of application
Pages 188–189

1 Students read the instructions and the model letter. Check their understanding of *grant*. Let them compare their opinions with a partner before eliciting answers from the whole class. Emphasize that they will lose marks if the tone of their letter is not appropriate.

Answers

- The target reader is the Director of St George's House.
- The effect would not be positive. As well as making several requests concerning the school and the class (Manchester, the class size, idiomatic expressions) the applicant gives rather frivolous reasons for wanting to go to England: meeting a relative, clubbing, a base for travelling. This does not sound like a serious letter from someone asking for money and the application would probably not be successful.

2–3 Students read the instructions and then plan their letter in pairs. Elicit some possible ideas. Students could refer to the answer key at the back of the Coursebook, if they have the answer key version, or you can make the suggestions below available to them.

Answers

Examples of other reasons:
- A course in the UK would help you pass the *First* exam.
- Your writing and grammar are fine but you would like to improve your fluency in speaking.
- You are going to study English at university next year.
- You are interested in meeting speakers of English from other countries.
- You will be working for two years overseas for a charity and English is a requirement.

Examples of further details:
- A period of study in the UK would improve your chances of obtaining a job in your own country.
  I would like to work in the travel industry but my job applications are repeatedly rejected because of my level of spoken English.
- A recent illness has caused you to fall behind in your studies.
  I was absent from school for three months after a car accident and this has affected my chances of passing the First exam.
- You are interested in learning about British culture and the British way of life.
  I believe that knowledge of the culture would increase my enjoyment of the subject and provide an important context for my study of the language.

4 Students read the instructions and the Don't forget! box. Explain that although all the information does not have to be true, it should not be overly strange. When you mark the letters, try to add a few tips on what they can do in the days before the exam, e.g. review indirect ways of asking questions in the Grammar reference, check rules for when to use gerunds and infinitives, etc.

Review 14 Answers Pages 190–191

Reading and Use of English — Part 1 — Multiple-choice cloze

1 C 2 B 3 A 4 D 5 A 6 C 7 C 8 B

Compound adjectives

1	twenty-pound	2	three-hour
3	short-sleeved	4	nine-to-five
5	high-speed	6	three-course
7	two-day-old	8	money-making

Reading and Use of English — Part 4 — Transformations

1 in order not to get
2 so as not to miss
3 in case it does not/doesn't
4 turned down an/the offer
5 make a complaint
6 made up your mind or made your mind up

Reading and Use of English — Part 3

Word formation

1	performers	2	traditionally
3	competition	4	successful
5	extinction	6	useful
7	survival	8	popularity

Alternative approach: Compound adjectives

Use the compound adjective exercise on page 190 of the Coursebook as a short quiz at the end of a lesson. Students work in pairs. Each pair uses a piece of paper as a score sheet to write down their answers. Explain that they are allowed a little time to confer for each question. Read out the descriptions and ask them to write the compound adjective. At the end of the quiz, pairs swap score sheets. Go through the answers as a class. Count the scores to find the winner.

Additional activity: Transformation revision

If you have prepared envelopes with transformations as suggested in earlier units, you should bring these into the final lessons and let students work through them in pairs. Remind them not to write on the cards.

 Progress Test 7

Ready for Writing

Content Overview

Writing paper

Part 1	Essay (2 examples)
Part 2	Article
Part 2	Email and letter
Part 2	Letter of application
Part 2	Report
Part 2	Review

Starting with an introduction of the different types of writing that students can expect to find in the exam, the unit then goes on to look at register, marking criteria, planning and checking. Annotated models of each task type are included as well as further writing tasks for each of these.

The general sections on pages 192 and 193 should be done in class towards the beginning of the course. The models on pages 194 to 199 are best used as the writing task type comes up in each unit of the Coursebook.

Introduction   Pages 192–193

Ask students to read Introduction and Part 1 and 2, but not Extracts. Then tell them to close their books, and ask the following questions:
How many writing tasks do you have to complete in the exam? (two)
How many choices do you have in Part 1? (No choices, just one compulsory task)
How many choices do you have in Part 2? (three)
How many words do you have to write in both tasks? (140–190)
What help are you given in Part 1? (some notes to guide your writing)
What are the possible task types in Part 2? (email – formal or informal, article, report, review).

Extracts

Books open. Students look at the extracts and do the activity in pairs. Check the answers as a class.

Answers

A 5b B 1 C 4 D 5a E 2 F 3

Register

Lead–in

Books closed. Write *formal* and *informal* on the board. Brainstorm the features of language which

are typical of each. Write students' suggestions on the board.

1–2 Books open. Students follow the instructions for exercise 1 and 2.

Answers

1

1 d informal   **2 e** formal   **3 a** informal
4 c formal   **5 b** formal

2

B Formal/neutral
The linker *however* is fairly formal, and there are no contractions or phrasal verbs.
C Neutral
There are no informal linkers, contractions or phrasal verbs, but neither is there evidence of any formal language.
D Formal
The linker *consequently* is formal, as is the use of language such as *gained experience, in this field, well suited to the position*.
E Informal
The writer addresses the reader directly with a question, and there are contractions in the second sentence.
F Formal
The language used for making recommendations is formal: *is certainly to be recommended* and *it is advisable to*. The linker *however* is fairly formal and there are no features of informal language.

Marking

Books closed. Ask students to think about what examiners would look for when marking their writing tasks, and brainstorm different features they think would be important. Write their ideas on the board. Ask students to open their books, and draw their attention to the features outlined in the box. They then do the exercise. Check the answers as a class.

Note

The criteria on page 193 of the Coursebook are all important points for students to bear in mind when preparing for the Writing paper in the *First* exam. While the official terms used by Cambridge English are phrased slightly differently, the same features are considered: Content, Communicative achievement (including appropriate register for the target reader), Organization, Language (including accuracy and range).

These headings are used in the analysis of the sample Writing tasks in the two practice tests which are on the Ready for First Practice Online site.

Answers

2 Content
3 Organization and cohesion
4 Register
5 Accuracy

Planning and checking

Students follow the instructions. Ask them whether they use a similar system when writing in their own language.

Answers

2 e 3 c 4 d 5 a 6 f

Part 1: Essay Type one   Page 194

Students look at the information about the type one essay. Before reading the model answer ask them to brainstorm their own ideas in pairs. Then students read the model and check whether any of their ideas are mentioned.

Task

Students read the instructions and brainstorm ideas in pairs. Then they join with another pair and give a mini oral presentation of the content of their essay using language from the Useful language box.

Part 1: Essay Type two   Page 195

Books closed. Ask students where they went on their last holiday and who they travelled with. Then in pairs, get them to discuss the advantages and disadvantages of travelling with family or friends. Books open. Students read the instructions and the model. Get feedback from the class. Ask if they agree with the opinion presented in the model.

Task

Students look at the task and prepare notes in pairs. Remind them to present one point of view and to back this up with reasons and specific examples.

Part 2: Article   Page 196

Books closed. Brainstorm ideas on how to make an article interesting, e.g. interesting title, lively informal style, direct questions, etc. Books open. Students read the instructions and model.

Task

Students should choose from task a or b and write notes individually. Ask them to present their ideas orally using some of the language from the Useful language box.

Part 2: Email and letter   Page 197

Students read the task and brainstorm advice for Emma. Then they should read the model and see if David gave similar advice.

Additional activity

Books closed. Write up some of the expressions from the Useful language on the board and get students to put these into the correct category, e.g.

All the best
Bye for now
It was great to hear from you.
Let me know what happens.
Hope to see you soon.
Make sure you …
You should …
Your holiday sounds wonderful.

Categories:

Beginning the email/letter
Giving advice and making suggestions
Ending the email/letter
Closing phrases

Answers

Beginning the email/letter
It was great to hear from you
Your holiday sounds wonderful.

Giving advice and making suggestions
Make sure you …   *You should …*

Ending the email/letter
Let me know what happens.
Hope to see you soon.

Closing phrases
All the best
Bye for now

Task

Students make notes in pairs and write the email

for homework. Remind them to include language from the Useful language box.

Part 2: Letter of application   Pages 198–199

Ask if students have ever had to write a letter of application in their own language or in English. Students read the task, but not the model.

Additional activity

Write the following categories on the board.

Beginnings and endings
Reasons for writing
Describing skills and experience
Personal qualities and suitability
Closing remarks

Ask students to cover the model, so that they can't see it. In pairs they should write possible expressions for each category, relating to the task in the question. After this, refer them to the Useful language box on page 199 and ask how many of their expressions appear. Then students should read the model and say whether they think the director of the summer camp will be interested in the application.

Task

Students make notes in pairs and write the letter for homework.

Part 2: Report   Page 200

✎ If you have students who are interested in preparing for the *First for Schools* version of the exam, turn to page 166 at the end of this unit for a short story model answer and task (photocopiable). Students read the task and model. Ask what they would recommend elderly people to visit in their town.

Task

Students prepare notes in pairs and write the report for homework. Remind them to use expressions from the Useful language box.

Part 2: Review   Page 201

Students read the task and model.

Task

Students read the task and decide whether they want to do a or b. Then they should refer to the Useful language box and write notes. In groups of three students could present their review orally. They should write their review for homework.

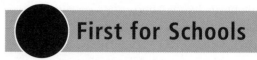

First for Schools

Part 2: Short story

Students read the task and model.

Task

Students read the second task and decide whether they want to do a or b. They can work in pairs to brainstorm ideas for how to include the two elements in their story. They should then plan their story and make notes individually, and write the story for homework. Remind them to use expressions from the Useful language box.

Part 2: Set text

This photocopiable is only relevant to those students who are preparing for the *First for Schools* version of the exam and who have read a set text. Apart from the wealth of language benefits students gain from the reading itself, doing a set text with your students can provide a welcome change of pace and focus. In the exam, it gives students an extra choice in Paper 2 writing. If necessary, reassure students that the examiner's judgement is based on the student's control of language in a specific context, and is not based on literary criticism.

Preparing students for this question

Here is a possible plan to follow, much of which students can do on their own with an occasional class discussion based on different features of the book. Ideally, students should read the book three times.

- Tell your students to read the book quite quickly the first time to understand the general storyline and familiarize themselves with the story and the characters. They should use their dictionary very little, if at all, at this stage.
- The second time, they should read it more carefully and take notes under headings, e.g. *events, setting, characters and relationships, ideas*. They should write down short, easily remembered quotations. They should use their dictionary for the words they cannot guess from context. Students could compare and discuss these notes in class.

- They should read the book quickly a third time before the exam, together with the notes they have made during their second reading.
1 Refer students to the instructions and the seven exam-style questions. Once students have ranked them, ask them to compare the list with their partner's, giving reasons for their choices.
2 The sample answer about *Animal Farm* by George Orwell answers question 4.
3 Students work together to answer the questions.

Answers

Has the writer answered both parts of the question satisfactorily?
Yes. The description of the place is brief (no more is given in the book itself) and the reader is fully informed of its importance in the story.

What is the purpose of each of the four paragraphs?
1 A brief description of the farmhouse and the animals' initial reaction to it
2 How the farmhouse comes to show the inequality between the pigs and the other animals
3 How the leader in the farmhouse separates himself from his subjects.
4 The final scene in the farmhouse and its importance to one of the themes of the book

Which words are used to link ideas?
Paragraph 1: *After, at the beginning, and*
Paragraph 2: *However, while, As (in Jones's time), whereas*
Paragraph 3: *Furthermore, In this way*
Paragraph 4: *At the end, then*

Has the writer quoted directly from the text?
Yes – 'the unbelievable luxury'. The quotation is short and relevant

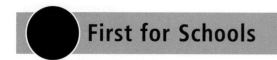

First for Schools

Part 2: Short story

> This photocopiable is intended for those students who are preparing for the *First for Schools* exam. It replaces Part 2: Report on page 200 of the Coursebook.

You have decided to enter a short-story competition. The competition rules say that the story must begin with the following words:

When Mark saw the weather forecast, he put his coat on and rushed out of the door.

Your story must include:
- a bicycle
- a shopping trip

Write your **story** in **140–190** words.

Model answer

Background	When Mark saw the weather forecast, he put his coat on and rushed out of the door. For the last few days it had been extremely cold and wet, and the pavements were very icy. Now, heavy snow was on the way, so Mark wanted to visit his elderly grandmother to ask if she needed anything from the shops.

a range of tenses and verb patterns

Development	He walked carefully along the slippery pavements and <u>headed for</u> her house, which was just ten minutes away. He almost <u>fell over</u> two or three times, but he managed to keep his balance. Then, just as he was crossing the road, a cyclist came past and knocked him over. 'Be careful!' shouted the cyclist, and <u>carried on</u> without stopping. He was listening to his mp3 player and didn't hear Mark shouting in pain. He had fallen badly on his arm and knew he had broken it.

use of phrasal verbs

some use of direct speech

Outcome	He was wondering what to do, <u>when</u> to his surprise, his grandmother appeared. 'I've been shopping,' she explained. 'It's going to snow and I didn't want to run out of food.' <u>So in the end</u>, it was Mark who had to be helped by his grandmother. She took him inside and made him a cup of tea <u>while</u> they waited for the ambulance to arrive.

a range of time linkers

Task

Either: **a** write your own answer to the task above in **140–190** words; or **b** answer the following question.

You have decided to enter a short-story competition. The competition rules say that the story must begin with the following words:

As soon as Paula heard the news, she took out her mobile phone.

Your story must include:
- an animal
- an unexpected visitor

Write your **story** in **140–190** words.

Useful language for stories

Surprises

To (her/our) surprise …
Imagine (my/their) disappointment/relief/surprise/shock when …
It was such a relief/pleasant surprise to see/find/discover …
(I) couldn't believe (my) eyes/luck when …

Endings

In the end …
(He/She) was wondering what to do when …
Just as things were starting to look bad/desperate/hopeless, (something positive happened).
(We) hadn't expected things to turn out the way they did.

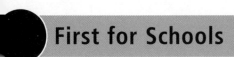

First for Schools

Part 2: Set text

> This photocopiable is intended for those students who are preparing for the *First for Schools* version of the exam and intending to take the set book option.

1 If you have read the set book, you may decide to answer the relevant question in Part 2 of the Writing paper. You may be asked to write an article, an essay, a letter or a review. Rank questions **1–7** below, from the one you would most like to answer about the set book you have read (1), to the one you would least like to answer (7).

  1 Write a **review** for your school's English magazine about the book you have read. Tell readers what you did and did not enjoy about the book and say whether you would recommend it.

  2 Write an **essay** explaining how the beginning of the book you have read is important to the development of the rest of the story.

  3 Your school magazine has asked students for articles on unpopular characters in literature. Which character in the book you have read did you like the least? Write an **article** saying who the person is and giving reasons for your choice.

  4 Write an **essay** briefly describing a place or building which appears in the book you have read and explaining its importance to the story.

  5 A friend has written to you asking about the book you have read. Write a **letter** to your friend explaining what you learnt from your reading about the time and/or place in which the story is set.

  6 'The ending of a story is crucial to the reader's enjoyment of a book.' Write an **article** for your college magazine briefly describing the ending of the book you have read and explaining how much it contributed to your enjoyment of the book as a whole.

  7 Write an **essay** describing the development of the relationship between two of the characters in the book you have read. Explain how the relationship affects the events of the story.

2 Look at the following example answer. Which of the above questions is it answering?

Animal Farm

After overthrowing Jones at the beginning of 'Animal Farm' the animals enter the farmhouse quietly and carefully. They are amazed at "the unbelievable luxury" of the rooms and the furniture, such as the horsehair sofa and the soft feather beds. They decide never to live there and it is turned into a museum as a symbol of the terror and oppression of Jones's reign.

However, the pigs eventually move into the farmhouse, and it soon symbolises the inequality between themselves and the other animals. They grow fat there, drink whisky and even sleep in the beds, while the others do all the work. As in Jones's time, the leaders live comfortably whereas the workers suffer.

Furthermore, Napoleon spends most of his time in the house, waited on by dogs in his own private apartments. In this way, the new dictator separates himself from the other animals, including the pigs.

At the end we see him talking to the humans as equals in the dining room. It is in the farmhouse, then, that we see best how Napoleon occupies Jones's position.

---

3 Has the writer answered both parts of the question satisfactorily?

What is the purpose of each of the four paragraphs?

Which words are used to link ideas?

Has the writer quoted directly from the text?

4 Choose one of the example questions and write your answer in **140–190** words, with reference to the set book you have read.

How to go about it
<ul><li>Underline the key words in the question to make sure you write a complete and relevant answer.</li><li>Write down as many ideas as you can which will be relevant to the question.</li><li>Check in the book that your information is correct and add any further ideas which might be useful. If you notice any short, relevant quotations, make a note of them too. [You will not be able to refer to the set book in the exam.]</li><li>Decide which of your ideas you will include in your answer. The word limit is 190 words, so be selective.</li><li>Organize your ideas into a paragraph plan which is relevant to the task type.</li><li>If you are writing an essay, four paragraphs should be enough.</li><li>If you are writing a letter, decide how you will begin and end it.</li><li>If you are writing an article, interest the reader from the very beginning.</li><li>If you are writing a review, make sure there is a balance of information and opinion.</li></ul>